❧ *The Last Days of Imperial Vienna* ❧

KEY

1. Hofburg
2. Parliament House
3. Town Hall
4. Palace of Justice
5. Opera House
6. University
7. St Stephen's Cathedral
8. Hotel Bristol
9. Grand Hotel
10. Hotel Sacher
11. *Votiv* Church
12. Burgtheater
13. Ministry of War
14. Franciscan Monastery
15. Rossau Barracks
16. Ringstrasse
17. Herrengasse
18. Kärntnerstrasse
19. Graben
20. Stadiongasse
21. Neuer Markt
22. Hörlgasse
23. Danube Canal
24. Elisabethpromenade
A. To Schönbrunn
B. To Wiener Neustadt
C. To the Hungarian border
D. To the Prater grounds

The Last Days of
Imperial Vienna

❧ Robert Pick ❧

THE DIAL PRESS
NEW YORK
1976

This work was originally published in Great Britain
by George Weidenfeld & Nicolson Ltd.

Copyright © 1975 by Robert Pick

Manufactured in the United States of America

First American Edition

Library of Congress Cataloging in Publication Data

Pick, Robert, 1898–
    The last days of imperial Vienna.

    Bibliography: p.
    Includes index.
    1. Austria—Politics and government—1867–1918.
2. Karl I, Emperor of Austria, 1887–1922.
3. Vienna—Politics and government.   4. European
War, 1914–1918—Austria.   I. Title.
DB92.P45   1975b   943.6′04   76–5386
ISBN 0–8037–4682–2

❧ Contents ❧

❧ *Acknowledgments* ❧

Grateful acknowledgment is hereby made for permission to quote, in English translation, from Otto Bauer, *Die öster-reichische Revolution* (by permission of Verlag der Wiener Volksbuchhandlung, Vienna); *Schicksalsjahre Österreichs 1908–1919; Das politische Tagebuch Josef Redlichs,* edited by Fritz Fellner (by permission of Verlag Hermann Böhlaus Nachf., Vienna); Franz Brandl, *Kaiser, Politiker und Menschen* (by permission of Johannes Günther Verlag, Vienna); *Vom Gestern ins Heute* by Heinrich Funder (by permission of Herold Druck- und Verlags-Ges. mbH, Vienna); *Österreich im Jahre 1918, Berichte und Dokumente,* edited by Rudolf Neck (by permission of Verlag für Geschichte und Politik, Vienna); and to reprint material from Arthur J. May, *The Passing of the Habsburg Monarchy 1914–1918* (by permission of University of Pennsylvania Press, Philadelphia).

❧ *1* ❧

Luncheon at Meissel and Schadn's

At 12.45 p.m. on 21 October 1916, the Austrian prime minister, Count Karl Stürgkh, left his office at 7 Herrengasse, and had himself driven to the Hotel Meissel and Schadn – a bare ten minutes' ride in the light traffic of wartime Vienna. A bachelor, fifty-seven years old, he was a man of set habits. He lunched regularly, and preferably alone, at the 'upper' dining room of that hotel, whose neo-Gothic structure occupied the north-eastern corner of Neuer Markt, an elongated square in the Inner City. (The hotel was destroyed by Allied bombing in 1944. The only other building in the Neuer Markt to be damaged in that raid was the Capuchin church, in whose crypt the later Habsburgs lie entombed in their sarcophagi.)

Meissel and Schadn's second-floor restaurant catered to the upper bourgeoisie and the higher ranks of the civil service. Unlike such *de luxe* places as Sacher's – or some new restaurants patronized mainly by war profiteers – it complied on the whole with rationing regulations. Stürgkh, so far from trying to evade those recently issued injunctions, made a point of not infringing them. His tastes were simple. His family's estates in mountainous Styria were small, and the comparatively restricted circumstances in which he grew up, received his education and started his career had left their stamp on his mode of existence. The emoluments of high office had not altered his plain living. He was a hard worker. Aristocratic hobbies were alien to him: he was not interested in thoroughbred horses, was never seen at a gaming table and avoided shooting parties: and even Viennese gossip had

not been able to link his name with that of some young
actress or ballet dancer. The local passion for the stage and
music had not touched him. There was something decidedly
un-Viennese about Count Stürgkh.

On his arrival at Meissel and Schadn's the prime minister
dismissed his chauffeur; apparently he planned to take, as he
sometimes did, a stroll after luncheon. Having entered the
lobby, he turned down the invitation to avail himself of the
lift – offer and rejection were part of the lunchtime routine –
and started mounting the wide staircase. Six feet seven
inches tall, he leaned forward slightly while walking.

No sooner had he been helped out of his greatcoat by the
cloakroom attendant on the upper landing, and handed over
bowler and cane, than the head waiter dashed out of the
short passage that connected the dining room with the hall-
way. The premier acknowledged the bow of the portly man
with a mumbled reference to the chilly weather, and began
advancing towards the table reserved for him daily at the
short end of the horseshoe-shaped room. To reach that table,
he had to pass five tables for two. The brevity of the walk
was known to please him. And so was the location of his
regular table: one of the slim columns supporting the ceiling
partly concealed him, once he was seated, from the view of
guests in the large right-hand section of the restaurant. Yet
Stürgkh was not misanthropic by nature. In his younger days
he had taken great pleasure in being talked to and in talking
himself.

I owe some of this information to Gustav Fruhmann, the
head waiter, who one evening in the early twenties gave me
an account of Stürgkh's luncheon on that day in October
1916. The facility with which the man told the story was no
doubt due to his having done so many times in the intervening years. According to his recollection, then, His Excellency, having exchanged distance glasses for reading pince-
nez, barely glanced at the menu, and asked Fruhmann 'what
he recommended', the point being that 'good old Meissel and
Schadn' still secured certain viands whose quality was not
harmed by the deficiencies of wartime cooking. Following
the head waiter's advice, Stürgkh ordered a bowl of mush-
room soup, a dish of boiled beef with mashed turnips ('Of

course boiled potatoes should have gone with that, too, but there were no potatoes to be had in those weeks') and a farina confection which 'wasn't bad at all'. A tumbler of dry white wine mixed with seltzer was served with the meal.

'His Excellency was a slow eater,' Fruhmann continued, before enlarging on Stürgkh's smoking habits. It seems that while the head waiter had helped him light a cigar he was asked to tell two gentlemen seated at a fair distance from Stürgkh that he would be pleased if they joined him. 'These were Count Toggenburg, then governor of the Tyrol, and Baron Aehrenthal,' Fruhmann said. 'Baron Franz Aehrenthal, the brother – you know, sir, don't you?'

The baron's older brother, Count Aloys, had been a person of great consequence. Foreign minister of Austria-Hungary, he had died in 1912, unshaken in his belief that he had done the right thing in 1908. When in July of that year the Young Turks compelled the Sultan to establish parliamentary government, certain legal problems arose in Bosnia and Herzegovina, two Ottoman provinces where the Congress of Berlin (1878) had installed Austria-Hungary as mandatory power 'on a provisional basis'. To forestall complications – or using their likelihood as a pretext – Aehrenthal proclaimed the provinces' annexation. Contrary to his and Franz Josef's expectations, that *coup*, which amounted to a breach of a great-power agreement, did not raise Habsburg prestige. Russia, dealt with clumsily, perhaps disingenuously, felt she had been duped: and in the ensuing international crisis the Habsburg state had to put itself under the patronage of the German *Reich*. As Bosnia and Herzegovina were inhabited largely by Serbs, the annexation considerably aggravated the friction that already existed between Vienna and the small kingdom of Serbia.

This was not admittedly the way in which Franz Josef's subjects in 1916 tended to look back to the 'Bosnian crisis'. Aehrenthal, if they thought of him at all, was recalled as the statesman who had averted war while gaining his own ends. People who were tempted to blame one single man for the war that had not been averted saw his successor, Count Leopold Berchtold, as the guilty party. But he, too – no longer in office – was rarely referred to. People were more interested in their present trials than in who, or what, had kindled the great conflagration. 'The longer the war lasts,' reported the German ambassador at the end of September 1916, 'the more strongly the simple question whether Austria-Hungary will be able to carry on the fight comes to the foreground. . . .'[1]

Did Stürgkh discuss the sad state of affairs with the two gentlemen at his table? Did he touch on the difficulty he had in discharging his duties? At a later date Toggenburg recalled only a 'conversation about various matters', while Franz Aehrenthal ('Franzi' to his numerous friends) dwelled on a trivial incident that had taken place. Fruhmann, too, mentioned this in our talk. He appeared to savour that memory.

It seems that the restaurant kept in the cellar some bottles of a liqueur that a friend had sent Stürgkh from somewhere behind the lines on the western front. He did not often ask for that French liqueur; and when he did so this time, the *sommelier* misunderstood him and brought a bottle of the house brandy that Meissel and Schadn served in those days. 'The man was new to the job,' Fruhmann explained. 'Our regular *sommelier* had been drafted into the army. And so I went to fetch the liqueur myself, and that took some time, but His Excellency didn't mind at all, and even made some humorous remark while I was pouring the drinks. It was 2.20 p.m. by then, as I well remember, for I was due to knock off at three o'clock, and as I was turning away from the table, I looked at the clock – that clock there over the sideboard.'

Except for Stürgkh's party, only a group of German army officers lingering over their wine were present in the left-hand section of the restaurant. 'Eight of them, as it later turned out,' according to Fruhmann. Some of the tables in the right-hand part of the dining room were still occupied. An unaccompanied middle-aged lady who had been at the table next to Stürgkh's had been leaving as Fruhmann went down to the cellar. There was no waiter anywhere in the room when a bespectacled youngish man – he had finished his meal nearly an hour before – rose to his feet. But instead of moving in the direction of the exit – as, incidentally, three other guests were – he walked towards the prime minister's table and, pulling a revolver from the right-hand pocket of his jacket, fired three shots in rapid succession at his head from a distance of less than four feet. Surely Stürgkh, who died within seconds, could not have heard the assassin cry out: 'Down with absolutism! We want peace!'

'The most harrowing thing', from Fruhmann's point of view, was that he had watched the stranger approach the premier's table. 'I was standing in the passage, answering a question from one of our regulars who was about to leave, and I distinctly remember thinking, "Now that fellow is going to accost His Excellency".'

It was eerie [Fruhmann went on] that a moment of complete silence followed the shots. It was as if all our patrons had lost their voices. I myself, bounding out of the passage, was not of course looking at them. I couldn't see His Excellency – he appeared to have slumped down in his chair. As I saw the assassin turn away as if to make for the exit, I got hold of his right arm, and then there were people about him – about us – waiters and kitchen staff among them, and while I was trying to wrest the gun from him, someone grabbed him by the collar, and someone else tore the glasses from his nose, and one of the German officers was brandishing his unsheathed sword. And there were shouts such as 'Kill him, kill the mad dog' from the people who'd rushed up out of nowhere, and Baron Aehrenthal was shouting over and over again, 'Hold him, hold him' – which, if I may say so, made little sense, for we *were* holding him and at any rate blocking his way. Up to the moment, that is, that his gun went off in the wrangle.

If we believe what the assassin was to say at his trial, he did not realize in the hubbub that the weapon, which he was still holding tightly, had discharged another bullet. He assumed that what had caused the sudden void about him was his shout of 'I'll turn myself in, I am Doktor Adler'.

Not until he was in the hotel manager's office, where Baron Gorup, the chief of police, confronted him within the half-hour, did he learn of the 'fourth shot' and the light wounds the projectile had inflicted on the head waiter and Baron

Aehrenthal. Neither Gorup nor any of his detectives told Adler that Count Stürgkh was dead.

The chief of the homicide squad, who escorted Adler out of the hotel, appeared to know a good deal about him. 'I always took you for an idealist,' he said to Adler as soon as they were in the police car. 'And now – this. . . .'

By the 'Compromise' of 1867 the Habsburg monarchy had been transformed into Austria-Hungary, a partnership of two countries, each with a parliament elected through limited suffrage. Each had its own administration, but defence, foreign affairs and treasury matters connected with both were still dealt with jointly. The renewals of the compromise every ten years were a nightmare to Franz Josef, Austria's emperor and Hungary's king. The Magyar governing classes constantly urged their demands for still greater independence and for a separate army. As Hungary's election laws discriminated widely against her large Slav and Rumanian minorities, and also against the workers, universal suffrage appeared to be a means of breaking the power of her stubborn magnates and squires. But Franz Josef could not possibly pursue that goal without at the same time aiming at a reform of the franchise law in the 'Austrian half' of his realm. Moreover, democracy recommended itself in Austria as a counterweight to 'nationalism' – a term that in this multinational country stood for the aspirations of its various ethnic groups. The 1905 revolution in Russia gave additional urgency to Franz Josef's decision to create a democracy. After a considerable struggle, a bill establishing universal manhood suffrage was passed in 1907. In Hungary the entrenched powers, renouncing the demand for a separate army, were spared any change.

Events in the Austrian parliament, or *Reichsrat*, did not work out as hoped. After a short honeymoon, national passions reasserted themselves in the Lower House. The German middle-class parties would not accept any whittling-down of the *de facto* privileges that Austria's Germans – the 'state *Volk*' in their parlance – had been enjoying since what seemed to them time immemorial. Nor did the vaunted supranational credo of the Social Democrats make the non-

Germans in their ranks impervious to the call of nationalism.

Stürgkh, who became prime minister in 1911, realized the momentum those forces had gathered. He did not exert himself to reconcile them. Early experience as a deputy to the Lower Chamber had imbued him with contempt for politicians. He came to admire Count Istvan Tisza, the Hungarian premier, who had dared to call in a platoon of soldiers to restore order in parliament. 'Count Stürgkh was filled with the deepest distrust of the masses,' Josef Redlich, an eminent university teacher and observant politician, was to note in his diary upon Stürgkh's assassination, 'and *a priori* credited only the Crown and its Ministers with the wisdom and the ability to shape the destinies of these lands and these peoples. . . .'[2] When the old German-Czech antagonism paralysed the provincial Diet of Bohemia in 1913, Stürgkh suspended her constitution. Thereupon the Slovenes and Ruthenes made common cause with the irate Czechs in parliament; and in March, 1914, Ruthenian obstruction handed Stürgkh a pretext for proroguing the Lower House. In November, it was 'suspended', though not dissolved.

It had not been called into session during the crisis that led to war, nor at its outbreak. Far-reaching changes had been wrought by 'emergency decrees' when war was declared. A War Supervisory Office had been set up and attached to the Ministry of War. Charged with protecting the armed forces against treason within the Dual Monarchy, as well as in occupied enemy territory, that office could interfere with all government departments. The army took over control of the 'operational zones', whose extent the Supreme Command alone determined. Civil liberties were ruled out of existence by *fiat*. Trial by jury was abolished, and 'extraordinary courts', or even courts-martial, empowered to administer criminal law.

Imperial emergency decrees were not a wartime innovation. Nor did they lack a legal basis. Article Fourteen of Austria's constitution gave the sovereign the power to issue regulations during the intervals between sessions of the Lower Chamber. These regulations could be voided by a majority vote upon re-assembly. True, such a majority had never materialized. But the virtual non-existence of parlia-

ment ever since its suspension removed even the possibility
of checking legislation by ukase. 'His Majesty and a very
small cabinet of his own choosing,' reported the American
ambassador in July, 1916, 'augmented by two or three military experts, govern and administer absolutely this land of
mixed races, wherein public expression of opinion, or discussion of state policy, is impossible. . . .'[3] The reference to
'two or three military experts' scarcely did justice to the
military dictatorship to which the authoritarian regime had
begun to degenerate.

A story current in Vienna had it that Count Stürgkh, one
day walking past Parliament House with a friend, had
boasted of having turned it into an army hospital – 'my
greatest accomplishment!' He could truthfully tell himself
that the spectacle of a deeply disunited House would
damage the prestige of the embattled country. He knew
enough of the rule of terror of the military in Slav border
regions during the first months of the war to dread parliamentary debate. Unlike some senior civil servants, he had
never tried to curb the army's interference in administrative
and judicial business. He did not doubt but that, except for
the Poles – for a long time government supporters (and
appropriately cultivated) – all Slavs were potential traitors,
and he considered their repression at home the only way of
blunting the seditious propaganda of the handful of Czech
and South-Slav *émigré* politicians abroad. He likewise feared
that Socialist deputies, using the privilege of immunity in a
re-assembled *Reichsrat,* might bring to public knowledge
newspaper stories, suppressed by the censor, of arbitrary
justice, dismal want, and profiteering.

While Stürgkh had remained in touch with the chairmen
of the parties in an informal manner, he had turned a deaf
ear to all requests for having parliament summoned. In
September 1916, pressure for re-assembly had grown to a
point where some high-born members of the Upper Chamber
(consisting partly of hereditary members, partly of imperial
appointees) tried to approach the emperor in a group;
Stürgkh blocked that attempt. Two weeks later the Social-
Democratic leadership – the party comprised one-sixth of
the membership of the Lower Chamber – resolved that

immediate convocation was 'absolutely necessary': Stürgkh gave orders that news of their conference, let alone their resolution, must not reach the public in print. The Speaker petitioned for an audience with the monarch; he was refused. On 15 October a spokesman from the War Supervisory Office summoned all newspaper editors to inform them that discussions of constitutional matters would not henceforth be tolerated. The Speaker invited the chairmen of all parties to meet, and asked the government to have its representatives present; Stürgkh let it be known that, as far as the government was concerned, the inter-party meeting would not exist, that no such person as a Speaker did exist, and that he himself assuredly would not confer with the gentleman who appeared to use that title.

Meanwhile, a number of Law School teachers at Vienna University had rented the largest concert hall of the city for a public meeting on 23 October, with Austria's foremost teacher of constitutional law as the main speaker. The police, asked for the necessary permit, would not hear of a public meeting, but agreed to let four of the group address 'invited guests'. That decision was reversed on 19 October, and the meeting prohibited in either form. The day after, an *ad hoc* committee of the law faculty asked Stürgkh to receive them: he refused, and, talking to his secretary, remarked that he 'did not have the time to see a bunch of professors'. Twenty-four hours later, time no longer counted for Stürgkh.

The unbending stance of the premier had affected Friedrich Adler in a particular way. As one of the four executive secretaries of the Social Democratic party, he had been working for some weeks on preparations for the *Arbeitertag*, or Workers' Day, scheduled for 5 November, at which delegates of the membership were to discuss the food supply of the industrial towns and labour conditions in the army-controlled war plants: debates on political issues had been ruled out by the party. Stürgkh's decision on the concert hall meeting doomed any hope that the *Arbeitertag* might be granted a permit. That realization brought Adler's plan to a head. The thought of assassinating one of the cabinet ministers or high bureaucrats had occupied him as early as the spring of 1915 – when he bought the revolver – but not before the summer of the following year had he decided to do away with Count Stürgkh himself.

Friedrich Adler was the son of Dr Victor Adler, the remarkable man who, abandoning his medical practice, had united Austria's splintered Socialist movement in the late 1880s. He had established a viable party and compact trade unions, and taught both to use strength wisely. Apparently, it was his son's lack of a similar bent for pragmatic action that caused the father to dissuade him from a career in politics. Friedrich Adler studied physics and mathematics, took his degree at Zurich, and became a lecturer there. He also contributed to Swiss socialist journals. He had been yearning for party work all along; and after the vacant university chair for theoretical physics was given to a friend of his (Einstein), he renounced the academic profession, and accepted the editorship of Switzerland's party newspaper. In 1911 he returned to Vienna to fill the vacant secretarial post. While living abroad he had been supporting wholeheartedly the tactics of the Vienna party, which were not impinged on by differing long-range views within the circle of its leaders. Dr Adler, once doubting the political gifts of his son, now cherished his presence. 'Hardest on me,' he wrote in his last will drafted in 1913, 'is [the thought of] the farewell I'll have to take from my work and the party. To the latter, I leave the best I have – my son.'[4] If anything set Friedrich Adler apart from his co-workers, it was an un-Viennese inflexibility, which was at variance with his gentle nature.

Throughout the spring of 1914, he was organizing the International Labour Conference that was to take place in Vienna in August. On 28 June Archduke Franz Ferdinand, the heir-apparent to the Habsburg throne, was assassinated in Sarajevo by a student whose contacts with radical circles in Serbia – though not with her government – were soon established.

The Socialist International had been debating the prevention of war for many years, and consistently rejected, by a large majority vote, the general strike as an instrument of achieving that goal. The congress of 1907 had adopted a resolution obliging each membership party to foil its country's going to war 'by any means each party will deem most efficacious'. In July 1914 the Social-Democratic executive in Vienna did not believe in the imminence of war. The ultimatum that the Foreign Office delivered to Serbia on 23 July took them by surprise, and their newspaper the *Arbeiter Zeitung*, hastened to criticize its stiff language.

The ultimatum expired on 25 July. The following day Friedrich Adler and his ailing father travelled post-haste to Brussels, where the International had called an emergency meeting. As Friedrich Adler was to recall, 'a sense of passivity permeated' the account that his father gave of the situation in his country. 'We are in a state of war,' Dr Adler said. 'Our press has been gagged. . . . Martial law is in the offing. . . . Do not expect action from us. . . .'⁵ The celebrated Jean Jaurès, taking the son aside, tried to convince him that no matter what happened the Vienna party must not relent in its demonstrations against war. Young Adler knew that there had been no demonstrations. 'Juarès' words made me feel ashamed, although I realized they were not aimed at me. I did not wish to dissociate myself from my father. For the first time in my life I felt strongly opposed to his views.'⁶

Before the week had run its course the Vienna Socialists had done more than relinquish any thought of opposing the war. On 4 August the powerful Social Democrats in the Berlin *Reichstag* cast their votes in favour of the war credits the Kaiser had asked for; and the following morning the Viennese party newspaper extolled that action in a bellicose outburst. In Friedrich Adler's words, 'the first defeat in this war was suffered by the Socialist International'. Otto Bauer, the foremost theoretician of the party – he had been called to the colours as a lieutenant in the reserves – was to write in 1923,

> Fear of a victory of the Tsar gripped the labouring masses, as it did all classes of German-speaking Austria. [The workers] did not think of Serbia or of Belgium. They gave no thought to the Habsburg and Hohenzollern dynasties. In the first months of the war, the workers' good wishes were with the imperial army, which was defending their native soil against the awesomely superior strength of

Russia. In those months ... the Austro-German Socialist party stood without reservation on the side of the Central Powers ... and put what influence it had at the disposal of the war effort.[7]

Still, Dr Adler called for an end to the slaughter as early as April 1915; in an article suppressed by the Vienna censor but published in Zurich, he spoke of 'peace without humiliation'. In May 1915, however, the Russian armies, which had advanced deep into Habsburg territory, were turned back by the forces of the Central Powers; and Karl Renner, the Socialists' right-wing planner, advocated with more strength than ever wartime 'co-operation of all classes'. Captivated by the imperialist German concept of *Mitteleuropa*, he did not object to annexionist projects. He also asserted that wartime government control of industry was a step in the direction of nationalization, and thus of socialism.

As casualties were mounting, and want and misery making their entry at home, the Social-Democratic leaders tried to alleviate the sufferings of the working population by whatever means were at hand. In Friedrich Adler's harsh words, they were 'transforming the political party into a large-scale philanthropic society'. He refused to give the benefit of the doubt to their avoiding conflicts and smoothing frictions with the powers that be. In a pamphlet published in several neutral countries at the beginning of 1916, he spoke of the 'wall of indifference and cynicism' he faced in executive meetings. He prophesied that the 'civilized world one day will shudder upon learning how the Austrian courts not only degraded themselves to an instrument of warfare ... but also became the harlot of political reaction. ... The constitution has been destroyed, free speech abolished, and the hangmen are at work. ...'

Friedrich Adler was a lonely man in these months. The discussion of 'every small matter led to an explosion between me and Karl Renner, my father, and others. ...' He did not champion insurrection, and in April 1916 explicitly rejected Lenin's idea of turning the imperialist world war into a socialist world revolution. What Friedrich Adler kept pointing out was the duty of the party not to ignore the tsarist methods at home while fighting the Tsar of Russia. They were, he reminded his peers, silencing 'the inner voice that told them that Austria had started the war, only to talk ever more loudly of the "self-defence of the German nation" '. He brushed aside as mere nagging such criticism of administrative excesses as the party press succeeded in getting past the censor, and went so far as to brand the Socialist leaders 'accessories to the war-prolonging policies of the government'. So bitter did the fight he was waging grow that his father, in the meeting of 18 October 1916, burst out, 'You're provoking us, Fritz! Apparently you want to be thrown out!'

Three days later Adler killed Count Stürgkh. 'Through my action,' he said at his trial, 'I wanted, on the one hand, to show to the rulers that patience and weakness in bearing injustice were not general. On the other hand, I was intent on trying to rouse those men in the proletariat who had preserved their pristine feelings, [intent] on making an attempt ... to restore their self-confidence and drive home that it was up to them, too, to shape the state of affairs. Seen in this light, the [planned] assassination appeared to me as an efficacious action.'

As it turned out, the shots at Meissl and Schadn's had been echoing not only in the proletariat. Josef Redlich, having taken a stroll along Vienna's boulevards late in the afternoon on the day of the assassination, confided to his journal, 'It would seem that the population is reacting mainly with a dazed kind of defiance.' And two days later, returning from a dinner party at which there had been 'a goodly number of ladies from higher civil-service circles', he noted their unanimous opinion that 'people show no indignation at the murder. . . '.

That same night the emperor appointed Ernest von Koerber to the office of the murdered count. That clever civil servant, who had served as prime minister half a generation earlier with great diligence and some success, was credited with the talent of reducing national tensions. These, rather than war weariness, imperilled the attainment of certain territorial goals that recent victories in battle seemed to have brought within reach. Koerber's premiership was short-lived.

On 21 November Franz Josef, in the eighty-seventh year of his life and the sixty-eighth of his reign, died a gentle death. According to Redlich, 'a deep tiredness, close to apathy, is hovering over Vienna. Neither sorrow for the deceased nor joy over his successor can be noticed.'

❧ 2 ❧

In the Calm Eye of the Wind

'The amazing ease with which the strongest monarchy in the world was overthrown must add to our apprehensions. . . .' Count Ottokar Czernin, the young emperor's foreign minister, wrote him in a memorandum after the March Revolution in St Petersburg. 'The responsibility for continuing the war is far greater for a monarch whose country is united only through the dynasty than for one whose people are fighting for their [common] national ideals.'[1]

Of all the Slavs in the Dual Monarchy, the Czechs were affected most by the events in Russia. What looked like the dawn of liberty for her masses could not but appeal to the Czechs, whose old grievances – precisely because some of these had been acted upon in the twenty years past – made them doubly sensitive to the high-handed policies of the wartime regime. Moreover, the war against Russia, the 'big Slav brother', had been unpopular among them from the beginning. A mutinous incident had occurred in 1914 at the departure of an army unit from Prague, and some months later an entire Czech battalion had defected to the Russians in the midst of battle – motivated, to be sure (as no less an authority than Masaryk has established) more by dislike of war than anti-Habsburg passion. It is true that the hold Germany was gaining on Habsburg affairs – a Germany whose chancellor had spoken of a 'struggle between Slavs and Teutons' – embittered the Czechs and alarmed their intelligentsia. Still, their overwhelming majority was not, by the time of Franz Josef's death, contemplating secession of their

nation from the Habsburg state. It was their place within it
that they were eager to see altered.

When the *Reichsrat* re-assembled in May 1917, their
deputies – two of them abstaining – declared that the 'transformation of the Habsburg Monarchy into a federal country
consisting of free and equal national states is necessary if . . .
the general development of all nationalities is to be secured
in the interest of the empire'. The Czech parliamentarians
were not isolated in referring to 'self-determination', or the
'natural rights of nations'. It was they, however, who now
formed the spearhead of the first domestic assault on the
basic structure of the Dual Monarchy.

The attack struck out at its Germans and Magyars (or, as
the Socialists put it, at the German bourgeoisie and the
Magyar feudalists). The Czechs were insisting on the inalien-
able historical rights of the lands of St Wenceslas's crown,
propounding as a matter of course Czech rule over the large
settlements of Germans who for centuries had been established in the border regions. At the same time the *Reichsrat*
pronouncement made light of the borders of the ancient
Hungarian kingdom, claiming union with the kindred
Slovaks, who had lived in Hungary's northern counties for
hundreds of years.

To the man in the street, more or less wilful demands on
the part of the various national *Reichsrat* factions had been
one of the facts of life for decades. He had watched successive governments test their skill (boasted of cynically by one
of Franz Josef's less inept premiers) of 'keeping all the
nationalities in a condition of even and well-modulated discontent', and had not learned to appreciate the growing
urgency behind the apparent mischief-making of Slav parliamentarians. In the first months of the war, lurid reports of
Ruthenian and South-Slav treacheries in the rear of the front
lines had shocked the man in the street, and hardened him to
rumours of drumhead justice. After the Italian kingdom,
bound to the Habsburg state and the *Reich* since 1882 in a
defensive alliance, breached that treaty and joined the Allies
in May 1915, he had few illusions about the sentiments of
Italian-speakers under Austria's rule. He grew inured to the
thought of disloyalty spreading on the fringes of the country.

What Vienna's next-door neighbours, the Czechs, were saying and doing stirred deeper emotions.

In the latter part of the past century, tens of thousands of
their artisans and labourers had settled in Vienna. True-born
Viennese had looked down upon and ridiculed them, albeit
without malice. Their offspring had adopted the German
language as a matter of course. Around the turn of the
century, however, the growing political strength of the
Czechs made that course less attractive. Much to the dis-
pleasure of Viennese of earlier vintages, the Czechs in their
city began building Czech schools. The municipality closed
them four years before the outbreak of the war.

In mid-1916 the death sentences imposed on four Czech
politicians were talked about endlessly in the homes and
coffeehouses of Vienna. The activities of the Czech *émigré*
politicians now were followed as closely as the trickle of
printed stories allowed. One did not have to have heard the
two maverick deputies in the *Reichsrat* subscribe to the
secessionist programme of the expatriates to be familiar with
the concept of an independent 'Czecho-Slovak' state. Thomas
Masaryk's name was becoming a household word in Vienna.
It was something of a symbol for a change one could not
conceive.

The 'break-up of the Empire once the Old Gentleman is
gone' had been a stock phrase not only of cynics long before
1914. But pronouncing it had been one thing; facing the
approach of a dire prophecy coming true was quite another.
The Viennese – of all classes – refused to imagine the Czech
'provincials', let alone backward Slovaks or Slovenes, or such
folk as Ruthenes, doing without metropolitan Vienna as their
natural centre. Also, people assumed that their beautiful city,
as much as the dynasty, gave a sense of cohesion to the
country. The proximity of the aged monarch seemed to
vouchsafe to Vienna the perpetuity which he himself
claimed for his House, and that irrational trust was at the
root of a quip which, springing up as the skies darkened,
called 'conditions hopeless but not serious'.

An American attaché, walking through one of Vienna's workmen's districts one morning in March 1916, noticed 'strings of

poorly dressed women and children held in line by police. [They] were waiting for milk, pitchers in hand, exposed to a slow but steady rain. Late-comers went home empty-handed, while lucky ones had obtained only half as much as expected.' Similar queues, the American reported, 'can be observed in the early hours in front of the bakers' shops. . . . The worst feature is the present scarcity of potatoes. . . . One stand-keeper told me that the great estates are hoarding potatoes with a view to obtaining higher prices; others blamed the market authorities for prescribing a maximum selling rate which excludes profits; while [still] others said there were [no potatoes] to be had because the provincial authorities would not permit their home population to be deprived of them. . . .'[2] 'The harvest is in,' the *Arbeiter Zeitung* wrote about six months later, 'yet we have no flour and no bread. Potatoes are not brought to market; sugar has been hoarded away; and kerosene is being looked for as though it were gold.'

By the time of Franz Josef's demise, food riots had occurred in Vienna. He is unlikely to have been told of the disorders, which had spread to the very heart of the city. Their cause was driven home brutally to his successor, Emperor Karl. No sooner had the Old Gentleman's mortal remains been laid to rest than Count Tisza began pressing Karl to have himself crowned as king of Hungary without delay; and behind the legal arguments Tisza adduced to shorten the constitutional six-month period between a king's death and the coronation of his successor, there loomed the threat of a curtailment of Hungary's shipments of foodstuffs to Vienna. The ancient ritual obliged the new king to affirm, in the oath of coronation, the integrity of Hungary's territory and her constitution. In other words, Karl was to – and on 30 December did – swear to renounce any plans of meeting the demands of Hungary's non-Magyar peoples in the course of a reconstruction of the Habsburg realm.

The bourgeois press of Vienna did not in so many words say that the shot-gun coronation had dealt a mortal blow to any plans for the country's reform along ethnic lines. Nor did the journal of Vienna's dominant party, the Christian-Socials, or the Socialist newspaper, dwell on that fact. The

Viennese themselves paid small attention to the coronation. Fond of spectacles as they were, they seemed not to begrudge the Hungarian capital the colourful pageantry; no such thing as an Austrian coronation had ever existed. There were some who found fault with the part that Count Tisza, a Calvinist, had been allowed to play in the Catholic service; but then, his power both in Budapest and at court had been well known for years, and the episode was shrugged off as just another piece of Magyar arrogance.

Photographs showing Karl with the regalia elicited wry comments on the over-large crown which apparently had slipped down on his forehead and was sitting slightly askew on his brow. Such observations differed in kind from the waggish stories about the senescent Franz Josef which had in effect merely complemented the sentimental emperor folklore. They had never made sport of the appearance of the Old Gentleman in his various costumes. Nor was there any true malice now as they pointed to Karl's small head under Hungary's crown, or his boyishly narrow shoulders weighed down with the ancient royal mantle. They simply gave vent to their discomfort in seeing a twenty-nine-year-old ruler who appeared to be ill at ease and nearly helpless.

Karl had promised 'an early peace' to his subjects upon his accession. A note had gone out declaring the willingness of the Central Powers to open negotiations. But when the American government, still neutral, invited the belligerents to state their conditions, Berlin's uncompromising terms put an end to the exchange. No further proofs of their young emperor's efforts to attain peace reached the public. His accession pledge was soon forgotten, or at any event scarcely believed more than the government's wordy assurance that ample grain supplies were ready for shipment in the recently conquered parts of the Rumanian kingdom.

Victories as such had ceased to fascinate the population. The part played in them regularly by the German army soured military triumphs even to people still tempted to glory in them. Neither were the Viennese turned jubilant by the *de facto* re-establishment of the constitution, brought about by a majority refusal of the Lower House to ratify the most ruthless of Stürgkh's Article Fourteen regulations.

However, the liberalization of the regime somewhat loosened the tongues of working men and women. The repeal of a punitive law that had empowered the army to cut out of hand a defence worker's wages to a conscript's pay restored some of the sense of civic rights that three decades of socialist education had been breeding.

The winter of 1916–17 was severe beyond the recall of the oldest Viennese. For many weeks pedestrians had to pick their way across soot-covered mounds of snow which the elderly men the city could hire had been unable to shovel on to the dump carts drawn by mules. With the shortage of rolling stock threatening to strangle the supply of coal and hence power production, the tram service had been reduced severely. Countless pipes had burst in tenement houses, and women could be seen fetching water from hydrants. To supplement the heating of flats, provided by cast-iron stoves, people in the outlying workers' districts would set out for the near-by woods on Sundays, trailing handcarts or sleds to load them with fallen branches; and not a few would return after nightfall, their haul carefully covered. In the dim lighting that the city managed to furnish, the 'rent barracks', so called, of those neighbourhoods looked grimmer still after sunset. As Vienna's prelates had turned over most of the church bells to armament plants, an unwonted stillness, punctuated by the clatter of wooden-soled shoes, hovered over the cobblestoned streets.

The Inner City – the district of Habsburg *palazzi*, noblemen's mansions, government offices, banking houses, luxury shops, and high-rent apartment houses – was growing shabby. The fumes of brown coal, brought from Styria, had begrimed the façades of buildings and their Victorian ornamentations. Taxicabs were at a premium, their business crippled by the shortage of petrol. The dashing horse-drawn *fiacres* of Vienna, which even men who could not afford their hire used to boast of as a feature unequalled in any other city, had all but disappeared.

For all that, quite a few well-dressed men and women would take the habitual midday walk along the cleared pavements of Kärtnerstrasse and Graben, and drop in at

Gerstner's tearoom for a glass of vermouth or sherry, dubious as its provenance had become. That promenade, known as the *Corso,* had been brought to Vienna nearly a century earlier by officers of the army stationed in what were then the Habsburgs' Italian dominions. The populace of mid-nineteenth-century Lombardy and Venetia had loathed those officers as fiercely as their latter-day successors were hated in war-occupied Serbia or Rumania. Youthful subalterns – such as the fellows likely to join the Vienna *Corso* on leave, with spurs on their boots, which they had no need of (for saddle horses were barely in use any more) and the tasselled guard of their sword (long discarded in the trenches) in the crook of the left arm – were not overly sensitive to the feelings the occupiers aroused in those parts. Yet nine out of ten were not professional soldiers. In peacetime, their likes, having volunteered for one year's service upon graduation from the *Gymnasium* (or its equivalent) would gain their reserve commission after training in officers' courses and a minimum of command experience. Sons of middle- and upper-middle-class families, they were from the start set widely apart from the run of conscripted young men, who had to serve for three years and could never be commissioned. The prolonged war had changed the pre-war reserve officers' corps called up for the duration. Duly promoted, they were put in command of units up to company strength. They got along well with the ranks who, mainly reservists themselves, relied on the common sense of such commanders to blunt the martinet spirit of career men in higher positions. The nineteen- and twenty-year-old lieutenants of wartime vintage invited no similar trust in the conscripts, as a rule their elders. Unmarried, as good as strangers to the responsible life of adulthood, such young men felt abashed by the unspoken anxieties of simple family men.

The 'volunteer's year' used to be regarded lightly in peacetime. Middle-class parents had been smiling indulgently at the 'volunteers' capers' their sons engaged in. The hardship and perils of warfare had not dislodged that attitude fully. They actually sharpened the young men's appetite for sowing their wild oats. However, the light-hearted world they had dreamed of did not meet them in the Vienna of 1917.

They could not fail to notice the reduced comforts in the homes of their parents, and on their faces apprehensions they had not themselves been aware of in the field. Having inherited the discord besetting the public life of their country, and watched the unwillingness of their fathers to face the roots of that discord squarely, Viennese middle-class boys were largely indifferent to its wartime ramifications. Asked about the loyalty of Czech, or Ruthenian, men in their units, they were prone to shrug off the queries; and of 'socialist elements', they would profess to know nothing. Yet they did not maintain that all was to the best in the army. They were inclined to complain about unequal distribution of combat medals, the blockheadedness of career men among superiors, or the high living at headquarters. There was a measure of fatalism in their low-keyed indignation. And they were convinced that the law of inertia, so often proved in the country's crises, would see it through its present trials That resilient confidence served for patriotism.

The young lieutenants were sincere when at nightclubs, drinking insipid Hungarian champagne – and little concerned about vulgar war profiteers and their ladies sitting close by – they applauded the band whenever it struck up the martial tunes of old. Those echoes of the long-silenced trumpets of glorious war seemed to conjure up the invincible empire of the textbooks. To be sure, nightclubs had to close early and the determined merrymakers, out again on the wintry streets, felt bored and lonely. Chances were that some crippled veteran in his threadbare greatcoat would approach them, hawking evergreen sprigs and paper flowers. The police ignored the hapless men loitering about places of amusement. Rather, they busied themselves stopping some of the young tarts who had taken to roaming the streets after nighfall without the permit the vice squad might grant upon application.

If the nightclubs of the Inner City were crowded, suburban wine-shops did not lack business either, although most of their customers were locals, because transport was scarce. As it was, upper-middle-class people who used to put in an appearance at those *Heurigen*[3] places if only to confirm to themselves their Viennese egalitarianism, no longer felt at ease there. They were not anxious to overhear, as they might in the cramped quarters, grumbling about the food situation, the black market, or the service deferments wealthy or well-connected families were said to secure for their sons. Similarly, army officers stayed away from the wine-shops, where enlisted men on leave could be expected to air their grievances in talking to other customers.

Gone were the days when front line soldiers, proud of their narrow escapes, would recount their feats under fire. The new weaponry and the mass destruction it wrought had discoloured the handed-down image of heroism. In the fourth year of the war the combatant had long learned that the endurance with which he bore life in the trenches and his burning wish to stay alive in combat were beyond the imagination of the home front. What the men spoke about over their cups were such matters as the quality of the war bread, the *ersatz* coffee all but unfit to drink, or the galling disparity of their own and their officers' fare.

Ironically, the 'solidarity of feeling' that patriotic writers, clergymen and middle-class politicians did not weary of extolling became a reality in the indignation that fired civilians and front line soldiers alike as they were exchanging tales of injustice and corruption. Scandalous gossip was abundant, and not all of it had reached the ears of the men at the front. Of the juiciest of those scandals, the partnership that one of the senior archdukes was rumoured to hold in a company producing dried vegetables (a staple soldiers detested), people spoke only in whispers. Archdukes belonged to the image of Old Vienna, and the wartime yearning for peacetime conditions tended to fuse with the pre-war nostalgia, nursed by the lower middle class, for the mythical golden days of Vienna. The mawkish tunes that the strings-and-accordion quartet ground out in *Heurigen* tap-rooms seemed to make the greyness that had crept into the life of the city doubly oppressive. Puzzlement stoked the angry sadness. Although people knew that a growing shortage of man and animal power was lowering farm production and that the Allies'⁴ blockade strangled the import of wool and cotton, they chose to believe in sinister forces that robbed them of food and offered them shoddy clothing. They had but the most nebulous notions, if any, of the money market. The word inflation had not yet drifted into their parlance.

Not the least of the vexations troubling their lives was the greed of the peasants they had to cope with when on Sundays, rucksacks on their shoulders, they themselves ventured into the countryside to purchase such treasures as eggs and butter, a smoked ham, or a couple of chickens. Political allies of the Little Man of Vienna, churchgoing folk, as hostile as he to social change and its Socialist champions, the peasants were nevertheless indifferent to the trials of the big city.

Vienna's lower-middle-class people had been taught to think of themselves as a class only in the late 1880s when an extraordinary man rose from their midst to tell them that progress, so glibly vaunted, had been shortchanging them all along. Karl Lueger made them recognize their own features in the portrait he drew of the wronged Little Man. 'Handsome Karl' offered him help against the powers that seemed to imperil both their traditional ways and their economic well-being – Marxist socialism on the one side, and modern capitalism on the other. The Christian-Social party, which Lueger brought into being with the support of the low clergy, soon won the favour of the prelates and even the Holy See, and was merged with Austria's various clerical groups. In Vienna the party thrived on the animus toward the Jews, which had grown in step with the expansion of their community ever since the 1860s. If Jewish bankers, industrialists and merchants were not the only exponents of the disturbing change that had overcome the city, they were among the most conspicuous.

Within ten years Lueger had put an end to the rule of the Liberals in the town hall and, as Vienna's burgomaster, opened an era of municipal socialism, which successfully challenged the utilities and public transportation magnates. By the time of his premature death in 1911 many affluent property owners had joined his party as had many bureaucrats and professional men, who had been estranged from the Liberals by their special-interest policies, their nagging anticlericalism, or merely their obvious attrition. As the

Christian-Socials, thus strengthened, concentrated their energies on blocking the advance of Labour, they ceased being only the Little Man's party, and in effect became Vienna's conservative political faction.

The dominant role of the German element in Austria's affairs had always been a matter of course to the people of Vienna. At the same time the Viennese believed they were far from being chauvinistic Germans. Some years before Lueger's rise, Georg von Schönerer, originally elected as a Liberal to the *Reichsrat*, had developed an eccentric pan-German doctrine and won much support, particularly among university students (who, on the one hand, watched Slav graduates compete for government jobs and, on the other, sons of Jewish immigrants flock to the professions). But his wild attacks on the dynasty and the Church had soon repelled the lower-middle-class people. Withal, the 'brotherhood of arms' with the mighty *Reich* had from the start of the war deepened the awareness of true-born Viennese that they were ethnically German. Lueger's successor in the town hall no doubt knew he spoke the mind of his voters when, in October 1915, he stated bluntly: 'The Germans of the country must hold a place commensurate with their history and their cultural achievements ... in the new Austria that will rise from the bloodshed on the battlefields.'[5]

What gave Vienna's upper middle class the semblance of coherence was a penchant for cultural manifestations – in particular, an almost inordinate enthusiasm for the stage and for music. Those men and women, remote in their personal lives from the urgency of the 'social question' and the acerbity of ethnic conflicts, believed in enlightenment and progress – progress, that was, within the framework of the *status quo*. Asked for their political beliefs, many of them were likely to wave off the query with a jaded air. Some would affirm their loyalty to Liberalism, or even refer to themselves as German-Liberals, even though the party boasting that name had shrunk pathetically both in parliament and the town hall.

It was significant of the weakness of Austria's representative institutions that the Liberal press exerted considerable influence on public affairs without a political base. The grandest of those journals was the *Neue Freie Presse*. The means by which its owner/editor, Moritz Benedikt, furthered the interests of banking and big business were as untainted by direct financial bribes as were the tactics by which successive governments managed to use his paper for influencing public opinion. His was an insidious kind of corruption. The profusion of sheer information he offered, the expertise, or merely the names, of the contributors he enlisted, and not least the busy concern of the *Neue Freie Presse* with the cultural life of Vienna came near to enthralling its subscribers. The rational stance of Benedikt's editorials kept them from plumbing the depth of his contempt for the masses and their political movements. His readers subconsciously welcomed the innocuous labels he attached to the pecking order of the nationalities in the Habsburg state. When, in the reassembled *Reichsrat* of 1917, the prime minister rebuffed the declaration of the Czechs by announcing that his programme was 'Austria', Benedikt 'rationalized' that statement by suggesting that 'Austria can be governed only in the Austrian manner, that is to say, as a state formed of minorities, among which the Germans, on account of their past, their convictions, and their culture are indispensable as the balancing political force'.

Meanwhile Vienna's culture had not remained unaltered. Wartime had rubbed off some of the gloss of the preoccupation with the 'higher things in life' the upper middle class claimed as its hallmark. The *haute bourgeoisie*, which prided itself on its good taste, was slowly losing its own discernment in artistic matters. Vienna's elite used to look down on operettas; now it was patronizing them, not least because it assumed that this approval strengthened the bonds with the lower classes who adored latter-day musical comedy. The young emperor's fascination with it did not harm his image in upper-middle-class circles. Their basic philistinism had not escaped all observers even in pre-war Vienna. The acidulous satirist, Karl Kraus, had been attacking the *Neue Freie Presse* ever since 1899 with an integrity amounting to obsession. His bourgeois readers merely allowed him to amuse them. As, from 1915, he was assailing the war policies of the country, they labelled him at best an apocalyptic visionary ignorant of what kept the modern world ticking.

The urgency of wartime business had curtailed the leisure time of men of affairs. Often it also restored to them the singlemindedness of their pioneering fathers or grandfathers. Moreover, the men who for two generations had served as a fulcrum, and been the backbone, of the upper middle class were drifting away from it. With the scarcity of goods grinding down the purchasing power of the salaries of senior public servants, and inflation nibbling at their savings, they found themselves – overnight, as it seemed to them – in more or less straitened circumstances. Their genteel pride bade them withdraw from the prosperous burghers they used to consort with. Now they retreated into the shell of their office, and often nursed their wounded pride by stressing the authoritarian spirit of the wartime regime. Much like the settled bourgeoisie, those cultured high bureaucrats had been irritated by the rise of *nouveaux riches* in Vienna, and had mocked their lack of refinement and their ostentation. But by mid-1917 a certain prejudice towards wealth for its own sake had developed in those quarters. Their bitterness seeped down to the lower middle classes, and frayed what respect for the rich *they* had salvaged from the anti-monopolistic policies of Vienna's early Christian-Socials.

Nor had the high nobility retained all of its aura. They had always been Viennese by courtesy only; most of their property was in Slav or Hungarian regions, and all, unless in public office, spent only late winter and spring in their eighteenth-century mansions in Vienna. Those families, numbering barely a hundred and inter-married over and over again, had played their part at Franz Josef's tedious court, were seen in its chapel on certain occasions, watched their thoroughbreds race on the Freudenau track, and dropped in at opera performances. For the rest, they engaged in intrigues and pursued their amours. Art collecting, a favourite pastime of earlier magnates, no longer seemed to allure their descendants. Neither, in general, did serious music, whose flowering their grandfathers had patronized with singular passion. Even though the upper middle class were not averse to adopting the mannerisms of that charmed

circle, they were equally ready to ridicule it. Intellectuals
were quick to brand all its members well-mannered block-
heads. Their affability in encounters with social inferiors – to
say nothing of instances of Tory democracy practised by
some titled politicians – had tended to perpetuate the rever-
ence accorded 'feudal' names in pre-war Vienna. The war
had reduced the popular regard for that 'first society'.
Though most of its scions held army commissions, few did
front line duty, while divisional headquarters were thick on
the ground with noblemen. One would have looked almost in
vain in the roster of generals for princely names such as had
given panache to the record of earlier Habsburg campaigns.
(Some archdukes had been put into high command; if not
mere figureheads, they had become notorious for their
blunders.) The Viennese middle classes, who even when
deriding bluebloods had felt the thrill of a vicarious participation in their mode of living, were asking themselves
whether such consistent self-protection in wartime was
within the privileges of a class whose escutcheons glorified
martial origins. They also began to question its ability to
serve the country and the Crown in high office.

In June 1917, Koerber's successor, Count Heinrich Clam-
Martinic, a Bohemian grandee, had resigned from the
Austrian premiership. Emperor Karl could not find a titled
man to fill the post and was reduced to entrusting it to one of
his childhood tutors, Ernst von Seidler, an undistinguished
bureaucrat. In his first speech in the *Reichsrat,* Seidler
announced that the government would set up a committee
of nationalities, and charge it with overhauling the
constitution.

The project fell into oblivion almost at once. About five
months after the prime minister's declaration, the army gave
a new lease on life to the Habsburg state as it was.

❧ 3 ❧

Thunder from the East

On 9 November the first news of the Bolshevik coup came to the Viennese. It made a deep impression on working people. The *Arbeiter Zeitung* called what had happened a 'revolution for peace' in its editorial, which went on to declare, 'The dictatorship of the proletariat has become a reality in St Petersburg. Our most passionate good wishes are with our Russian brothers. Issues that concern us ourselves, above all the issue of peace, are at stake in Russia.'

'Not for another hour must Austria prolong the war!' Victor Adler called out in the mass meeting arranged by the Social-Democratic party in Vienna's largest concert hall on 11 November, after he had considered the Russian suggestion of a peace without annexations or indemnities. 'We on our part must do our share ... in parliament, if possible, outside it, if necessary....' Those were fiery words, and a good many listeners must have thought them at odds with what they had for some time tended to call the pussyfooting of the party leaders in dealing with the government. In fact, several hundred of the eight thousand people the police estimated had come to the concert hall proceeded to march to the nearby Ministry of War and staged a noisy demonstration. The brief account Vienna's bourgeois papers carried of it, as of the meeting itself, was crowded out by the news of the great offensive that had started on the Italian front about two weeks earlier – the Twelfth Battle of the Isonzo, as it was called in Vienna, the Battle of Caporetto, as the appalled Allied capitals were to name it.

What looked like a decisive victory over 'treacherous Italy' worked like a tonic on the middle classes. Its impact on their mood was incomparably greater than the effect that the defeat of Rumania had produced ten months earlier, although that country, too, like the Italian kingdom, originally had gone over from alliance with the Central Powers to warring against them. What made Vienna's middle classes actually gloat over the rout of the Italian army was mainly the disdain they harboured for such Italian-speakers as they had met in their own city.

The mid-nineteenth-century liberation of the peninsula from virtual Habsburg domination had been won despite respectable successes of young Franz Josef's armed forces. The new kingdom of Italy had not united all Italian-speakers – there remained the *Italia irredenta* under the Habsburg flag. Of the inhabitants of those areas, latter-day Viennese by and large had seen only the poorest. They would come as road workers and street pavers, and out of that seasonal labour offer their brawn on doorsteps with the humble words *lavoro tutti* (I do any kind of work). True, informed people knew that Austria's Italian-speaking districts could boast of a sophisticated intelligentsia (whose irredentism exercised politicians in the Alpine provinces). But no Viennese was thinking of that group when catching a glimpse of some *Lavoratutti*. Even less would he recall the Italian architects, painters and musicians who in centuries past had enriched life and embellished the city. By the turn of the century that aloof contempt of the Viennese for the Italians in their midst had transferred itself to Italy herself – to her pretences as a great power, her trustworthiness as an ally, her military prowess.

That her troops had withstood Habsburg arms for two and a half years had embarrassed the military and set tongues wagging with censure. For a few days the triumphant breakthrough at Caporetto and the swift advance into enemy territory revived some of the robust self-assurance sweeping Vienna at the start of the war against Serbia. Moreover, the expected annihilation of the Italian forces seemed bound to stop the appalling bloodshed on the south-western front. With Russia knocked out of the war, and the German army undefeated in France, hopes for general peace no longer seemed a pipe-dream.

Harbingers of a life of plenty were making their appearance in Vienna. Families of fighting men were receiving by post parcels of rice, or sugar, or coffee, or a length of woollen or silken fabric – plunder garnered on the victorious march. The town of Udine with its apparently well-stocked shops and markets became a byword in Vienna. The quality of the gifts surprised the recipients and those who heard of the windfall. The newspapers had told the public over and over again that manpower shortage had crippled Italy's farms, and German U-boats strangled her supply of raw materials. The proof, now at hand, of those untruths was not alone in paling the pleasure. By the time the Caporetto campaign had ground to a halt at the River Piave, it became evident that not all of the soldiers' presents had reached their destination; and soon it was said that many parcels had been stolen by shady traffickers in collaboration with employees of the railway.

One was inured by then to under-the-counter offers of goods such as had vanished from the shelves of shopkeepers and, according to their accounts, were out of production. Most of the merchandise that was for sale on the black market was supposed to have changed hands several times in a process referred to as chain trade (*Kettenhandel*), and its secrecy embittered frustrated consumers nearly as much as did the exorbitant prices of such goods. Sometimes anger found an outlet in tales, true or invented, of the adventurous methods practised in that 'sneaking commerce' (*Schleich-handel*) and in the sardonic humour that spiced those accounts. Less playfully, lower-middle-class people took to blaming a conspicuous group of recent arrivals to Vienna for at least part of that trade.

'Polish' Jews, natives of Galicia or Bukovina, had by no means been unknown in pre-war Vienna. A fair number of them had settled in the town since the 1870s and gradually exchanged their Yiddish for the language of their new surroundings. Most had remained poor, a drain on the community of true-born Viennese Jews, sons or grandsons of immigrants from Bohemia, Moravia, Hungary, or the Rhineland. They considered the Polish Jews backward in their habits and unreliable in business. Ironic as this sounds today, the 'old' Jewish families frowned on intermarriage with them.

In the first weeks of the war hosts of Galician Jews fled their homes on the approach of the pogrom-happy tsarist battalions, and were shipped all the way to Vienna at the behest of the army anxious for manoeuvring space on its retreat. Even though the indigenous Jewry did not welcome the sudden influx, its charity, supplementing makeshift government help, kept the needy among the refugees from starving during the winter of 1914–15. Without employment, they tended to escape their overcrowded lodgings, and clusters of them could be seen sitting for hours in the small coffeehouses of Leopoldstadt, a traditionally Jewish neighbourhood, or simply standing about on street corners. Their Yiddish puzzled passers-by: portions of it sounded familiar, while the whole was apt to remind them of Lueger's demagogic suggestion that the 'Jews [had] invented a special kind of German for secrecy's sake'.[1] At the same time, those visibly anguished strangers were the first noncombatant victims of the war the Viennese saw with their own eyes; and pondering what might be in store for themselves, they could not help looking at the fugitives as a portent of calamities they might be fated to experience themselves.

After the army had recovered Galicia with German assistance in the spring of 1915, those ambivalent sentiments crystallized soon in plain aversion. Quite a few of the Galicians lingered on in Vienna, notably those who had nothing to return to in the war-torn province. They used to eke out a living as petty traders or middlemen in their home towns – and as middlemen they had been drawn into the nascent traffic in scarce goods in Vienna. Whatever their participation in it may have amounted to, their activities courted generalizations. From blaming the newcomers as such for that trade it was but one step to blaming them as Jews. Once that step had been taken, Jewish businessmen who had been settled in Vienna for a long time did not escape censure. Much as the small tradesmen of the preceding generation had regarded Jewish merchants and bankers as the embodiment of the vexing changes overcoming Vienna, so their sons now appeared as exponents of an economy that seemed to be running wild. Its disregard for the needs of the home front was but one source of resentment. As an ever larger part of manufacture became engaged in army contracting, and its profits and rumoured lack of scruples emerged as a topic of lower-middle-class talk, the 'Jewish army contractor' was a handy catchword in passing strictures on all businessmen, Jewish or Gentile, making their fortune in deliveries to the armed forces.

The animus toward banking and big business that had furthered the rise of Lueger's party, and which had weakened during its growth to respectability, did not as such come into the open again. But men who again felt that hostility stirring found some satisfaction in condemning mercenary industrialists and smart traders.

The Austrian harvest of 1917 had fallen below the most pessimistic predictions. Provincial governments, notably that of Bohemia, abetted hoarding on the large estates, and were deaf to requests from the central authorities to succour Vienna. The Office of War Supply, established under the presidency of Prince Ludwig Windischgrätz, a reputedly energetic man, was trying to induce the Hungarian administration to seize part of the harvest and ship grain and cattle to Vienna. In the countryside surrounding the city itself farmers more and more often refused to part with their produce. A chilly sense of isolation was creeping up on the urban population.

To provide a bottle of skimmed milk for one's children, push them into the queue at one of the volunteer-staffed bread centres the municipality had set up, persuade a cobbler to mend the family's shoes, or set out once again on the wearying search for a length of cloth not made wholly of shoddy material – those and countless similar errands sapped the strength of the undernourished women of both the lower middle class and the labouring population. No reasonable hope for relief lightened the burden of the men. The admonition of the government to stick it out (*durchzuhalten*), repeated over and over again, had long ceased affecting their

spirit. Whatever working men heard of disloyal acts on the
part of Slavs, or of the treacheries of their politicians abroad,
formed but an indistinct *obbligato* to the grind of their own
sordid lives.

The news from Russia was of a different kind. The first
trickle of released prisoners of war had come home, and even
though the military authorities, quick to appreciate the
menace of revolutionary infection, tried to keep them out of
industrial centres, tales of the new order in Russia had begun
to penetrate Vienna's workmen's districts. While official news
stressed the chaos in the Russian army, the proletarians
savoured instances, reported by soldiers on leave, of frater-
nization in the front line. Their own attention was riveted on
the peace negotiations that had opened in the Polish town of
Brest-Litovsk. They seemed to be getting under way too
slowly for the taste of the undernourished masses. At least
some of them had seen the inflammatory broadsheet a small
group of radical socialist dissenters had put out; and a great
many were getting tired of the admonition, emphasized in
scores of peace meetings organized by the Social-Democratic
party, to refrain from disturbances of the domestic peace. It
would appear that Vienna's middle classes were widely
ignorant of the smouldering restlessness among workers.

They themselves had been in a dazed state of dejection
ever since the offensive in Italy petered out on the Tyrolian
mountains and at the River Piave in the first days of
December. The record of hundreds of thousands of prisoners
taken and hundreds of heavy guns captured could not miti-
gate the sense of failure. The *Neue Freie Presse* itself con-
ceded that the Dual Monarchy was 'yearning for peace', and
added that it was 'the only belligerent whose population is as
one in that respect'.

The great newspaper regularly gave pride of place to the
most bizarre innovations within defeated Russia. The threat
of 'exporting revolution' which Trotsky had thrown into the
Brest-Litovsk talks appeared as but a tactical move to the
editorialist in Vienna. He could see no sign of approaching
world revolution. And neither could his readers. That spectre
worried the middle classes less than did the ever more
forward pronouncements of the expatriates, the accounts of

which in the press only served to keep anxieties in a state of confusion.

It was not unknown that the 'wretched' Masaryk (as the foreign minister called him) had made a trip to Russia in the past spring. But little had filtered through to the public of the main purpose of his journey – the recruitment of Czech and Slovak prisoners of war as volunteers for a legion under Allied command. The first stories of the existence in Russia of an army of Austrian defectors were brought to Vienna by soldiers who had faced one of its battalions in battle in August (and seen captives of that unit summarily hanged). Soon rumours of hundreds of thousands of those 'armed traitors' were springing up. The Viennese did not learn for a long time of the incidents that brought the Czechoslovak Legion into conflict with Bolshevik forces; and thus the Legionnaires were spoken of as bloodthirsty revolutionists, as well as traitors to emperor and country.

While the lower middle class were dynastic-minded as a matter of course, the upper middle class also felt that such was the course of reason. So closely interwoven were the economic interests of the various parts of the country that men accustomed to take the primacy of economic life for granted were unable to imagine its ties as no longer existing. The realities of the Habsburg state, its highly developed communications, its increased industrialization, its largely self-supporting farm production, were too obvious and too strong to be made a shambles of by 'mere' treason!

A sensation was caused in July when an amnesty freed all civilians military courts had sentenced for sedition or treason, including the four Czech politicians who in May 1916 had been sentenced to death. If some Viennese had hoped that the show of royal mercy might help resolve the country's dilemma, the unabated manifestations of Slav particularism threw them into deeper dejection. So did the abusive reception most German deputies gave their amnestied colleagues in the Lower House of the *Reichsrat*. Practically no one agreed with Heinrich Lammasch, a distinguished university teacher of unswerving pacifist persuasion, who in a French-language periodical published in Vienna asserted that the Habsburg state had 'made extraordinary progress in the therapeutic treatment of nationalism'. Yet, paradoxically, that scepticism did not displace fully the old trust in the intrinsic strength of what Vienna's savants had long before termed the 'Austrian idea'.

The lower middle class nurtured a simpler faith. Whatever their tribulations, its members believed in the return, no matter how slowly, of the 'normality' of peacetime. As if to ward off the shadows closing in on them, they made a point of not letting go of the trappings of Old Vienna. Such musicians as still performed in the winehouses of the outskirts in the winter of 1917–18 were asked regularly to strike up some of the exuberant, or maudlin, pieces of nineteenth-century vintage. Likewise, the sentimental song that had assured the 'heavy-hearted Old Gentleman in Schönbrunn' of 'how glad the city is to have you' (popular in 1915), could still be heard rising from the throats of *Heurigen* patrons, half a dirge, half something like a defiant local anthem. . . .

The Red Cross had as early as 1915 organized distributions of Christmas presents, complete with candle-lit tree and carol singing, to children of soldiers killed in action. The bourgeois press devoted a good deal of space to those celebrations. In 1917 the empress herself made an appearance at one of the pre-Christmas fêtes. To the dismay of her suite considerably fewer children turned up than had been expected. Trams ran at very long intervals only, and the worn-out shoes of the children had not allowed them to walk the snow-swept streets all the way from the outlying districts to the Inner City mansion the court had chosen for the occasion.

On 31 December Josef Redlich recorded in his diary the appointments he had kept during the day, bewailed the inclement weather, speculated on 'technology, natural science, and capitalism which have robbed men of their souls', made a nostalgic note on two early Victorian novels he had finished reading, and closed as follows : 'No one knows where the maelstrom of sanguinary events will drift us. But I am certain that we will have to live through the worst to make all of us on this earth lastingly better and more reasonable.' Redlich is unlikely to have opened his journal that night to the entry of 26 July 1914. On 25 July his brother had visited him and the two had agreed that 'Serb acceptance [of Austria-Hungary's ultimatum] would be a disaster. The enthusiasm of the Viennese would turn out to have had nothing to be enthusiastic about.' Redlich's brother, on that fateful day, stayed with him till 7.15 p.m. Calling him shortly thereafter, he reported that, 'according to what I just heard, Serbia has rejected everything'. (The hearsay was inaccurate, but that even the professor, well-informed as a rule, was to learn only a week later.) Within five minutes the telephone in his study was ringing again. 'It was Count Kinsky. He said, "[Our ambassador to Serbia] has left Belgrade." "Hurrah!" I rejoined.'

On 15 January 1918, the Austrian government reduced the daily flour ration from 200 to 150 grams. No sooner had the news reached the shops of the Daimler plant at Wiener Neustadt than the 10,000 men employed there laid down their tools. At 11 a.m. they had assembled for a demonstration, and soon after were joined by the workers of the other factories of the town, one of the industrial centres of the country, twenty-five miles south-west of the capital.

While the Social-Democratic executive in Vienna, caught by surprise, was trying desperately to reason by telephone with the union leaders at Wiener Neustadt – who confessed to be helpless – an ominous report from the local police was received by the government: the excited strikers, marching on the town hall and loudly demanding the repeal of the 'hunger edict', were also shouting for the election of councils from their ranks. The authorities had no doubt but that some repatriated P.O.W.s from Russia were among the demonstrators. Cooler observers suggested that it was peace the workers clamoured for – immediate peace.

The labouring masses of the country were as uninformed as the rest of the population on the day-by-day conduct of the negotiations in Brest-Litovsk. But though they were ignorant of Count Czernin's growing subservience to his German colleagues at the conference table, working men had grown suspicious of the sluggish progress of the talks. Back in October, their leaders had shocked them by approving, with only mild qualifications, the policies of the government;

and their altered pronouncements since the outbreak of the
Russian revolution had grown less and less forceful since the
mass meeting of 11 November. A radical broadsheet had
been circulating in some of the workshops, and not the least
of its demands was for the election of peace delegates 'by the
people'.

The party executive now made haste to catch up with the
mood of the strikers. Within twenty-four hours, the movement had spread to Vienna, and before another three days
were over, Lower Austria, Styria and the Tyrol were in its
grip, and Moravia's capital was strike-bound; even in
Budapest, where no reduction of the flour ration had been
decreed, the armament workers had walked out of their
plants. Nor was the stoppage of work confined to industrial
enterprises. By 17 January the sales and clerical personnel of
some of Vienna's retail merchants had halted work, as (to the
indignation of upper-class women) had the employees of the
fashionable custom tailors.

Tempers were running high, if less so in Vienna than in the
industrial towns of Lower Austria. But there were no acts of
violence. Victor Adler, convincing the Austrian premier that
no revolutionary situation had developed, wrung from him
the pledge that the censor would not interfere with the
publication of a party manifesto likely to lead the strikers
back to work. Printed in the *Arbeiter Zeitung*, it not only
stated that the war must be ended forthwith, but also
warned the government against any attempt to extort territorial concessions from prostrate Russia. To the surprise of
the workers, who surely had given no thought to the
'nationalities problem' when quitting their workshops, the
manifesto also declared the party to be in agreement with
the principle of self-determination for all nations, big and
small, as proclaimed by Woodrow Wilson on 8 January.

As early as 1899 the Austrian Social-Democratic party had
enunciated something akin to that doctrine with regard to
the 'nationalities' of the Habsburg state. Without taking
issue with its right to exist, that resolution had suggested
their union in a 'federation of free peoples'. Later, a rather
quixotic interpretation of that idea had surfaced in the
scholarly writings of Karl Renner. Otto Bauer, for one, had

attacked Renner's blueprint for offering 'mere administrative reforms' as a panacea for the gravest ill of the country.

A few short weeks after his return from Russian captivity in September 1917, Bauer presented his blueprint to his colleagues. He advocated the convocation of constituent assemblies by the various nationalities, and professed to be certain that those gatherings would need no prodding to set up the machinery for regulating the affairs common to them all. The idea found reluctant acceptance. 'We also arrived at the conclusion,' Bauer writes in his memoirs of those weeks, 'that, should national revolution[s] break out, the working-class must under no circumstances align itself with the counter-revolutionary forces – the dynasty, the Austro-German bourgeoisie, and the Magyar gentry – in a defence of the Habsburg state against the rebelling nationalities....' Recalling that thought, Bauer also outlines its far-reaching implications. 'If we thus recognized the claim of the Slav peoples [of the Monarchy] to self-determination, we [Austro-Germans] could claim justly the same right for ourselves. If the Slav peoples gained freedom and unity in new nation-states, we must likewise try to make a reality ... of the idea of [ethnic] unity through *Anschluss* to the *Reich*.'[2] It may be safely assumed that, throwing out the contingency plan, Bauer was not forgetful of the two powerful socialist factions in the German parliament.

The great strike, erupting with such suddenness, brought the Socialist leadership face to face with a concern more pressing than the future disposal of the abandoned German-Austria that Bauer foresaw. Should radicals get the upper hand, and their wild talk of 'councils' panic the government into a separate peace with 'the first socialist country in the world', Germany's generals would not hesitate to transfer the bulk of their eastern army, now expendable in Russia, to Habsburg territory. The party executive in Vienna may have felt relieved watching the swift application of the time-honoured Habsburg nostrum for upholding public order in moments of crisis. Six divisions of 'foreign' troops – Bosnians, Ruthenes, and Rumanian-speakers – were dispatched into the strike-ridden, German-speaking towns. Their mere appearance broke the momentum of the movement, which had failed to grow into a country-wide general strike on account of the half-heartedness of the Czech sister party. On 19 January the executive, in a stormy conference with the strike-born 'workers' council', received its approval for having the strike called off on 21 January.

When the week-long nightmare was lifted from Vienna's middle classes, they awoke to the fact that the worst of their fears had not come true: although 200,000 men and women had stopped work in Vienna, no demonstrations or marches on government buildings had taken place, no harangues had been heard in the streets and no property had been harmed. True, heavy snowfalls had clogged thoroughfares and squares, and the municipality had been slow in calling out its removal squads. Yet the apparent self-restraint of the strikers was remarked on with some appreciation. That frame of mind also tempered the amazement when it was learned that the prime minister had received a delegation of the workers' councils on 19 January and, in addition to promising an improvement in the supply of defence workers' food and a reform of the army control of war plants, had handed those extraordinary representatives a letter in which Count Czernin pledged a speedy conclusion of the Brest-Litovsk negotiations, unhampered by territorial demands on Russia. While the upper middle class resented what amounted to workers' interference with government decisions, humbler folk merely wondered at the apparent ease with which the foreign minister had yielded to such pressure. They were asking themselves whether Czernin's solemn promise, 'extorted' or not, might not indeed bring peace closer.

With the spectre of revolution receding, the lower middle class also became conscious of the grain of satisfaction in the curiosity that made it listen to tales of generals humiliated and rich men chastened in the new topsy-turvy Russia. Vienna's Little Man, too, was growing impatient with the meddlesome bureaucrats, the ubiquitous military, and the high-living profiteers. He did not realize that such feelings were straining his patriotism. But less than three weeks after the strike had ended, his patriotism was buoyed by a sensational turn of events.

On 8 February the Central Powers signed a treaty of peace

with the Ukraine, Russia's south-western province which
was outside the Bolsheviks' grip, and whose sovereignty had
been recognized on 7 February by Czernin and his German
counterpart at Brest-Litovsk. The puzzling Russian reaction
to that coup – Trotsky left the conference, declaring the war
ended – did not spoil the exultation of the Viennese over
the agreement with the newly created republic, whose
reportedly bulging granaries a commercial treaty promised
to throw open. Tens of thousands of middle-class men and
women took to the streets of the Inner City to hail the 'bread
peace'. Flags had been hoisted on public buildings and
apartment houses; student fraternities donned their colourful
costumes to march in parades; and on 10 February the
archbishop celebrated a Thanksgiving Mass at St Stephen's
in the presence of the imperial couple. Spontaneous out-
breaks of jubilation lasted for days. The military band that
performed in the courtyard of the Hofburg at noontime, and
which had been losing much of its public over the past year,
found itself playing to a large audience again. If workmen
thought that Czernin had gone back on his promise of 'no
territorial demands upon Russia', they kept silent. In their
homes, too, there was much talk of the grain from the
Ukraine.

Meanwhile, the German army had begun marching deeper
into Russia, ostensibly to 'force the defeated enemy back to
the conference table'. To knowledgeable men it was obvious
that the establishment of the Ukrainian client state had not
sated the expansionist appetite of the German generals. The
Neue Freie Presse, which had rarely, if ever, questioned the
strategic wisdom of the great ally, expressed the hope that
the new offensive, in which some Habsburg divisions participated, would be 'restricted to operations necessary for keeping open the lines of communication with the Ukraine'.
Much significance was also seen in the evident self-restraint
of the censor who did not red-pencil the *Arbeiter Zeitung*
when it declared in a blunt editorial, 'This is no longer a war
of defence ... and Austria is not willing to wage a war of
conquest for the benefit of an ally.' Russia was brought to her
knees on 3 March. She renounced roughly a third of her

arable and nearly all of her industry and coal mines, and lost a good third of her population.

The signing of the treaty did not halt the movement of the victors' army. On 13 March its Austrian wing reached Odessa. It was from that Black Sea port, so the bourgeois papers in Vienna reported some weeks later, that Marie Jeritza, its darling opera star, who had journeyed there to entertain the troops, shipped a quantity of provisions to her relatives in the capital. These were among the few Viennese ever to see anything of the much-heralded Ukrainian cornucopia.

❧ 4 ❧

'A Catastrophe
for the Dynasty . . .'

The number of men wounded in combat, as well as the
legions of fatalities, had overtaxed the imagination ever
since the great battle that had swept the tsarist army from
Galicia. People who themselves had no hospitalized son or
husband had come to avoid thinking about the outlandish
mutilations modern warfare inflicted. The press touched but
lightly on the painful subject. Stories of the rehabilitation of
handicapped men by novel means met with a good deal
of scepticism; paradoxically, lower-middle-class Viennese,
while not ignorant of the world-fame of their Medical
School, were doubtful of its discoveries. Rumours of what
was going on in a particular hospital kept tongues wagging
in the winter of 1917–18 – the rumour-mongers were reluctant to mention by name the venereal disease for whose
treatment the rooms of the old building had been equipped,
and were prone to condemn the novel therapy of inducing
high fever as unscrupulous experimenting. It was in those
months also that a special medical-corps commission set up
to comb hospitals for malingerers became notorious. There
was a trace of romantic enjoyment in the stories current
about the 'green cadres', smallish bands of deserters who
roamed and poached in the forests of Bosnia, south-eastern
Hungary, or Styria. Working-class people could be heard
suggesting that, whatever the transgressions of those
marauders, they at least had had the good sense to take
themselves out of the slaughter. A whiff of that attitude had
been noticeable in the ambivalent way in which the Socialist

press had reported the great mutinies in the French army the past summer. The bourgeois press had gloated over them. Once it turned out that the abortive rebellion had not broken the fighting spirit of the French army, men of the middle-class satisfied themselves that, like the French generals, the Habsburg commanders would know how to deal with muti-nous troops.

They did. On 1 February, the crews of the Fifth Fleet mutinied in the Gulf of Cattaro (Kotor). At noon, its flagship fired a cannon shot, the band struck up the *Marseillaise*, and red flags went up on all vessels. Although the sailors took over the ships' command smoothly, the rebellion was never-theless to collapse within forty-eight hours. As the coastal guns were being trained on the mutinous men-of-war, and the Third Fleet was steaming into the gulf, the rebels surrendered.

The government managed to suppress the Cattaro story. Only after courts martial and hangman had done their work did the Socialist executive hear of the mutiny through a party member who happened to do army duty on the coast. The Socialist leaders refrained from giving pub-licity to the events of Cattaro – they were, it would seem, dreading an upsurge of radical elements. (Not until 10 October did the *Arbeiter Zeitung* print a report.) Yet rumours of restlessness in the navy were circulating in Vienna during the fortnight that followed the Ukrainian 'bread peace'. The euphoria those glad tidings produced stifled the untoward gossip. The navy had not been much in the thoughts of landlocked Vienna ever since Allied flotillas bottled up the Austro-Hungarian warships in their ports late in 1916. (They were in the main manned by South-Slav conscripts; few Viennese were in the crews.) That near-indifference may have helped the conspiracies of silence, and these, in turn, spared the middle class a shock certain to have weakened its confidence in the Habsburg forces as a dependable instrument of the state.

Strange to say, the multinational Habsburg army had retained a life of its own throughout the decades of national bickerings and the nationalities' struggles. Although German was the 'language of command', its slim vocabulary, in effect a handy code, did not offend the ethnic sensibilities of non-German soldiers. Ethnic considerations did not affect the recruitment for the officers' corps, or promotion in it. Young Slavs who had gained reserve commissions in the course of the war nevertheless were wary, for discipline's sake or to protect their status, of letting co-national soldiers appeal to brotherly sympathies. Nor, from late 1917 on, were such Slav subalterns, as middle-class boys, altogether impervious to the German middle-class notion of a Bolshevik element in lower-class Slav chauvinism.

It has often been asked what checked its thrust at a time when the exiles' messages and their echoes at home were becoming familiar to Slav front-line soldiers. Scholars in Vienna loved to speak of the army as the embodiment of the 'Austrian idea' whose essence was 'supra-nationalism'. The facts were less grand. The sense of cohesion in low-echelon units was still strong enough to ensure that personal dissatisfactions were kept in check, and continued to give the men a feeling of security, however illusory, amid the perils of warfare. Moreover, commanders made no secret of the bloody vengeance brought down on apprehended defectors. Be that as it may, the ethnic tensions within the army were given priority at supreme headquarters only to the extent of trying to keep enemy propaganda away from the troops. The authorities' satisfaction at the performance of the army during the great strike had been heightened by the fact that Slav regiments had executed the ordered actions.

If soldiers and workers had united to topple the dynasty in Russia, no similar union appeared to be nascent in the Habsburg realm. And Emperor Karl decided to use his soldiers to ward off a renewed upsurge on the part of the workers. Without consulting anyone, he summoned a high-born general and offered him the virtual dictatorship of the country, based on the army. 'I had to talk to the emperor without equivocations,' Prince Schönburg-Hartenstein recalls in his memoirs, 'for I had heard from different sources that the emperor, after conferring with [a succession of] personages, was likely to follow the last advice he had been given.'[1] Whoever Karl may have listened to after the prince had submitted to him 'efficacious means for restoring authority in the centre', nothing came of the royal project (and no one in wartime Vienna was ever to learn of it). As it turned out, no *coup d'état* was needed to have the home front policed *de facto* by ever larger army formations.

Vienna's *haute bourgeoisie* had misinterpreted the breakdown of the strike. They mistook their vested interests for the actual power they themselves commanded. The dreaded social revolution had not come to pass; why, then, should 'national revolutions'? Transferring their own lack of imagination to the Slav malcontents, upper-middle-class people kept deceiving themselves about the portents of rebellion that came to their attention. After the audience in Prague's opera house had staged a nationalist demonstration at a new production of Smetana's *Libuša*, Vienna's music lovers deplored eloquently that 'defiling of art' and few disapproved of the authorities' decision to forbid further performances of the Czech classic.

On 28 February the *Neue Freie Presse* printed an odd little story on one of its back pages. During the *Reichsrat* debate of 27 February an army captain had risen to his feet in the visitors' gallery, and interrupted the proceedings. The Speaker, overruling shouts of protest, encouraged the officer to go on with what he wished to say.

> I am a German [Austrian] the man declared, and I have been doing service with a Serbo-Croat regiment for more than three years. I am proud of my German heritage, and worried about what the future may hold in store for the Germans [in Austria]. For a long time I've been burning with the desire to speak up – to say that, having come to know Serbo-Croat men, I came to realize their worth. The stance my own people has assumed toward them torments my thoughts. I have been waiting for the [Austro-] Germans to give that nation its due at long last. Instead, Serbo-Croats could not possibly be treated worse than they are.

Turned over to the army authorities, the lonely demonstrator, so the journal reported, had been put under psychiatric observation.

Directly the first news of the opening of a great German

offensive came to Vienna, Josef Redlich confided to his journal, 'Despite the mighty successes of Messrs Hindenburg and Ludendorff, the prevailing mood here is one of glum discontent. The populace no longer expects any good to come from the shedding of blood. They simply don't believe that German victories can bring peace.'

Not that they themselves would have known what could bring peace. A definite lassitude had begun to enter their reactions. Behind the Viennese garrulity, there had always lurked inertia. 'Under the circumstances there's not a thing one can do', had been a saying ever-ready among them. Only once in the past fifty years had the lower middle class acted – they had given their votes to Lueger. Not much had been left of his original gospel save the aversion to Jews and a sentimental dynasticism blending with parochial pride. Gritting their teeth as they watched the selfishness of the Hungarians in provisioning their city, they loved to quote Lueger's sardonic catchword of 'Judeo-Magyars'. His authority could not be adduced in the increasingly bitter talk about treacherous Czechs. Nor had the lower middle class ever acknowledged the fact that the Ruthenes in eastern Galicia constituted a nation; as now, referring to their kinship with the 'liberated' Ukrainians, the Ruthenes, too, put in a claim to national self-determination, the Little Man of Vienna threw up his hands in incomprehension. He scarcely took any notice of the vanishing prospect of the creation of a Greater Poland with an Habsburg prince as its king, hinted at for months by the press.

The tradesmen, small-property owners, schoolteachers and lowly bureaucrats, huddling over their cups of barley-and-chicory *Kaffee* in surburban coffeehouses, showed in their eyes, as in their very frames, the listlessness that less than adequate nourishment produces. A faint smell betraying the shortage of soap hovered over the groups of those late-afternoon regulars in the rarely aired places. The cafés of the more privileged districts still offered their patrons, free of charge, a choice of periodicals and newspapers fastened to bamboo poles. Educated people flattered themselves that they could cull the truth from neutral countries' journals or, conversely, from their not reaching Vienna on certain days. In actual fact, the circumspect reportage of their own press, alongside its harping on the 'lying Northcliffe propaganda', had reduced the credibility of all printed stories, and threw the reader back on rumours and guesswork. There was no dearth of either in upper-middle-class Vienna in early 1918. On the whole those circles had found no fault with the draconian treatment of defeated Russia. It had eliminated her as a great power for the foreseeable future. One could also say that the creation of 'independent' states on former Russian territory conformed to the doctrine of the self-determination of all nations.

Its applicability to the nationalities of the Habsburg state seemed to have become less urgent with the British prime minister's declaration on 5 January that 'the break-up of the Austrian-Hungarian Monarchy [was] no part of the war aims of the Allies'. To be sure, there was little secret about the convention called together in Prague on 6 January. But though its attendants – the Czech *Reichsrat* deputies, the Czech members of the Bohemian and Moravian Diets and a number of Slovak politicians – had demanded a 'sovereign state of our own, including [Hungary's] Slovakia', Vienna's upper middle class persuaded themselves that such an autonomy might be squared somehow with Lloyd George's reassuring declaration. The stress he had put on the 'genuine self-government' to be granted to the nationalities of the Habsburg state did not really upset men who for a long time had been talking, no matter how casually, about federalization.

Yet, to use a contemporary expression whose vagueness did justice to the prevailing sentiment, Vienna's middle classes were 'German-minded'. At that juncture, that cast of mind fitted a renewed confidence in a *Reich* whose triumph would safeguard the permanence of the Habsburg state. 'We will, for we must, be victorious' (*Wir werden siegen, weil wir siegen müssen*) had its own specious reasoning. The 'peace without annexations and reparations', a concept suspicious enough through its advocacy by Socialist spokesmen, could not be seen as one that would heal the wounds suffered by the economy, and keep Austria-Hungary viable as one of the great powers. Business men knew only too well that oceans of paper money had been printed, and were cognizant of the alarming quotations for the Austro-Hungarian currency on

Swiss and Dutch bourses. They did not care to doubt the assertion of their press that Germany's great offensive represented the turning point of the war. It was not a fanatic pan-German, but a Christian-Social deputy who exclaimed in the *Reichsrat,* 'We are the victors, and we demand victory's prize.'

On 2 April, Count Czernin delivered himself of a speech at the town hall in response to a mayoral address thanking him for having concluded the 'bread peace'. In the course of his oration, Czernin touched on the prospects of a general peace settlement, and mentioned certain overtures received from Clemenceau, the French premier. 'I replied immediately that, as far as France was concerned, I could see no obstacle to the restoration of peace except for her claim to Alsace-Lorraine. The French answer, alas, made it clear that negotiations were not feasible on that basis.' Four days passed before the French news agency put out a notice reminding Czernin that 'some time ago a personage of far higher station than he had approached Paris with a definite proposal for peace.' Yes, Czernin admitted promptly in a press release, there had been earlier exchanges : 'but these had proved just as futile as the later ones did, inasmuch as France at that time, too, had refused to drop her insistence on the return of Alsace-Lorraine [ceded to Germany after the war of 1870–71]'. Clemenceau lost no time retorting. On that matter, he declared, no less a person than Count Czernin's master had spoken the last word. 'His Majesty, Emperor Karl, writing to Prince Sixtus of Bourbon-Parma', one of the empress's brothers, had 'expressed his own unconditional support of France's just claim to Alsace-Lorraine, and in a subsequent communication made it clear that he was acting in agreement with his minister [of foreign affairs].' Some days later, the text of Karl's letter, dated 24 March 1917, was published in Paris, and when Czernin – who had been incompletely informed to begin with and upon the French revelation had compelled the frightened monarch into prevarications – branded the letter a forgery, Clemenceau had a photostat reproduced in a Paris weekly.

It was not seen by the public in Vienna. But the circumlocutions of the bourgeois press, echoing increasingly

awkward government declarations, only served to aggravate
the sensation. The lower middle class reacted to it at first in a
surprising manner. Recalling the emperor's pledge on his
accession to bring peace, unsophisticated people felt grati-
fied to learn that he had at least tried to redeem his promise.

The upper middle class reacted differently. As Vienna's
police headquarters put it in its routine report to the Ministry of the Interior on public opinion, 'the contents of the
[emperor's] letter have filled educated German-minded citizens with indignation.'[2] The disclosure of Karl's attempt to
present the Kaiser with a *fait accompli* shocked even those
who had been irritated by what was known of the pressures
that his generals had brought to bear on Czernin at Brest-
Litovsk. To make things worse, Karl's faithlessness was
divulged in the very days when the thrust of the German
army in the west seemed to have lost its momentum, and the
arrival in France of the first American units gave the lie to
the oft-repeated assurance that U-boats would play havoc
with their transport. 'Anyone who has spent the last months
in Austria cannot but wonder at the effect on public opinion
here of the Sixtus affair,' the German ambassador reported
from Vienna. 'Before, criticism of the German ally was
plentiful . . . [and] one could believe that there was a strong
desire to break away from the *Reich*. Now, however, when
the alliance is in danger, protests against such a policy are
being raised. . . .'[3] Wits, in a play on words based on the
designation of Dual Monarchy widely used for the Habsburg
state, suggested that Emperor Karl had now proved to be a
'dual monarch' indeed, allied with Germany and at the same
time dickering with the French. In actual fact, what agitated
educated men and women was not moral indignation. It was
the angry amazement at the dilettantism, now revealed, that
had marked, and doomed, Karl's personal foray into foreign
affairs. To quote police headquarters' pointed allusion to the
twenty-three-year-old empress and her brother, there was
'widespread grumbling about the influence that irresponsible
persons have gained on the conduct of foreign affairs'.

Karl's consort, Zita, was one of the numerous daughters of
the late Duke Robert of Parma, whose dynasty had been
compelled, in 1859, to cede its duchy to the new Italian

kingdom, and who had spent much of his life in comfortable
retirement in the Austrian countryside. Upon Karl's accession, Vienna's middle classes had welcomed the comely
young empress. It was the high aristocracy that first took her
full measure, and behind the poised demeanour espied a very
strong will, together with a desire for a share in royal
business. Nor was that all. The 'three foreign ladies' – Karl's
Saxon stepmother, his Italian-born wife, and her Portuguese
mother – became a common phrase in the rooms of the
Jockey Club. Its pedigreed members had grown concerned
about the inexperienced women whose closeness to Karl
some of the noblemen had been observing in their ceremonial offices at court. Apprehension had been mounting lest
the ladies' counsel should harm the prestige of the Crown.
The Sixtus scandal confirmed the worst fears. And, as it
happened, another discreditable story was making the
rounds at the Foreign Office, a department staffed chiefly
with aristocrats.

It would seem that the Dowager Duchess of Parma had
purchased large quantities of coffee and cocoa in Spain
through some local agent, and was planning to have these
goods – commodities unobtainable throughout the Monarchy – shipped to the port of Trieste. Czernin, having got
wind of the matter, ordered one of his subordinates, Count
Demblin, to apprise the monarch of it. Karl was taken aback,
and instantly promised to talk to his mother-in-law. In a
following audience he informed Demblin that a coffee and
cocoa purchase had in fact been made, and the shipment
earmarked for charitable distribution. Within a few days,
however, an Hungarian officer belonging to the entourage of
the duchess ran into Demblin in the corridors of the Foreign
Office, and told him that the Parma family expected 'to make
a profit of millions on the transaction'. At Czernin's request,
Demblin now warned the emperor that the duchess
appeared to have fallen prey to some swindlers in Spain, and
Czernin himself, although by then in acrimonious conflict
with Karl over the Sixtus correspondence, implored him to
have the harbour command of Trieste seize the cargo upon
arrival. Whatever the truth may have been – there is no
evidence that any such goods were landed at an Austrian or

Hungarian port at that time, and the whole story rests on a
memoir published by Demblin after the collapse of the
Habsburg state – the tale was retold freely in noblemen's
mansions, and soon reached the drawing rooms of the middle
classes, and even seeped down to common people. It
coloured their view of the weak young emperor and his ill-
fated search for peace. It was asked whether he might not,
after all, have succeeded, if he had not entrusted the mission
to his young brother-in-law, and become enmeshed in what
may well have been a self-seeking Bourbon intrigue. Sixtus's
service in the Belgian army, before then unknown to humble
folk, seemed ominous in the context of the miscarried 'peace
offensive'. *Six d'es?* they would pun, in broad dialect, on his
name. (Do you see that?)

The upper middle class saw no occasion for joking. The
more they learned about the Sixtus affair, the more its messy
record appalled them. The announcement of Czernin's resignation meant more rumours. Whether one viewed Karl's lack
of candour *vis-à-vis* Czernin as a concomitant of his inepti-
tude only, or as duplicity pure and simple, Vienna's bourgeoisie were agreed that he had gambled away the mystique
of the Crown. Only now did they grasp how much of that
mystique had been tied to Franz Josef's person – to his
uncanny reserve, to his stubbornness in keeping his family in
its place, and to the aura of probity, at once comfortingly
philistine and impressively aristocratic, he had attained in
the loneliness of old age. It is significant of the preoccupation with scandals in high quarters that an event of
great moment, which nearly coincided with the Sixtus and
Parma imbroglios, gave rise to hardly any discussion in
Vienna.

Late in April, the expatriate politicians assembled in Rome
to iron out their internecine differences, and consolidate the
forces determined to dismantle the Habsburg state. Their
fiery oratory reached the Allied governments while the consequences of Clemenceau's disclosure of Prince Sixtus'
mission were destroying their last hope for a separate peace
with the Habsburg state and its preservation as a post-war
counterpoise to the *Reich*. Czernin's successor, Count
Stephan Burián, an Hungarian of limited scope, may have

had some sombre thoughts of his own on the 'Congress of Oppressed Nationalities' and its influence on the shaping of Allied war aims; public opinion in Vienna was taking both in its stride. The farthest the *Neue Freie Presse* went in commenting on the speeches in Rome was to admonish the German deputies in the *Reichsrat* to 'guard their language so as not to pour oil on the flames of hostile propaganda'. A Berlin journal came fairly close to speaking the mind of Vienna's middle classes when it called the Rome assemblage 'the traitors' congress gathered together by the Italian gallows birds', in other words, the statesmen who in April 1915 had abandoned the Central powers and turned against them.

Some apologists during the Sixtus controversy recalled that *volte-face*. Had not the Kaiser's diplomats, bargaining on its eve for Italy's neutrality, admitted the justice of her claim to the Trentino part of Austria's Tyrol? And had not Karl now merely repaid the Kaiser in kind by recognizing the French claim to Alsace-Lorraine? Such rare defenders of Karl were promptly reminded that, unlike the Kaiser in 1915, Karl had left his ally in the dark about the price he was expected to pay. 'Catastrophe is the least of the words on everybody's lips today', J. M. Baernreither, a former cabinet minister and member of the Upper Chamber, wrote in his diary on 15 April. 'It is a catastrophe for the dynasty and the country, for the alliance and for our domestic situation.'[4] No one in Vienna had any illusions about the savage mood at the Kaiser's headquarters when Karl and Zita set out on 10 May to call there upon urgent invitation.

The *communiqué* published three days later left no doubt about what had been arrived at there. Not only had the Germans bullied Karl into forswearing all further unilateral moves toward peace; they had also extracted from him the promise that he would have his foreign office sign a number of new agreements with the *Reich* drafted to deepen and strengthen the alliance in every field. Little acumen was needed to foresee that those agreements reduced the Habsburg state to little more than a satellite of Germany.

That prospect did not as such mortify the middle classes. Only when it dawned on them that the *Reich*'s dominance could not but antagonize the Slav Habsburg subjects still more, did educated men gauge the mortal dangers to the country's survival. The supercilious, if not indeed wilful, lack of attention to its 'nationalities' problem' that the men in Berlin had never concealed may still have appealed to some diehards among Austria's German middle classes. It only served to compound the pessimism of their majority. Nearly every day brought still another story of Slav sedition. None exercised men of affairs more than the indictment for high treason of the president of Prague's largest bank, who stood accused of having advised its clients against purchasing war bonds. Having always thought highly of that man's financial judgment, Vienna's bankers could not persuade themselves that Czech chauvinism alone had motivated the action deemed criminal by the administration.

The imperial couple had not yet returned from German headquarters when news broke in Vienna of a serious, if small-scale, disturbance in an army training camp in Styria. The mutineers, punished without delay or mercy, had been Slovene recruits. Whether national passion, insufficiency of food, or Bolshevik propaganda, had caused the riot was left unanswered in the truncated reports. When another, larger mutiny occurred in a camp in northern Bohemia, and the story came to Vienna, complete again with the hangman's record, it was rumoured that the mutinous Czech battalion had in fact consisted of returned prisoners of war from Russia. A new term coined by the army had by that time entered the public's language – 'politically unreliable men', or 'p.u.s' (*politisch Unverlässliche*).

The most telling episode of the mutiny in Styria remained unreported in Vienna, and gossip failed to relate it. 'Up with the Bolsheviks', the Slovene soldiers had been chanting and 'Down with the war!' But they had also shouted, 'Long live bread!' The outcry would have been understood by all classes in Vienna. Even households who now and then were provided under the counter with meat by their butcher at exorbitant prices had to make do with a greyish, tough-grained kind of *ersatz* bread. As the days grew longer, a good many lower-middle-class people took to staying away from work on a weekday to look for provisions outside the city

before the numerous Sunday competitors arrived. More and
more often they encountered farmers adamant in their
refusal to part with produce in exchange for legal tender.
Tales of Oriental rugs, pianos or fur coats, acquired by
peasants from townsfolk in uneven barter were in circulation, and became no less provocative for their being
accompanied by ridicule heaped on the new tastes of the
G'scherte (literally, round-heads), as the Viennese had called
rustics since time immemorial.

As property became less and less secure in the countryside,
gendarmes tended to blame stray army deserters for the
pilfering from farm barns. Some enlightened officials
referred to the large number of urban adolescents who had
grown up during the absence of soldiering fathers and were
poorly controlled by mothers who did factory work. In some
cases, small-time black-market dealers could be apprehended for having organized thefts of foodstuffs. But the
authorities knew quite well that a sullen disrespect for the
law and its enforcers had started to take hold of all sorts of
ordinary people gnawed at all the time by hunger. On 18
June, several of Vienna's newspapers carried a four-line story
under the heading 'Lynching of a Potato Buyer'.

> In Stammersdorf-near-Vienna [the story read] an as yet
> unidentified woman who had purchased a quantity of
> potatoes in that community was attacked and beaten to
> death by some people who, also having come from Vienna,
> had been unable to buy anything. The assailants appa-
> rently kicked and trampled the [prostrate] woman, for her
> corpse was found horribly mutilated.[5]

That notice very probably did not arrest the eyes of many
readers. On the day of its appearance everyone was scanning
the papers for the latest news from the Italian front. On 15
June Emperor Karl as commander-in-chief had unleashed
there a large-scale offensive. It would 'strike the final blow at
the perfidious enemy, and bring about peace', he had fore-
told in a proclamation read to the troops in the languages of
the various units. He had also reminded them that 'glory and
honour await you beyond the Piave River . . . and abundant
spoils and good food'.[6]

❧ 5 ❧

The Last Offensive

Tales of a most extraordinary kind started making the rounds in Vienna a fortnight after the collapse of the Piave offensive. The news of its initial success had been too glowing and the avowal of failure too sudden not to cry out for a convincing explanation. The heavy rainfalls that had swollen the Piave and swept away bridges as soon as they were built, or the novel poison gas employed by the British contingents which had led the Italian counter-advance, were not allowed to account for the swift reversal of fortune. Speculations about insufficient supplies of ammunition and food during the attack were abundant. But so insistently had the home front been persuaded that its sacrifices were sparing the fighting men privations that the theory of their reduced stamina was angrily rejected. Reports of the unbroken morale in which they had retreated to their pre-offensive positions, frustrating pursuit, compounded what seemed to be a puzzle. The suspicion of treason in high places entered the impatient search for the author of the fiasco. And who seemed less unlikely to have trafficked with the Italians than the Italian-born empress, the 'instigator of the Sixtus intrigue'? No one stopped to consider that the daughter of the duke of Parma would be the last to succour the Italian kingdom, whose patriots had driven him out of the duchy.

The government promptly issued a 'solemn declaration' that denied 'any truth in a certain malicious gossip set afloat by enemy propaganda', and proceeded to arrange public meetings of 'all sober-minded citizens' to voice their protest.

That is probably the greatest stupidity I have ever encountered in court-directed policies [Josef Redlich noted on 7 July]. I hadn't known much of those rumours until I learned today that people on the streets, in coffeehouses, or on the tram, have been telling one another that the empress, having been present when . . . the Chief of Staff submitted the final plans [to her husband] passed them on to the Italians; that [upon the breakdown of the offensive] she was on the orders of Kaiser Wilhelm put into a convent, together with her mother; and that her car was pelted with rocks during the journey, and she herself injured. The emperor has lost all willpower, will be forced to abdicate, Austria annexed by Germany, etc. etc. No tittle-tattle more idiotic can be imagined. And against that sort of nonsense the government has opened a regular campaign!

On 15 July, Redlich recorded the 'curious reception late last Saturday night of the chairmen of the parties' at the royal palace, and added, 'The exalted lady cannot face the prospect of harsh words being uttered against her, her mother and her brothers in the *Reichsrat*.'

None were. The Socialist deputy, Karl Leuthner, who took the floor in the secret session of 24 July, did not even mention the name of the empress or her Parma relations. He had bigger fish to fry:[1]

From the first week of the war the government has waged a war against its own people [Leuthner said]. . . . Even as [the army] was preparing for the offensive on the Piave, whole regiments, nay whole divisions were being concentrated in every large city and every industrial town in order to forestall strikes, or in cases of mutiny create a balance of forces through those 'loyal soldiers' the Minister [just] referred to. Well, it just isn't possible at one and the same time to wage war at the country's border and make war on its population. The least one can ask a government that considers such domestic operations its primary task is to spare us offensive actions the gentlemen are neither mentally nor morally equipped for.

Leuthner proceeded to give a shattering account of the

belated retreat which had 'exposed thousands of our sons and brothers to the kind of tortures that religion at its most insane could not think of in depicting hell'.

At that point a Polish deputy interrupted Leuthner, exclaiming, 'Those criminals [the generals] must be indicted in a court of law. I move that the House so resolve. If the law doesn't call them to account, revolution will!'

The interjection made Leuthner turn to the subject of military justice. 'Judges in army officers' tunics! Throughout Austria they are being looked upon with the utmost contempt as wretched careerists....' And after the applause following his words had subsided, he went on to speak of the treatment of returned prisoners of war, who were

> interrogated as though they were criminals.... Does the government assume that that procedure ... can secure order and calm in the ranks? Or that the inhuman methods used in quelling mutinies can? The gentlemen are mistaken. They and the army officers, not Bolsheviks, are preparing for rebellion in the army.
>
> Alas, the end of the war is not yet within sight. But we are on the eve of the end of a system.... It is felt in all quarters that that system cannot go on functioning, that its collapse is approaching. It is not to seek revenge but to look for deliverance that I am urging the government to apprehend the criminals and rid us of them. Stop talking of subversion and revolt.... Understand that we [Social-Democrats] abhor, that we loathe the kind of revolution bound to seize the country in an all-devouring conflagration.... It is the incompetence and frivolity of the government that are engendering that kind of revolution.... The men who kindled the war must not be allowed to use it as an excuse for their inability to wage war with success.

Did that speech amount to a call for deposing the dynasty as the hub of the discredited system? It may well have been understood as such in the *Reichsrat*'s Lower Chamber. Among Socialist constituents generally, rumours of Leuthner's oration do not seem to have stirred anti-dynastic passions. The story of the empress's 'treason' did not fill working men and women with the same kind of anger that was informing the middle classes. Over the past decades, the Social-Democratic leaders had kept the romantic republicanism of the earliest socialists dormant. Even those politicians who no longer believed in a feasible co-existence of the reformed body politic they envisaged with the archaic Habsburg court had not openly questioned its *raison d'être*. Upon Emperor Karl's accession, one of them, the highly respected Karl Seitz, had gone so far as to remark, 'We could wish for no better president of a republic. . . .'[2] Only as Karl's shortcomings and blunders became notorious did working people tend to look upon him as the main exponent of the forces that were unable to make peace. When, on 25 June France recognized the Czechoslovak Council in Paris as the 'basis of the future Czechoslovak government' – a step on the road to a settlement which, however much fraught with new problems, would at least end hunger and bloodshed – the *Arbeiter Zeitung* had pointed out that the emperor had been passed over in silence in that pronouncement.

Meanwhile veterans of the Piave offensive who had been delivered to hospitals in Vienna displayed to their families copies of the leaflet Italian flyers had scattered over the trenches on the eve of the ill-starred crossing of the Piave. 'Your loved ones are starving', it ran in part. 'Starving for what? Your officers talk to you of duty and honour. Is not a man's first duty to keep his children from starving? Does not his honour urge him to do so?' Police made the rounds of hospital wards to seize the 'fabrications of enemy propaganda'. They could not prevent them from being quoted. Embroidering them, people pretended to know that some of the leaflets had promised a share in Italy's abundance upon surrender.

A succession of hunger riots erupting in Vienna's outlying districts in the course of July was quelled by police without injuries to the demonstrators. The weather had grown oppressively hot.

> No one can recall such temperatures [Redlich recorded]. Vegetables, potatoes, and maize are being roasted to death. We are facing complete destruction of the harvest.

The Fruit and Vegetable *Zentrale*[3] is buying, or requisitioning, for the armed forces, whatever there is to be found. . . . Workers in the tenth and eleventh districts of Vienna are living on cucumbers, and intestinal diseases have been spreading. . . . There is chronic unrest among Prague's workingmen, martial law has been declared in [the industrial towns of] Pilsen and Witkowitz, and in Salzburg a new middle-class association is protesting noisily against the influx of tourists. And Berlin continues to recommend 'sticking it out'! . . .

So much had the Viennese become used to thinking of Hungary as the land of Cockaigne that news of a wave of dissatisfaction disrupting Hungarian life took them by surprise. The wheat harvest there threatened to fall well below expectation. But when one of Budapest's newspapers declared that 'the country must gird itself for a . . . terrible winter', not a few Viennese suggested that such dire statements were most likely printed simply as a warning to Vienna with regard to its hopes for assistance. At the same time, upper-class diehards in Vienna derived not a little satisfaction from the fulminations of Count Tisza, no longer Hungary's premier but still her most influential politician. 'We might well have ended the war by now,' he had told the Budapest parliament in July, 'if it were not for certain unscrupulous men in Austria, and in Hungary as well. . . . Does not the shameless treachery of the Czechs surpass imagination? They brazenly admit to their plan of destroying their Austrian fatherland, and have even cast their eyes on [the] thirteen [Slovak] counties of the Hungarian kingdom. The voices of South Slav traitors can be heard in our own Croatia. . . .' Even though knowledgeable people in Vienna could not help sensing the lack of reality behind such language, it sounded refreshing to their ears, if compared to the insecure pronouncements of their own Austrian statesmen. The mere word 'treachery', used so forcefully by Tisza, seemed to lend a new soundness to the Habsburg state to which those Czechs, those South-Slavs, or those Rumanian-speakers were traitors!

'If there are some who detect the tendency toward a German course in the government's abandoning its long and patient endeavour to reconcile the nationalities,' the Austrian prime minister declared on 16 July, 'I don't feel like contradicting that view. . . .' That remark from the government bench was Herr von Seidler's swan song. His successor, Baron Max Hussarek, originally a teacher of canon law, hastened to emphasize the 'reconciliation of the nationalities' as his policies' main aim. When he proceeded to dwell, in his speech, on the 'home, not to be lost ever, of all of Austria's peoples', the Slav deputies in the chamber interrupted him, chanting, 'Too late, too late!'

Yet Baron Hussarek, unlike his predecessor, had conceived a plan of breaking the deadlock. He meant to satisfy the aspiration of the Croats and Slovenes as a counterweight, alongside the Poles, to the irreconcilable Czechs. The Croats had furnished the Habsburgs with staunch supporters and fierce soldiers for a very long time. Churchgoing Catholics, as were the Slovenes, they might still be imagined to deny their sympathies to the Orthodox Serbs and the concept of an independent Croat-Slovene-Serb 'Yugoslavia' as championed by the emigré politicians. As the ancient kingdom of Croatia-Slavonia, for all of its trappings of semi-autonomy, was part of the Hungarian kingdom, a 'sub-dualistic' reform of the latter was considered by Hussarek – in effect, a 'trialistic' organization of the Habsburg realm. 'Why, perfect order reigns in nine-tenths of our Hungary,' her premier told his Austrian colleague when he came with the project to Budapest on 30 August, 'and here you are suggesting that we upset that order for your sake!' That very day the Hungarians also reminded Karl of the oath he had sworn at the Budapest coronation.

News of Hussarek's 'Greater Croatian solution' was not withheld from the public. It learned nothing, however, of Karl's refusal to support the design. To be sure, what he did and did not do was of dwindling interest to people. His humiliation at the Kaiser's hands had turned him into a mere figurehead of Habsburg tradition. It was to that tradition, rather than to him, that the dynastic-minded were loyal in the face of threatening disaster.

He was travelling a good deal that summer. He and his wife sailed down the Danube to Pozsony (today's Bratislava), the principal town of Hungary's Slovak counties, and according to Vienna's great press, were given a rousing welcome by the peasants assembled there for their harvest festival. He travelled to the Tyrol, that heartland of Habsburg devotion. He paid a state visit to Constantinople, and photos showed him reviewing a Turkish crack unit by the side of the visibly ailing sultan, his ally. But above all, he visited front line troops. He pinned medals on deserving soldiers brought to the rear for that purpose, and used deftly enough his smattering of the languages the occasion demanded. On one of those trips his motor car happened to slide off a dirt road and into the muddied bed of a shallow stream; and dramatic reports of the sangfroid of the monarch and the heroism his suite had shown in rescuing him from mortal danger exercised Vienna's middle classes for a day or two.

Habsburg troops did not stand only on the River Piave and in the mountains of the Tyrol. They were fighting French and Italian formations and native partisans as well in Albania; they were trying to keep order in the Ukraine, now 'pacifying' armed bands of peasants, now skirmishing with Bolshevik units; they were busy in the hills of Macedonia and on the shore of the Black Sea; they were mounting guard against the untrustworthy Rumanians; they garrisoned large tracts of what had been the Tsar's Polish province; and three Habsburg divisions had been transferred to the Western front to take part in the great German offensive.

It was from their midst that the Viennese received a peculiar piece of word-of-mouth information. A Vienna-based gunnery brigade on its arrival in Flanders had run into German soldiers jeering the arrivals as 'war prolongers'. The painful episode, which did not remain isolated, revealed fissures in the German army that its admirers and its critics alike had not been aware of. Even though they had both known for some time of the pacifist language of radical socialist politicians in Berlin, the morale of the German forces in the field had never been queried by Vienna's population. Its divisions had come to the rescue of the Habsburg military too often – and Germans, in uniform or out, had boasted too loudly of that support – not to silence doubts about the ability of that army to 'stick it out' come hell or high water. From late 1917 onwards, commanders of the two allied armies had been interchanged for limited periods on the company level, and that innovation had set many tales of 'Prussian' martinetism afloat in Vienna. The self-assurance of those officers, at once ridiculed and fumed at, had still appeared as a corollary of the steely backbone of the German army. By mid-August 1918, it was no longer taken for granted. 'On the Western front the backward movement of the German armies has come to a stand-still', Redlich wrote on 8 August in his diary, and the pithy terseness of that entry reveals the alarm with which he for one was viewing Marshal Foch's counter-offensive.

The reports from the artillery men in Flanders of their reception was not the only surprising news. Food supplies there, they also wrote, were much superior to those in Venetia. Although furloughs from Venetia remained restricted, being granted only to soldiers deemed reliable politically, there was general talk in Vienna of the catastrophic food situation in the south-western army. The new manner of bread distribution made for an outlandish story: enlisted men had to queue up, helmet in hand upside down, to collect the lumps into which the loaves were crumbling. Meatless days were becoming the rule, for all the slaughter of horses. Accounts of the growing shortage of clothing and shoes were peppered with hostile remarks about army contractors. In some units there were uniforms only for the men in the trenches, while those in reserve wore but underclothing under their greatcoats – or such was the story sworn to by lower-class Viennese. 'We're not heroes, sir, we're beggars',[4] a much-decorated Croat soldier had burst out as a staff officer singled him out for commendation; and that retort had somehow become known in Vienna.

Its people were sliding into a kind of beggary themselves. 'Purchase of the most necessary victuals ... has again posed a grave problem to housewives this week ...' the *Arbeiter Zeitung* reported on 7 July. 'As there is an extreme dearth of meat, sausages and fish, the demand for vegetables has been extraordinary, but the quantities available have lagged far

behind that growing demand....' (The *Neue Freie Presse*
carried an almost identical story.) Nearly every day some
greengrocer, butcher, or baker, was indicted for selling
some of his wares under the counter at inflated prices. In
June a couple of landowners had been hauled into court for
breaches of price regulations. Hardly anyone spoke any
longer of such tokens of law enforcement. Its inadequacy
was taken as a matter of course, as was the venality of low-
echelon officials. Workmen and impecunious lower middle-
class people alike were cursing the rural producers, as well as
the urban middlemen, day in and day out. Invectives aimed
at the customers of the black market – the rich, the profiteers, the speculators, the takers of bribes – vied with
enraged tales of soldiers contending that officers in the rear
still ate and drank to their hearts' desire.

The misery of the south-western front was capped by the
ravages wrought by malaria. 'Because of the shortage of
quinine prophylactic measures could not be given the
necessary attention...,' a general staff officer recalls in a
memoir. 'Moreover, enlisted men would evade preventive
treatment, making malaria in effect a kind of self-mutilation.
To counteract that tendency we employed the ruse of insert-
ing a mounting number of fictitious cases of death from
malaria into the order of the day.'[5] Rumours of an epidemic
were spreading among Vienna's lower-class people, whose
information on malaria, a disease unknown in the prewar
city, was sketchy at best. Also, malnutrition had weakened
their resistance to tubercular infection – an ailment practically endemic in Vienna's tenements for decades. The
afflicted were quick to blame the 'Italian malaria', and to ask
why the army did not quarantine its carriers. The appearance of a vicious kind of influenza (to become notorious as
the Spanish *grippe* only too soon) deepened the puzzled
concern about exotic dangers to health.

Discussions of the miscarried Piave offensive had not been
dropped. Veteran officers of it tended to speak endlessly of
the fiasco of the gas ammunition, assurances of whose effii-
cacy had on the eve of the forward movement apparently
raised their spirits to the point of blinding them to the rot
setting in all about them. Or the survivors would reminisce

at length about the crush and confusion on the pontoon bridges thrown across the swollen river, or about the ruthless despair of drowning men who tried to hold on to the make-shift craft launched after the collapse of the bridges. But none of the horrific details of the campaign made a deeper impression on the Viennese than the tale of the Capronis, Italian biplanes equipped with machine guns. Had army intelligence, it was wondered, been unaware of the development of those planes since Caporetto? Why had the Germans, who were priding themselves on mastery of the air, not sent some of their fighter squadrons to combat the Italian fliers?

For all that, upper-middle-class people did not greet with undiluted satisfaction the dismissal of the general said to have urged the Piave offensive on Emperor Karl as a repeat performance of the glorious campaign of Caporetto. As they pointed out, Baron Conrad von Hötzendorff was not the first Habsburg general picked by the dynasty as the scapegoat for a disaster; and cynics suggested that the blame for the calamity had been pinned upon him to squash the lingering rumours about the empress's 'treason'. In the last years of peace Conrad had been a much-talked-about person in Vienna. Then chief of the general staff – he was removed from that post in March 1917, to take command of the Italian front – he had been said to bring his influence to bear on high-policy decisions. There had been some disapproval of his meddling. But large sections of the middle classes had looked nevertheless at his rumoured advocacy of preventive wars, against Italy and Serbia, as a sign of the country's self-assertion as a great power. Conrad's arguments with Franz Josef, and his disagreements with the old monarch's unpopular heir, had added colour to the image of a stiff-necked soldier sure of his goal. 'The god of battles has not smiled upon Conrad', remarked the *Neue Freie Presse* on the morrow of his discharge. Although the public had long ceased to believe in the miracles Conrad would work, his disappearance engendered in Vienna's bourgeois circles a feeling of loss – the loss of yesterday's dreams. The mere thought of the baron's well-known trim figure and his moustachioed and rosy-cheeked face seemed to belong to an age light-years removed from the drabness that had closed in on Vienna.

Early in the morning of 8 August seven Italian airplanes appeared over the city and scattered leaflets bearing the name of Gabriele d'Annunzio, the famous poet turned soldier and aviator. 'People of Vienna', his message read, in part, 'the whole world has turned against you. . . . Your prolonging the war would amount to suicide. . . . The victory you are being told of is like the bread from the Ukraine – you are dying while waiting for it!'[6] Under pain of stiff penalties, citizens were ordered to turn the leaflets over to the police. Compliance did not, however, prevent the swift burgeoning of a d'Annunzio-over-Vienna saga. Unfounded stories of bombs unloaded by the raiders on their approach to the city were passed round for days. Tempers flared up in reiterating the text of the poet. 'The whole world has turned against you. . . .' Not against the Viennese *qua* Viennese?

'The "bread-peace" has brought us neither bread nor peace,' the *Neue Freie Presse* lamented. But there were new fantasies being spun. A team of chemists was said to have succeeded in extricating fat from horse chestnuts, or a sugar substitute from God knew what. When the municipality organized a large-scale extermination of rats – the dearth of refuse in poor districts had made the animals aggressive – it was widely assumed that the rodents were killed to gain fat for human consumption. No story was too far-fetched, no rumour of a new invention too silly, not to be taken up. Rather like children who have stopped believing in Santa Claus without having their expectation of his gifts shattered, so the Viennese clung to a trust in science, above all German science, which would come to their help. At the same time, gossip about hoarded pre-war stocks was widespread again, and people contended that newspaper advertisements for *ersatz* goods were in actual fact code messages of black-marketeers soliciting offers. There was no end to stories of corruption, and no longer was it the low-echelon bureaucracy alone that such stories dealt with. 'Another two months of the confusion that prevails now,' the *Arbeiter Zeitung* wrote, 'and those who are counting on the collapse of the Habsburg Monarchy will be jubilant.' Did the Socialist leader count on it? While Karl Renner was refusing even to discuss a Central Europe without the Habsburg state, Victor Adler dreaded its break-up and the chaos he foresaw in its wake and which he feared would destroy the social gains of the workers. Otto Bauer held that nothing could stem the centrifugal movements of the country's non-German peoples, and that even the distinction, beloved by Vienna's historians, between 'historic nations' (Magyars, Poles, Czechs, Italians) and ethnical groups 'without a history' (Slovaks, Ruthenes, Slovenes, Rumanians) had lost its meaning. What the masses knew of Wilson's Fourteen Points may have been superficial, but the voice behind them, so different from the voices of their own great personages, sounded like the harbinger of a change that might extricate them from their misery at long last. If having self-determination granted to the nationalities of the country was the price to be paid to the Allies for lifting the *Hungerblockade,* working men and women saw little reason for objecting. It is probably fair to say that not many of them at that juncture worried about the economic dislocations the country's break-up would cause, and that fewer still wondered whether the radical demands of the nationalities were just.

Middle-class people, on the other hand, had not ceased talking of their ingratitude: it was Vienna that had educated them, was it not? That kind of indignation lent a new strength to the stories of treason on the part of the Czechs or the Italians in Trieste and Trentino and to new tales of underground contacts that the 'green cadres' were supposed to have established with Allied agents. Meanwhile, the *Reichspost* had begun preaching to the nationalities. 'In reality [the editorial ran] there is no such thing as absolute self-determination. Just as every person's freedom of action is limited by considerations for the welfare of his fellow men and the society he lives in and is tied by the bonds of civilization and common tasks ... so the individual state cannot exist in isolation.' A solution resulting in full independence for the nationalities would 'not be consonant with natural law and hence *wrong!*' That word was apt to appeal to the readers of the *Reichspost*: had they not been wronged for years – wronged by shady operators pushing up the cost of living, wronged by meddlesome or even corrupt bureaucrats? Now the working class felt, in addition, wronged by that foreigner, Wilson, who appeared determined to block the return of the country and of Vienna, to pre-war conditions!

In lecturing to Wilson the *Neue Freie Presse* was more down-to-earth than the *Reichspost*. On 19 July it had given pride of place to a speech one Herr Forscht had delivered in the Upper Chamber. An elderly Czech civil servant of moderate views who had held a post in one of Franz Josef's cabinets, Forscht had risen to answer the challenge of one of his peers in reference to 'certain occurrences in Czech units of the army in the field'. If such lamentable instances [of defection] in fact should have occurred, Forscht said, he did not hesitate to condemn them. That qualified answer was derided by Moritz Benedikt, who pointed at the activities, hardly covert any longer, of the recently organized Czech National Committee in Prague. And reflecting on national self-determination, he roundly declared that an independent Czech state, such as that mooted by 'the friends of the Masaryks and the Benešes' would not be viable anyway; as one-time minister of trade, Forscht should be the best man to tell his fellow-Czechs that an independent Bohemia, cut off by tariff walls from the high seas, would find herself unable to dispose of her industrial surplus.... It may well be assumed that that kind of argument, meant to impress the Czechs, also convinced, or at least comforted, many educated people in Vienna. The potency of Czech national passions was still beyond their full comprehension. They were equally uncertain about the South-Slavs. The independent state of which their politicians – not only those in exile – were talking ever more loudly would have its own outlet to the high seas.

By mid-August, bad news from the south-east could be no longer ignored. Ever since Serbia's belated conquest in October 1915, the Viennese had paid virtually no attention to her. The retreat of King Peter's ragged army to the Adriatic Sea had lived on as a saga of just retribution. His government-in-exile on French-occupied Corfu might as well not have existed for all the Viennese cared. The rumoured split between him and the South-Slav *émigrés* had reinforced the notion that the Yugoslav movement could be kept under control in the Habsburg Monarchy. As for occupied Serbia, the benevolent rule there of the military had been made much of for close on three years by the press, while the guerilla fighters who continued to plague the occupying army had hardly ever been mentioned. The sketchy accounts of the 'traitors' congress' in Rome had done little to shake the complacency with which the Viennese had been viewing defeated Serbia. Thus the 200,000 Serbs who by mid-August were reported to be in the ranks of the Allied army which had just assembled in Saloniki, took on the appearance of so many revenants itching to take their revenge and to make common cause with the restless Croats and even the docile Slovenes. Overnight the name of Frenchet d'Esperey, the commander of the five-nation Saloniki army, had become a household word in Vienna.

Stories of Bulgarian defeatism were circulating. Bulgaria, which had aligned herself with the Central Powers upon their crushing Serbia, had been a weak ally in the years since. Her wily German-born king had never been popular with the Viennese. Whether or not the press had heard of his attempts at a separate peace in the past summer, no indication of them had been printed. There were scattered stories, though, of a failure of crops in Bulgaria, and virtual famine in her cities. Nor need Viennese with a map before them be told that that country held a position of strategic importance: the collapse of its defence line would not only open Serbia to the thrust of the Saloniki army, but also invite an attack in Southern Hungary, and a march upon Budapest! No less frightened of that prospect than the Supreme Command, Vienna's press joined the government's silence not only to evade censorship interference. Much as a desperately sick person might acquiesce in his family's disinclination to tell him the truth, the public does not seem to have been anxious for full information.

On 29 August it was disclosed that detailed studies of federation were under way. Some days later the name of Heinrich Lammasch was on all lips: he was said to be trying to gain the support of certain Slav politicians. An authority

on international law, an erstwhile judge at the arbitration
court at The Hague, and a member of the Upper Chamber,
he had been opposed to the war from the start, and had
condemned annexationist ideas wherever he could throughout the conflict. He had been shunned by the *Neue Freie
Presse* and rebuffed by the *Reichspost.* Now the bourgeoisie greeted the rumour of Lammasch's involvement in
the studies of federalization with a sigh of relief. Whatever
else he might be, he was known as a man of conservative
views – and blue-prints for Austria's federalization would not
be worked out only by Socialists such as Karl Renner in
conjunction with 'moderate' non-German politicians! Even if
Lammasch's integral pacifism had been disturbing to think of
in the past, the bourgeoisie now did justice to the service he
might render the cause of peace – peace at any price short of
the dismemberment of the country.

Even usually well-informed middle-class men do not
appear to have been unduly discomfited by the arrival in
Vienna of a Russian commission for the exchange of
prisoners-of-war. But neither did their appearance disturb
the leaders of the Social-Democratic party. In fact, the latter
seem to have remained ignorant of the contacts the commission established with the few radical socialist dissenters
the police had failed to apprehend during the January strike.

For the trip home [from a visit with a wealthy merchant
who was dabbling in 'peace projects'] I boarded the
Trieste-Vienna express [Josef Redlich recorded on 3
September]. I found a seat in a compartment reserved for
army officers. Soon I was engaged in conversation with the
gentlemen – two first lieutenants of Slav extraction, an
[Austro-]Italian ensign from Trieste, an Austro-German
captain, and an Hungarian first lieutenant. All of them . . .
spoke with cutting bitterness about the Supreme Command, its incompetence and its deceptive methods, the
corruption rampant in the supply corps, the numerous
shirkers on the general staff, the scandalous behaviour of
the army's women clerks. . . . [The officers] also spoke
disparagingly about Conrad, and even more so about the
'true instigator' of the June offensive.

It may be assumed safely that Redlich's fellow-travellers, with the possible exception of the captain, were reservists – four-fifths of commissioned officers were by that time – and as such hailed from the middle-class families. They no doubt talked with equal freedom to their relations and friends once they had arrived in Vienna. Ever since the January strike, the army authorities had been apprehensive lest defeatism at the home front should infect the fighting forces (and indeed had been careful not to return to them regiments employed in quelling workers' demonstrations); now it was the anger in the front line that spread to the civilian population.

To be sure, the depressing stories told by officers from the front and its rear did not affect all middle-class people alike. There were those who spoke of malicious gossip exaggerating instances of mere *Schlamperei* (sloppiness), that peculiarly Austrian muddle which for decades had been referred to with a paradoxical mixture of disapproval and self-love. That half-hearted criticism, however, had not as a rule included the military; and talking now of the *schlampige* army gave a cutting edge to the old condemnation. Still, whatever Vienna's upper bourgeois may have cared to know of the crumbling morale of the army, the tales of corruption in it failed to mortify them. An insidious kind of corruption had corroded their own sense of fairness in the course of the war. 'Connections', social in origin, had become increasingly important to their self-interest and sense of survival. Businessmen of patent probity had been walking a tightrope between wartime patriotism and the temptations of wartime commerce. A supercilious laxness towards wartime ordinances had been permeating well-to-do households. (Redlich's diary entries of 1917–18 bristle with jottings of 'peacetime-style' meals at aristocratic and upper-middle-class homes or at Sacher's.) They would soothe their social conscience by increasing charitable donations. But the comparatively minor discomforts their families had to endure, had made them less and less sensitive to the unmitigated misery in the 'rent barracks' of Vienna's workers. Civil-service families recently impoverished could be heard complaining, in a blend of Viennese caste consciousness and

Viennese xenophobia, that they were virtually no better off
than Slovak construction workers.

Even though their own sons had been killed or maimed by
the thousand in proximity to enlisted men, the upper middle-
class knew painfully little about them. Their own imagination had always held the common soldier at arm's length.
He was assumed to be no less malleable than the peasant
conscript fighting Habsburg wars had been half a century
earlier. 'Bolshevik propaganda' was a handy catchword to
disparage the mounting despair of the men at the front.
Actually, the thought of workers' and soldiers' councils did
not occupy front line soldiers. They were simply hungry and
deadly tired of war.

As it dawned on Vienna's middle classes that the great
offensive of the Germans was failing, they persuaded themselves that they had never put much store by its prospects.
They shifted all their attention to the prospects of peace. On
19 September, Wilson's reply to the Austro-Hungarian note
of 16 September was published in Vienna. In answer to the
suggestion of a secret and noncommittal exchange of views
of all belligerent countries to deal with the basic principles
of a conclusion of peace, the President curtly referred
Emperor Karl's foreign office to the Fourteen Points. Four
days later the *Neue Freie Presse,* which until then had
treated them with the benevolence due to high-sounding
utopian ideas, hit out at the man in the White House,
castigating the 'humanitarian whose speeches overflow with
protestations of love of his fellow men and who yet no longer
conceives of peace without victory and without his enemies'
total destruction'. Benedikt went on to enlighten the
'American professor' on some of the consequences of its
break-up. 'The Austrian Alpine lands cannot possibly exist
without the Adriatic littoral which has been as one with
them for many centuries. The fact that South Slavs and
Italians live there constitutes no reason for separating that
littoral [from the Alpine lands and Vienna].' Or ceding
Galicia to an independent Polish state? How could the
Monarchy be expected to help form a Greater Poland at its
own border without knowing how that new country would
order its relations with Vienna? The editorial did not touch

on the Czechoslovak state, even though its sovereignty had been recognized by the United States two weeks before, as by France, Italy and Great Britain. Surely even the man in the White House did not have to be convinced that the Alpine provinces could not exist without the German-speaking industrial centres in Bohemia and Moravia which that would-be country claimed as its own! The people of Vienna were as incensed as the *Neue Freie Presse*. They had fooled themselves believing that Woodrow Wilson would leave them a way out of the mortal dilemma.

The scarcely disguised accusations of perfidy that the non-Socialist German press had levelled at Emperor Karl in the spring no longer exercised Vienna's upper classes in September. With bad news from the Western front emerging ever more clearly from the circumlocutions of the press, the great ally appeared bereft of his aura of irresistibility. What anti-German bias had accumulated over the war years – side by side with a grudging admiration of the war machine of the Kaiser – came to the fore, and a good many people gave credit to Karl for having made the right move after all. Nothing daunted by Wilson's rebuff, they were eager to have the young emperor take another step in the same direction. As it was, his foreign office was preparing a new proposal to Wilson. But before its drafting was completed, the Saloniki army had begun clearing the road to peace for the Habsburg state via the defeat of its weakest ally. Four days after Frenchet d'Esperey had started his offensive, Bulgaria lay open to conquest. On 2 October her army had been routed, and she had concluded an armistice which made her territory available to Allied operations.

❧ 6 ❧

Vienna Abandoned

In the days of the Piave disaster the government had cut the bread ration once more. Although the new ordinance contained a promise of preferred treatment for manual workers, they had given instantaneous notice of their dissatisfaction.

In about 120 industrial plants . . . [Vienna's chief of police reported on 26 June], 47,000 workers laid down their tools. Sizable groups of strikers elbowed their way into workshops to force those still doing their jobs to join them. Rocks were hurled, and a number of windows broken. The demonstrators also attacked lorries laden with bread or flour, stopped trams, and maliciously inflicted some damage on them. . . . Police, who had been attacked by a hail of stones . . . were compelled to advance with sabres unsheathed, and only their quick and energetic reaction prevented those large groups from inflicting greater damage on property. . . . Work was resumed between 24 and 26 June.

Those revolutionary elements the bourgeois press had noticed among the January strikers did not appear in the disorders of June. In fact, it was the Vienna Workers' Council – suspected of revolutionary tendencies by the middle classes – who, together with the union leaders, had calmed the workers.

While the authorities did not hesitate to call out the army to deal with disorders in Bohemian mining districts, or the Budapest munition plants, no such intervention was practised in German-speaking places. The lingering unrest there caused some local middle-class politicians – first in the Tyrol and then in Wiener Neustadt – to embark on a peculiar project. Certain Christian-Social associations let it be known that their ranks would be open henceforth to all Christians irrespective of church affiliation. In other words, those politicians were trying to put together an extra-parliamentary coalition of Christian-Socials and German nationalists (many of whom had severed their ties with the Church) to oppose the Socialists on a local level.

> The first meeting, sponsored by exponents of the German-National Association ... [the governor of Lower Austria informed the Minister of the Interior], attracted a large audience. Besides personalities of both parties, numerous civil servants and businessmen were present.... Common action to strengthen the middle class was dicussed. The speakers made no mention of the Social-Democratic party so as not to prevent individual workers ... from attending future meetings. Next to a stimulation of general activity, the plans envisage the setting-up of welfare establishments such as a home for single working women. In that and other humanitarian projects, her Royal Highness the Duchess Maria Antonia of Parma [Empress Zita's mother] had expressed a lively interest. Probably it is that interest that has set afloat a ... rumour according to which her Royal Highness has been promoting the action. Further circulation of that rumour will be opposed by appropriate enlightenment.[1]

The governor gauged the damage which the undertaking was bound to suffer if public opinion should connect it with the name of the duchess who had become a favourite topic of critical gossip.

Actually, Vienna's middle classes put little store by what the *Arbeiter Zeitung* called an 'anti-Socialist coalition of provincials'. They knew too much of the sullen strength of organized Labour to assume that such a haphazard undertaking could so much as dent it. And the sobriety a Victor Adler or a Karl Renner had shown during the great strike was giving rise to the hope that they and their like would

spare the city the violence of social revolution. If his inter-
party antagonists dubbed Renner a 'black and yellow Socialist' in allusion to the Habsburg colours, that epithet pleased
the middle classes.

Nor were he, Victor Adler and Karl Seitz 'vicious
destroyers' such as Masaryk or Beneš, or the evangelists of
the Yugoslav movement, 'those wretched creatures and political condottieri', according to the *Reichspost*, 'who fill the
simple mind of Slovene rustics with radical passions . . . and
alienate them from their traditional loyalty to the emperor.'
It had taken the man in the street most of the war years to
grasp the fact that the Yugoslav movement claimed, besides
the Serbs (both in Serbia proper and on Hungary's territory),
the Croats and the Slovenes. His eyes riveted anxiously on
the faithless Czechs and the Slovaks whose allegiance the
Czechs appeared to have gained, he had been slow to
appreciate the waxing strength of Yugoslav sentiments.
When in September one of the Slovene bishops was reported
to have received some overtly Yugoslav-minded Slovene
politicians, the *Reichspost* admitted to being dumbfounded.

The Lower House reassembled on 1 October. 'Events in the
south-east have no doubt created a serious problem. . .' the
prime minister said, opening his speech. 'But I am far from
calling it critical. Adequate military measures have been
taken . . . and based on reliable information I am able to
declare that we can look forward with equanimity to further
developments in the Balkans.' Then Baron Hussarek turned to
his programme for Austria's transformation.

A discussion, indeed a solution of the problem of
[national] autonomy, is in order. Considering certain
unpleasant manifestations in public life, I can with a
certain consoling feeling of trust say that the exceedingly
fruitful principle of national autonomy can be made use of
still further, and that we are entitled to look forward to no
mean improvement and in fact a clarification through
systematic use of that principle. The difficulty lies only in
its implementation [the baron admitted before he
assured] all of Austria's peoples of self-determination in

national and cultural affairs under the aegis of the government, whose business it will be to prepare for and set in
motion that great work so rich in prospects.... The
strength of our future lies in conciliation and unity, not in
division and decomposition.

On 2 October the spokesmen of the Polish, Czechoslovak and
Serbo-Croat-Slovene nations rose to answer Hussarek. 'We
reject any unilateral and partial solution of our problems,
and protest efforts to deny them their international character.
The regulation of all questions relating to our future and to
the co-existence of all European nations may be left to the
peace conference. Our nations will be represented there....'
Certainly, those problems had grown beyond the framework
of the Austrian half of the Habsburg state: 'Czechoslovak'
regions lay in Hungary, as well as Austria, South-Slav territories in Hungary, Bosnia, Herzegovina, Serbia and
Montenegro, and too in the Austria the prime minister still
spoke for.

The determination of the Crown not to touch on matters
Hungarian would have made the secessionists inaccessible to
any compromise. The Hungarian parliament had recently
passed a new suffrage law which through gerrymandering
had managed to keep most of the kingdom's Slavs and
Rumanians disenfranchised.

The sanction [that the emperor as king of Hungary] put
on that law [said the Czech deputy, Staněk] proves once
again that every gesture of the Monarchy devised to show
its submission to the rule of European civilization is utter
hypocrisy.... What a disgusting farce! Sham democracy
is supposed to salvage autocracy. In periods of danger
Austrian governments succeeded repeatedly in calming
the people through solemn promises. Once the danger to
the autocrats had passed, they did not hesitate to go back
on their word. Small wonder that the Central Powers and
their exponents are no longer taken seriously. No one
wants to negotiate with them. The nationalities of Austria,
too, are tired of negotiating.... It is not among them that
you will find allies once the war is over. If there was still a
shred of hope that the Austro-Hungarian monarchy might

be looked upon as a [reliable] signatory to a compromise
peace, that prospect has been smashed for good by the
provocative arrogance of the Hungarian government. . . .
If we still needed a warning as to the worth of promises on
the part of this monarchy, the abandonment of the
Hungarian Slavs and Rumanians to the tender mercies of
the Magyars would suffice all of Austria's peoples. . . . Not
only in the name of liberty and democracy, but in the
name of basic decency, we don't wish to have anything to
do with the Austro-Hungarian Monarchy and its political
system. . . . A free South-Slav state, an independent
Greater Poland, and our own Czechoslovakia are rising out
of this dismal mire. . . . We pity Herr Hussarek and the
rest of you for having come to this pass. If you agree to
President Wilson's terms and gain his confidence . . . you
can have peace. No other way is feasible. We advise
you to capitulate.

As Staněk was laying the arbitrary action of the Hungarian
government and its parliament at the *Reichsrat*'s door, the
German deputies were no less stunned than enraged. Had
they not, along with the Crown, often enough taken exception to the lengths to which Hungary had gone in her
insistence on rights supposedly flowing from her separate-
ness? They had indeed. But at the same time they used to
avert their eyes from the iniquities that the Magyar ruling
classes had imposed on Hungary's non-Magyar peoples with
unabated harshness.

'When the Czechs demanded a seat at the negotiating table
at Brest-Litovsk,' Staněk concluded his speech amid mounting turmoil, 'the Germans [of Austria] threatened them with
the hangman's rope. Now those gentlemen will have to
accept Czech delegates at peace negotiations, after all – not
as Austria's Czechs, but as the representatives of the Czechoslovak Legion.'

'Traitors! Rascals!' German deputies shouted. 'A bunch of
scoundrels, that's what your Legion is! How dare you speak
like this in the Austrian parliament!'

Staněk and his Slav fellow-deputies were well aware of the
long-range significance of the Legionnaires in the eyes of the
Allied statesmen: anti-Habsburg and anti-Bolshevik at the

same time, the Legion, 100,000 strong, had shown them an anti-German alternative to the Habsburg state. The Germans in the *Reichsrat* could not help realizing that the Allied recognition of the Czechoslovak National Council as a 'trustee of the future Czechoslovak government' – or, as Washington put it, the '*de facto* government of Czechoslovakia' – had been more than a stroke of enemy propaganda, more than a stratagem to force the country to its knees. Hence their boundless fury, the abuse and the inkwells that some of them hurled at Staněk, while others prepared to engage in physical argument with the traitors.

Yet the German deputies had had plenty of warning. 'Privately voiced opinions of Czech leaders,' the *Neue Freie Presse* reported two days before parliament opened, 'make it clear that the Czech parties will declare their total lack of interest in intra-Austrian affairs, and will stay aloof from discussing them. The *Reichsrat* will assemble . . . at a crucial time in world history.' That calm tone hardly did justice to the mood of the public, which thus was told that the destiny of the Dual Monarchy was at the mercy of uncontrollable forces, and had ceased to be one of the determinants of world history. Unlike the German-National deputies, the Viennese bourgeois did not shout 'Treason!' Rather, they began branding Woodrow Wilson as the 'gravedigger of the venerable country'. Even the level-headed among them did not grasp the thought that had ripened the aversion of the Allied policymakers to preserving the Habsburg state. It was not understood that the Allies now thought of the Habsburg state as a satellite of the *Reich*. This conjured up the spectre of a German sphere of influence vastly enlarged even upon the Kaiser's defeat. As the Viennese middle classes were turning against the 'American schoolmaster' as a man misguided by the paucity of his knowledge of Central-European affairs, tales apt to denigrate him personally were being heard. One of those – accepted by no less a person than Emperor Karl – labelled Wilson a Mormon, a member of a religious sect that until quite recently had practised polygamy.

'Austria has a prime minister residing in Washington,' the *Neue Freie Presse* commented bitterly on 9 October. 'His name is Woodrow Wilson, and the executor of his policies is

Baron Hussarek. . . . The proceedings of yesterday's session
of the Lower House leave us with sombre impressions.' The
foreign office (as its *Reich* counterpart) had asked
Washington for an armistice based on the Fourteen Points.

> Yet in these crucial days of decision [the *Neue Freie*
> *Presse* continued] . . . a large part of the House no longer
> feels for the country. Many seats were empty, all the
> Czechs absent . . . Poles, South-Slavs and Czechs are wait-
> ing for the guidelines Wilson's answer will give them.
> They keep silent about their own intentions. They do not
> wish even to hint at what their future relationship to
> Austria-Hungary might be. . . . Meanwhile they nurture
> fantasies about a Slav community that – never mind ethni-
> cally German territories – would reach from Danzig [on
> the Baltic] to the Adriatic. They have made their own the
> mood of the Allied camp, its loves and its hatreds, while
> Austria[-Hungary] has embarked on a depressing errand
> to Washington to stretch out her hand to a man who has
> been inflicting untold sorrow on her.

The 'mature people of the country, after exercising their
right of self-determination,' Hussarek had told parliament
the day before, 'must find a way of mutual co-operation for
the pursuit of common goals.' The *Neue Freie Presse* found it
'unheard of in Europe that a state should reduce itself to a
mere spectator of developments [on its territory]'.

Thoroughly outstripped as such arguments were by what
was happening in Prague, Zagreb, Warsaw, or Trieste,
Moritz Benedikt's editorial may yet have appealed to its
readers who were as anxious as he was to hold fast to the
fiction of a 'state'. Proceeding from the general to the particular, he tried to impress, less upon them than on the enemy
chancelleries, how totally unfeasible the new order would be
if shaped without the guidance of the state and outside its
framework.

> The Poles of Galicia are clamouring for union with a
> Greater Poland . . . and [according to Hussarek] the
> [Habsburg] state would not influence the decision on
> whether the inhabitants of Galicia, eight millions of them,
> and her arable, her petroleum and her salt mines would

remain with us. . . . Austria is supposed to turn into a commonwealth of States. But not one of the official or covert Czech leaders has mentioned that plan. . . . It is the state which has to create such a federation. . . . No answer from Woodrow Wilson has been received as yet, and the right of [national] self-determination he wants to be put into practice may be very different indeed from Baron Hussarek's notion.

Josef Redlich called Hussarek's speech the 'fiasco of an academic'. Actually, it was the muffled outcry of an old man who could not for the life of him break away from his own rules. In that respect, he differed only in degree from most middle-class people.

I talked at some length with the Czechs [in parliament] [Redlich continued]. They are courteous enough, but I cannot perceive any way out. Staněk said to me, 'Austria [-Hungary] has to disappear. We don't need the dynasty. Poland, Bohemia, Slovakia and Yugoslavia will unite. We don't care what you Germans will do.' It makes no sense to me, for that programme presupposes the defeat of Germany, and the destruction of Hungary, as well as the end of the Habsburgs. Still, as things look now, such a development is not impossible. The German troops are retreating, Turkey will go the way of Bulgaria soon, and Rumania will enter the war again. I talked to Victor Adler. He no longer believes in Austria's survival, but thinks some kind of reconstruction will follow her downfall. . . .

Vienna's bourgeois had never taken the full measure of the mediocrity of the latter-day statesmen of their country. Franz Josef's confidence in them, however short-lived in most cases, had insidiously weakened critical judgment. The growing number of senior civil servants among cabinet ministers had by no means been unwelcome. Their abhorrence of radicalism in any form seemed a guarantee against drastic change. Hussarek was only the last of the statesmen, titled or not, whose love of the *status quo* had appealed to Vienna's bourgeois, no matter how harshly they would judge the 'illiberalism' of some, or wonder about the qualifications of others. While the *Neue Freie Presse* took exception to

Hussarek's *Reichsrat* speech of 1 October, he himself in the privacy of a cabinet meeting confessed that he deemed it 'utterly impossible to tie himself down to the idea of an *actual* federalization of the realm'.[2]

In the afternoon of 5 October the authorities were taken by surprise as frenzied demonstrators, most of them women, were pouring into the streets of Vienna's suburbs. It turned out that rumours of an armistice had been spreading, along with a story of municipal hoards of foodstuffs to be released. The subsequent let-down did not lead to any large-scale violence. A baker's shop or two were plundered by young people and a pile of rubbish set afire.

The following morning the newspapers announced that a National Council of Serbs, Croats and Slovenes had been set up in Zagreb with the declared purpose of uniting them in a sovereign state under the dynasty of Serbia. And within twenty-four hours the Regency Council in Warsaw – a body that had, albeit fitfully, co-operated with the Central Powers for months – re-established Poland as an independent republic. So preoccupied were the Viennese with what by that time had happened in Prague – the National Council there had taken charge of Bohemia's administration without meeting any resistance – that the pronouncements from Zagreb and Warsaw did not sink in at once. Everyone was waiting for Wilson's reply. . . . It was assuming an almost magical connotation in the thoughts of the middle classes. When a special edition of the *Wiener Zeitung*, the government organ, published an imperial manifesto on 16 October, sophisticated men rightly assumed that it was directed more at Wilson than at the 'faithful Austrian peoples' Emperor Karl was calling upon – fashioned to frustrate the radical interpretation of the Wilsonian programme. 'The population in general is discussing His Majesty's manifesto, if it is discussed at all, with a view to its possible contribution to a speedy attainment of peace . . . and the influence Austria's planned reconstruction could have on provisioning Vienna,' police headquarters reported to the minister of the interior on 18 October. 'There is a growing concern that the German-speaking parts of Austria, unless special arrangements are made for them, will be ravaged by actual famine. They are unable to support themselves. . . .'

This, in part, was the text of the manifesto.

Ever since I succeeded to the throne I have tried to gain the longed-for peace for all my peoples, and to show [them] the ways by which they could cultivate their individual national identities [*Volkstum*] free from all hindrances and tensions, and devote themselves to their cultural and economic well-being. . . . The reconstruction of the fatherland must be commenced now. It must be based on its natural and hence dependable foundations. . . . In accordance with the will of her peoples, Austria shall be organized as a federal country in which each national component in its territory of settlement shall form its own state. . . . This reconstruction, which shall in no way affect the integrity of the Lands of the Holy Hungarian Crown, will guarantee independence to each of those states. But it will also safeguard common interests wherever co-operation is vital to their needs. . . . Until the reorganization is completed through legal means, the existing institutions will remain in force unchanged to ensure the general interest. I have charged my government to start work without delay. To the peoples, on whose right of self-determination the new commonwealth will be built, my call goes out to help implement the great work through National Councils which, made up of the *Reichsrat* deputies of each nationality, shall represent the peoples' interests in relation to one another and in contact with my government. . . .

A police report of 18 October suggested that the failure of Vienna's masses to appreciate the importance of His Majesty's manifesto must be accounted for by the 'conditions of supply which are occupying the lower classes to the exclusion of all other considerations'. Turning to other strata of the populace, the report continued:

People of German-National leanings see themselves faced with the non-German peoples' interpretation of the right to self-determination as an invitation to outright secession.

Hence they are admonishing their fellow Austro-Germans to think of themselves, and work for [their territories'] union with the *Reich*. It is worth noting [the official went on], that the Social-Democratic press, taking the Austro-Germans' desire for such a union for granted ... is stressing its economic advantages, as well as national sentiments. Among Christian-Socialists it is argued that Austria's reconstruction, as outlined in the ... manifesto, could be viable only if the Lands of the Hungarian Crown, too, carried through a reform based on the same principles.

The upper bourgeoisie was passed over in silence in that public-opinion summary. But surely they were the first to perceive that Hungary's exemption from the reform plan made a mockery of it. Perhaps some people upon opening that morning's newspaper had been hoping against hope that the Crown's apparent conversion to Wilson's principle of national self-determination might work a miracle still; once they grasped that Hungary's Slavs and Rumanians should, in a reformed Habsburg state, be left under Magyar hegemony, even such optimists could imagine the utter derision with which Austria's Slavs would reject the emperor's proposals. The role of the villain was transferred from the Czechs to the Magyars when a certain dramatic story filtered through: the Hungarian prime minister was said to have hastened to Vienna, along with Count Tisza, and threatened Karl to his face with a stoppage of all supplies unless their kingdom was in so many words excluded from his manifesto. But side by side with that account, there was melancholy talk about Karl's oath at the Budapest coronation – his pledge to uphold the integrity of Hungary's territory. Only twenty-two months had passed since that day. It seemed light years away in mid-October 1918. The memory of young Karl wearing Hungary's crown and holding the ancient sceptre amid the Hungarian nobles threw their true intentions into profile to the minds of the Viennese who commented on the 'latest Hungarian blackmail'. While the image of the helpless sovereign in Schönbrunn no doubt moved them, there were also some who recalled that the young Franz Josef had often found pretexts to disavow what to most men would have appeared as a pledge. Curious to say, the *Neue Freie Presse* did not touch on the crucial Hungarian issue.

Its comments on the manifesto came close to a condemnation of it.

> The independent states are as good as ready but the [Austrian] confederation is no more than a phrase at this writing. . . . Austria, which in the course of four centuries succeeded in developing, slowly but consistently, the power of governing, is supposed to divest herself of that result of traditional wisdom, and beg Czechs and Slovenes to form a federation with her. . . . No guarantees are stipulated for securing common foreign policy, common defence, freedom of movement, tariff union, and the servicing of the public debt. People who in the years of wartime emergency invested their savings in [war bonds] could have expected not to be forgotten when the manifesto was drafted. . . . A confederation consisting of nations that as a rule cannot abide one another, differ in language and thinking, and have long been looking for separateness as a nostrum for their own domestic problems, will not easily be brought into existence. Why did the prime minister suggest that course despite the failure of his talks with the chairmen [of the *Reichstag* parties]? A federal country, the 'United States of Austria' – the very name amounts to a bow to Mr Wilson. . . .

Wilson was still biding his time. Only on 20 October did a note signed by his country's Secretary of State arrive in Vienna. It stated that the President was 'unable to entertain proposals from the Austro-Hungarian Government because certain events of the greatest importance which have occurred since his statement of 8 January have necessarily changed the attitude and the duty of the United States of America'. Referring explicitly to the tenth of the President's Fourteen Points – the doctrine of the right of national self-determination – Mr Lansing bluntly continued,

> Since that sentence was written . . . the government of the United States has recognized that a state of belligerence

exists between the Czecho-Slovaks and the German and
Austro-Hungarian Empires, and that the Czecho-Slovak
National Council is a *de facto* belligerent government
clothed with proper authority to direct the military and
political affairs of the Czecho-Slovaks. It has also recognized in the fullest manner the justice of the national
aspirations of the Yugo-Slavs for freedom. The President
is therefore no longer at liberty to accept the mere
'autonomy' of these peoples as a basis for peace, but is
obliged to say that they, and not he, shall be the judges
of what action on the part of the Austro-Hungarian
government will satisfy their aspirations and their conception of their rights and destiny as members of the
family of nations.

Mr Lansing's note did not come as a thunderclap to Vienna's
educated classes. They had known before its arrival that the
country was breaking up. At the same time their subcon-
sciousness refused to realize that it was theirs no longer. The
proprietary feeling with which they had looked for so long at
the Habsburg state – refractory Hungary not excluded –
could not be dislodged overnight. In their speech, 'we' still
stood for the Austro-Hungarian Empire.

We often lost wars [the *Neue Freie Presse* wrote on 22
October]. The gravity of the present crisis calls to mind
the days when the Winter King [the Palatinate son-in-law
of James I of England] was residing in Prague [after the
Bohemian Estates had deposed the Habsburgs] or those
later days [of the Thirty Years' War] when Swedish troops
were approaching the Vienna Woods. But the present peril
is more serious still because the monarchy ... being
undermined from within, is disintegrating into daughter
states partly hostile to one another. What is to be
done? ... The most important question facing us is
whether a community does not, after all, exist between
them. ... Proof is at hand. Vienna is ill supplied, and
everybody knows the possible consequences of such a
situation. It is preferable not to pursue that thought. ...

To gain leverage for new demands on the Crown, Hungary
had restricted her supplies to Vienna almost from the hour

Karl's manifesto was published. 'Let us concentrate on immediate exigencies rather than complex problems, of which a stroke of Wilson's pen can make nonsense anyway tomorrow,' the editorial closed. 'Surely Hungary, too, is anxious to preserve law and order [and] protect her citizens' property. That much we have in common. Vienna must not go hungry.'

It did. Countless households had to make do with a gruel of rye flour cooked in salt water without any fat. It was useless to queue up for one's puny ration of fat at the grocer's – he simply had none. Butchers were selling, if anything, horsemeat; most of them put their shutters down after 10 a.m. Such bread as was on sale early in the morning would crumble to sticky bits in the customer's hands. Rather than railing at the *Diktat* of Mr Wilson, or guessing about what was really going on in Schönbrunn or in the government's councils, the Viennese would burst out in anger at Hungarian railroad workers who were said to have blocked the shipment of wheat. Gossip about the food of the rich was rampant among the lower classes. This being the shooting season, the game which, it was assumed, came to the table of noblemen and wealthy folk from their preserves was discussed endlessly even by people who had done without such delicacies in peacetime. There were also stories of large-scale poaching practised by army deserters.

In fact, 'green-cadres' bands had turned up near Vienna. Legend had it that escaped prisoners of war were roaming the countryside. The dread of such lawless gangs penetrating the city was joining the fear of imminent famine. The *Arbeiter Zeitung* wrote on 20 October, 'If we do not get relief soon, we are threatened with a catastrophe. . . . Every single family is living in fear of grave social convulsions.' The Socialist leaders, deeply embarrassed by the part that Hungarian fellow proletarians played in the virtual embargo of foodstuffs, knew only too well that in certain plants of Wiener Neustadt and Vienna extremists were busy insinuating to their fellows that all of them take to the streets, force the doors of army warehouses, or get at the 'blood-sucking rich' and their 'bulging larders'.

As it was, the larders of even moneyed households were no longer full. Rural producers were less and less willing to sell,

and as the mood of the outlying districts posed bodily
danger to the small-time black marketeers these families had
come to rely on; they were more often than not waiting in
vain for their 'contacts'. Also, an instance of food poisoning
that occurred in a privileged home late in August had given
a bad name to such wares as black-market traders still had to
offer. The scarcity of everything had become the prime issue
of talk even in circles that used to pride themselves on the
refinement of their conversation. It barely ranked second to
the fears of social unrest, and was not outstripped, after 16
October, by discussions of the emperor's manifesto.

Withal, the opera had not closed down, and its orchestra
had not discontinued its Sunday morning concerts of classi-
cal music in the unheated concert hall. Franz Lehar's latest
operetta, premiered in March, went on packing the *Theater
an der Wien* in October. At the imperial-royal *Burgtheater* a
new management had taken over headed by Herr von
Andrian, a minor diplomat who in his younger days had done
some writing, and Hermann Bahr, a playwright, novelist and
critic as well known as he was prolific. 'In the afternoon
Hermann Bahr called on me,' Josef Redlich noted on 20
October. 'His relationship to Andrian is such that [Bahr]
thinks he will get out of the mess within a week. . . . I'm
afraid the management will end with a crash.' That same
day's diary entry also records the

> deep indignation of the public about the Hungarian
> swindlers. Wekerle [the premier] and Tisza have come
> out with a proclamation establishing, as of 1920 [in place
> of the dual-monarchy arrangement of 1867] a mere
> personal union [between Austria and Hungary]. The
> Magyar gentlemen have the cheek to declare that Wilson's
> Fourteen Points do not concern them, as [non-Magyar]
> nationalities enjoy full liberty in Hungary anyway. The
> Viennese almost like Wilson now, so great is their hatred
> of the Hungarians.

Two days later Redlich was told by one of his many well-
connected acquaintances that the emperor was planning to
flee to Gödöllö, his Hungarian summer residence.

❧ 7 ❧
'Cockades Down!'

'The German people of Austria has resolved to determine its own future, establish an independent German-Austrian state, and regulate its relations to Austria's other nationalities by mutual agreements.' These were the opening words of a resolution unanimously adopted by the *Reichstag* deputies of all German-speaking constituencies who on 21 October had assembled in the Landhaus of Lower Austria on Vienna's Herrengasse. At least some of these men must have been conscious of the irony in their declaration: except for the Socialists, they, as their predecessors, had opposed 'mutual agreements' as long as self-determination had implied the surrender of German domination over Austria's non-German races; now they adopted German self-determination with alacrity. 'The [new] German-Austrian state assumes sovereignty over all Austrian territory of German settlement, including the German lands of Bohemia and Moravia, and will not tolerate any annexation by other nationalities of territory German peasants, workers and burghers live in. . . .'

A great deal of speech-making had preceded the resolution. Victor Adler had reminded the assembly that what was

> happening today under the pressure of unparalleled events [had been] fought for by us [Social-Democrats] for two decades. . . . Our new state will form a free federation of nations with the other peoples provided such is their will, also. If it is not . . . or if they come out with conditions contrary to our economic and national needs, then German-

Austria – which, thrown back on its own devices, would
not be viable economically – will be compelled to enter
the German *Reich* as one of its states. . . . German-Austria
shall be a democratic country, truly of its people. . . . The
time of Upper-House gentlemen, of bureaucratic rule, and
of feudal-capitalistic privileges has passed. We demand
that the German people of Austria, following the principle
of its own sovereignty, draft the constitution of its body
politic through a Constituent National Assembly. . . . We
[Social-Democrats] will fight for making the German-
Austrian state a democratic republic.

Pointing out that the assemblage he was addressing no
longer mirrored the popular will – the deputies had been
elected seven years before – Victor Adler yet hailed it as the
'first parliament of our German-Austrian country. We Social-
Democrats are participating in its debates because this is the
only possible forum. Mind you, we have no desire to form a
. . . coalition with you men who are enemies of our class. We
will remain your adversaries. We will continue our struggle
for the proletariat, for democracy and for socialism. . . .'

The Christian-Social spokesman opened his remarks by
stressing the 'adherence of [his] party to a monarchical form
of government', and closed them by expressing his 'party's
inalterable gratitude to both the heroes of the front line and
the long-suffering populace at home. We implore them both
to persevere till peace is achieved.'

'We Germans worked for, and carried the burden of
the [Habsburg] state and frequently sacrificed our own
interests,' said the German-National speaker. 'We have lost
the flower of our nation on the battlefields for that Austria.
The force of events writes finis to old Austria, and we
Germans enter the new in unity. . . .' Curiously, he made no
reference to *Anschluss*. He admonished old Austria's 'government and parliament to . . . establish guarantees that the
citizens who put their savings at the disposal of the state be
spared ruin, that public servants, invalids and the families of
dead soldiers will get what the old state committed itself to
paying them. . . .'

It was left to the spokesman of the once-powerful Liberal

party to inject Vienna's future into the debate. 'No doubt, this centre of the old Austria will be the loser through the break-up. . . . But we are convinced that the capital of the free German-Austrian nation will flourish as brilliantly as it did before.'

While those speeches were in progress at the Landhaus, the Upper House of old Austria's parliament had convened. The seats of the Slav and Italian members were empty. It may be surmised that most of the men of outstanding merit appointed by the Crown – one-time cabinet ministers, former civil servants, scholars – who were there had come to dispel the feeling of isolation taking hold of each. The hereditary titled members still felt incredulous. They were all listening patiently to the premier, Hussarek, as he enlarged on his Croat project – that kernel of the plan for federation he had worked out. 'No vacuum must be allowed to develop while old formations are disappearing,' he said in the course of his speech. 'The beloved fatherland must suffer no harm. We should take comfort in the thought that the Austrian idea and the Austrian mission are indestructible. Something like a current of hope is noticeable throughout these much-tried lands of ours. The dawn of a new epoch is rising over the dark of a long night.' Whereupon one of the members remarked dryly, 'The reddish hues that his Excellency perceives on the horizon do not, alas, herald a new era's dawn, but the sunset of a passing age.' Prince Fürstenberg rose to quote the great Czech historian, František Palacký, as having said in 1848 that 'if no Austria existed, surely it would have to be invented'. Today he, Fürstenberg, believed in a 'mighty whole, a confederacy of peoples in which each can live according to its own individuality and prevail in happiness'. Indeed, said another peer, there 'does exist a tendency toward union among the nations of Austria, the venerable Austria we all love so deeply. Stirred up as they are, they do not dare say so'. The session was drawing toward its close when Rudolf Sieghart, the *éminence grise* of Franz Josef's declining years (dubbed the 'corrupter general' by Redlich in the intimacy of his journal) took the floor to submit that 'the peoples will find their way home to the

[Habsburg] state as soon as the excitement of novelty has evaporated'.

Some days earlier that controversial upstart had asked the editor-in-chief of the *Reichspost* to call on him.

I had not seen Sieghart for a long time [Funder reminisces]. Only the year before, Emperor Karl had forced him to resign from his position as president of the Bodenkreditanstalt [to which lucrative banking job he had been appointed in 1910 as reward for many services behind the scenes]. His involuntary resignation ... had caused a sensation. ... He now started our conversation by sketching the present situation with all the precision of a political general-staff mind. Not everything was lost yet, he said. Conditions being what they were, the [Vienna] press was the most powerful instrument for shaping public opinion. Certainly the *Neues Wiener Tagblatt,* with its big circulation ... was ... firmly anchored to the life of the middle class. ... The paper thus far had shown restraint. However, he, Sieghart, was now determined to make it lead the fight against the enemies of the state and the dynasty. 'Listen to me, Doktor Funder', he continued, raising his voice, 'I own ninety per cent of the stock of ... the *Neues Wiener Tagblatt,* and I am at liberty and have the firm will to have the leftish tide of public opinion stemmed. ... I am attaching one condition to it, though. When I was compelled to resign ... I was neither informed of the reasons nor granted an audience [by the emperor] in which I could have answered possible accusations. What I am asking for is merely to be given that chance by His Majesty now.'[1]

Emperor Karl, whose secretariat was informed by Funder, postponed a meeting with Sieghart. He and his wife left Schönbrunn on 22 October bound for Debreczin, where in 1849 the ill-starred revolutionary Kossuth had declared the Habsburgs to have forfeited Hungary's crown for ever. Karl now came to inaugurate the new university. Vienna's bourgeois press printed brief descriptions of the truly Magyar enthusiasm that welcomed the king. At the time he entrained for Budapest, the Hungarian prime minister had resigned,

and the streets of the capital were reverberating with calls
for Count Michael Károlyi, the radical maverick, to be put in
his place. It was in nearby Gödöllö Lodge that Karl had to
realize what men of sound judgment in Vienna had foreseen
since the sixteenth of the month: his manifesto, useless as an
appeal to Wilson, served to give a semblance of legality to
secession. One nationality after another staked its claims for
full independence, and the monarch's hope that they would
remain under his sceptre as autonomous nations was dwindling rapidly.

In Vienna, Hussarek's cabinet had tendered its resignation
even while the debate in the Upper House, which dragged
on for three days, was in progress. When Karl returned to the
capital on 27 October, Heinrich Lammasch, designated by
him, at last succeeded in forming a cabinet. At the same
time, the emperor appointed Count Julius Andrássy as
foreign minister of Austria-Hungary. He lost no time notify-
ing Wilson that Austria-Hungary was prepared to conclude a
separate peace based on the Fourteen Points. He was never
to receive a reply. 'In Prague the Czechoslovak state has
been proclaimed without the dynasty', Franz Brandl, a senior
police official, wrote in his diary on 28 October.[2] 'Union
with the Polish state has been announced in Galicia ...
Andrássy has sued for peace. The German ambassador was
most astonished.' Was he ignorant of the telegram Karl had
sent the Kaiser the day before? ('Even the closest brotherly
feelings of alliance have to yield to the consideration that I
must save the existence of those lands whose fate divine
providence entrusted to me. For that reason etc. etc.') People
of German-National persuasion, though as profoundly weary
of war as the rest of the populace, promptly spoke of 'that
ultimate perfidy of the Habsburgs'.

In Austria proper the mood of the public has turned
against the dynasty [Brandl noted]. The emperor is
denounced as a tippler, his wife as a traitress, the Parmas
as having lined their pockets; and people seem to be
certain that the regalia have been spirited abroad. Today
the emperor, who is not ignorant of those wild rumours,
decided to test his popularity. At noon Their Majesties had

themselves driven out of the Hofburg in an open car. It
advanced at a slow pace toward Ballhausplatz, where
hundreds of people are regularly milling about [in front of
the foreign office] in expectation of news. . . . The imperial
couple were greeted by warm ovations on their drive. Such
is the ancient magic of their station. But what importance
do [such reactions] of fortuitous passers-by have if
weighed against the aloofness of the apathetic masses, and
against the malice of the few activists who know how to
whip up indifference into hostility?

The following day at about 5 p.m. the crowd on Ballhausplatz, waxing vociferous, succeeded in having Count
Andrássy step on to the small balcony of his office to address
them. 'Amid the difficulties and responsibilities of my position I cannot now deliver myself of long speeches, [he said,
according to the police report]. I appreciate your coming
here, gentlemen. I pledge my honour to do whatever is
humanly possible to conclude, as circumstances will permit,
a prompt and good peace. Our country and our peace
emperor. . . .' Catcalls interrupted the count. There were
shouts of 'Down with Andrássy!' and 'Long live the republic' and '*Anschluss, Anschluss!*'. As Andrássy could not prevail over the din, he hastened to finish his speech. 'I am
counting on the Viennese,' he finally managed to say. 'My
compliments.' But even before he withdrew from the
balcony in visible indignation, renewed shouts of 'Down with
Andrássy' had gone up. It would seem that the form of
farewell he had chosen, pronouncing it with his upper-class
Magyar accent, impressed the gathering as a scornful allusion to Viennese usage.

Ironically, Andrássy, to believe Brandl, had himself
arranged what he wished to amount to a popular ovation.

And strange to say, the same Viennese democrats [among
the *Reichstag* deputies] who a few days ago had gone all
out for the establishment of a [German-]Austrian republic
. . . brought their people to Ballhausplatz. Police headquarters, asked for help to get 'the whole' of Vienna there,
had warned against the plan, public opinion running
against Andrássy. . . . Massive crowds are at this moment

marching along Ringstrasse, shouting, 'We want the
republic, down with the Habsburgs!'

In the late morning of the next day, 30 October, about a
thousand students assembled in the great hall of the university. These were mostly reserve officers happening to be on a
two-month furlough for studies such as the army had instituted in mid-1917. 'With the *Rektor* at their head, they
adopted a resolution demanding that the [newly formed] . . .
[Provisional] National Assembly proclaim union with
Germany. Then they started marching . . . in the direction of
Ballhausplatz, chanting "Andrássy must go, Andrassy must
go". But as soon as they learned that the well-known German-
National deputy, Dinghofer, had entered the university, they
turned round to rush into the great hall again, where
Dinghofer made a speech, at whose conclusion the students
bared their heads and began singing *Deutschland, Deutsch-
land über alles. . . .*'

In the afternoon a throng of many thousands in front of
the Lower-Austrian Landhaus and all along Herrengasse
and its side streets, expressed deep concern about the
political developments, [the *Neue Freie Presse* reported
on 31 October]. Perhaps that demonstration, which lasted
from early afternoon to dusk had better be called a great
open-air assembly of Vienna's population. Liberals,
German-Nationals and Social-Democrats were present,
and it is significant that the Socialist speakers, too, addressing the massed people from the balcony of the Landhaus,
called on them as 'Viennese', rather than 'comrades', as is
party usage. A number of deputies spoke, but also others,
including an army officer in field uniform, and all of them
pointed out that while the old Austria was being carried to
its grave, a new German-Austria was being born. They all
implored people to preserve order, shelve differences of
party allegiance, and be careful not to sully with violence
or bloodshed the greatest revolution our fatherland has
ever experienced.

The word 'revolution' harked back to the tumultuous scenes
in March 1848. But unlike the demonstrators of 1848, those

of October 1918 never got out of hand, did not break into the Landhaus to wreck its rooms, and made no attempt to push close to the nearby Hofburg.

Some demonstrators took umbrage at the presence of police, [according to the *Neue Freie Presse*] and cries of 'Police go home' grew ever louder and more vehement. . . . The windows of all the buildings on Herrengasse were occupied by spectators. The mansion of the prime minister's office was the exception, and its apparent aloofness seemed to live up to pre-1848 standards. For the rest, the apartment houses and aristocratic *palazzi* had their great day; and inasmuch as remnants of a deeply conservative group, however outdated, still linger on in that neighbourhood – and more than one family may have lived on the same premises for generations – one can easily imagine a grandson standing at the same window from which his grandfather had watched the exciting events of March 1848 . . . witnessing the birth of a new epoch, an epoch which has now grown old and weary.

While those 'stiff-necked noblemen' of 1848 had seen troops firing at the revolutionaries after themselves being pelted with stones, their grandsons were spared the sight of such bloody scenes. The only soldiers in view were isolated men without arms making common cause with one or some other group of demonstrators. The vociferations which partly interrupted, partly followed the speeches, ranged from '*Heil* the German nation' to 'Long live the International', and the songs intoned, from the *Wacht am Rhein* to the workers' anthem. More frequent and more insistent than all chants, however, was the cry 'Peace and bread, peace and bread' echoing in the narrow street. As Brandl's diary notes report,

Socialists exchanged with German-Nationals such compliments as 'Hohenzollern flunkies' and 'international rabble'. Not one single voice was raised in support of the emperor. Yet there are hundreds of thousands of Christian-Socials in Vienna. Where were they? . . . There were more speeches [from the Landhaus]. Finally the [Christian-Social] mayor, Weiskirchner, appeared on the balcony. But no sooner had he opened his mouth than he was silenced by a thousand-fold 'Down with him, down!' and he had to retreat. Are there really no Christian-Socials left in Vienna?

More alarming incidents occurred toward evening.

Communists roved the streets calling, 'Free the political prisoners, liberty for Friedrich Adler! ...' At night a wild mob of some 2,000 men approached the Rossau barracks, where the army keeps its prisoners, and tried to storm the building. They had just about broken down the bolted door when mounted police managed to push the crowd off and disperse it. At the same time another mob, several thousand strong ... converged on the War Ministry and began chanting, 'Peace peace peace!' About fifteen hundred people demonstrated in front of Parliament House for Lammasch's resignation ... and about three thousand were standing on Michaeler Square [in front of the Hofburg] demanding the emperor's abdication. It took the exhausted police until after midnight to restore order. No military assistance was given. ... There may be no more than ten [army] companies in Vienna. The others have melted away,

Brandl closed his diary entry, and then, as an afterthought, wrote, 'Meanwhile the political prisoners, including Friedrich Adler, have been released.'

Rumours of scores of wounded in the barracks incident — unfounded rumours, as it turned out — were all over town the next morning. Only some smallish motley groups had taken to the streets. Those men and women looked oddly forlorn in the drizzle coming down. 'Peace, peace and bread' they were shouting in intermittent attempts at unison. Now advancing in one direction, now in another, and then again standing still as if to start a meeting, they called out, 'Up the republic', or 'Long live the republic', or simply, 'Hoch, hoch!' They appeared to be uncertain as to whether the gentlemen in the Landhaus had actually proclaimed the republic during the past night. (They had not. They had elected a State Council and entrusted it with 'assuming governmental powers in all

German-speaking territories of the Monarchy'.) A fanatical-
looking middle-aged man carrying an opened umbrella was
rushing from one knot of people to another, shouting 'Down
with Andrássy, down!' and eliciting curiously half-hearted
insults directed at the foreign minister whose professed
endeavours to bring peace seemed suspiciously slow-moving
not only to the demonstrators. They were increasingly angry
at the police known to have cordoned off Ballhausplatz and
locked the gates of the park stretching from that square to
Ringstrasse.

It was along that famous tree-lined boulevard circling the
larger part of the Inner City that more sizable groups started
promenading once the rain had stopped at noontime. Working people were arriving from their suburbs, unaccompanied
by such party marshals as used to keep order in the ranks of
Socialist marchers. There was no tendency towards violence
among them. Only when more and more juveniles joined
them – and also many soldiers, who marked their unilateral
separation from the army by rakishly sloppy outfits – did the
assemblages deserve the name of 'mob' which the police
report was to apply to them without discrimination. That
Liberal middle-class element the *Neue Freie Presse*'s
reporter had noticed the day before in the crowds on
Herrengasse was absent. At about 2 p.m. one group of
excited demonstrators grew impatient and started converg-
ing on the War Ministry.

> They blocked a motor car in which the Minister was riding
> with Lieutenant Field Marshal Bardolff . . . and demanded
> that they remove the cockades from their hats, and when
> the gentlemen said they'd do no such thing, rocks began
> flying, the windows of the car were shattered, and the
> Minister sustained injuries on the back of his head. . . . The
> police, numerically weak and splintered, could barely
> prevent worse excesses. Time and time again they had to
> shield army officers who were refusing to yield to the
> terror of yelling mobs.

By mid-afternoon knots of them were in many places of the
Inner City. They were drumming with their fists on the iron
shutters the shops had rolled down, or tearing vainly at the

knobs of the locked doors of apartment houses. On Neuer Markt an intoxicated army sergeant, brandishing a revolver, stormed into the lobby of the Hotel Meissel and Schadn and demanded to be handed over a certain captain who had taken refuge there after declining to divest himself of his cockade. The sergeant was subdued by police.

Even during the demonstrations in front of the Landhaus, smallish groups had approached army officers and peremptorily asked them to remove the cockades, even though they, too, having come to Herrengasse, signalled their yearning for a new order. About twenty officers and enlisted men styling themselves the soldiers' council, managed to enter the *pro tem* office of the First President of the Provisional National Assembly [it had elected three].... They had no cockades on their hats and no longer wore any war-service medals. In leaving the Landhaus they jeered at the uniformed guards in the entrance hall who still sported their rank insignia. 'You fellows will be through soon, now we're taking over.' On 31 October such demonstrators had grown more forward. Whenever they came upon an officer, they ordered him to turn over his cockade, and ripped the stars from the standup collar of his tunic. Those little gilt stars denoting rank had become overnight a symbol of all the iniquities the common man, in uniform or out, was certain he had suffered at the hands of his betters.

Of course, cockades worn by the servants of a crumbling regime had been a provocation to its assailants at least since the French Revolution. The rioters in Vienna surely were not cognizant of historical precedents. They had got wind of the 'cockade-down!' wave started in Prague on 28 October. To Czechs, the emperor's initials into which the gilt yarn of the cockade was braided had been as much of a challenge as had the Habsburg flags they had lowered in their bloodless national revolution, or the sculptured Habsburg eagles they had severed from the façades and rooftops of public buildings and defenestrated in accord with age-old Bohemian custom. The 'off-with-the-gilt-stars' movement was a Viennese refinement.

A large soldiers' meeting took place at night at

Lembacher's tavern, where the draft board used to assemble, [Brandl noted on 31 October, late at night]. The soldiers were making some efforts to agree on leadership and organization.... Pretty radical words were being used. Despite all the senselessness of the speeches, a leaning towards Bolshevism could not be ignored.... Calls for a 'red guard' were heard. No doubt, a 'council of soldiers, workers and peasants' on the Russian model is being considered. [Finally] some two thousand men, led by officers, marched to the War Ministry, waving red flags.

Those officers had 'de-cockaded' themselves and got rid of their rank insignia, as had many army officers with no radical sympathies whatever during the night of 30–31 October.

The cockade-and-stars hunt was to continue for weeks. It was to lead to many ugly scenes, not least around railway stations where the troops arrived from the field in varying degrees of discipline or in wild disorder. For good measure, the hunters would also manhandle Slav officers in transit through Vienna who had covered their cockades with bits of cloth in their own national colours. Nor, in those earliest days of the Austrian Republic (or German-Austrian Republic, as its statesmen called it) would *its* red, white and red colours satisfy those roving bands. Nothing short of a cockade-less hat and a star-less tunic collar would please their egalitarian mood and the pleasure in humiliating yesterday's privileged men. In the memory of Viennese contemporaries, that chase was to remain easily the most rebellious aspect of the first days of the republic.

It was a thing of the past when the scarcity of jobs and the reluctance of disbanded officers to fill positions they deemed beneath them created a special class within the mass of unemployed Viennese, and undisguised *Schadenfreude* gave birth to a doggerel sung to the tune of an old *Heurigen* refrain. It may be translated into this quatrain:

> Now who's going to sweep the streets?
> The gents without stars,
> Without medals and bars,
> Now they'll be sweeping the streets.

What was liberated Friedrich Adler up to – Count Stürgkh's assassin whose name had remained a symbol of revolutionary martyrdom to the proletariat even after his death sentence had been commuted? Was he planning to put himself at the head of a Russian-style communist party? (Unknown to the public at large, including most workers, the two small groups of radical leftists set up clandestinely early in the war had each sent a messenger to Adler upon his release from prison. Both urged him to break with the Social-Democrats, whose war policies he had censured bitterly at his trial, and assume the leadership of a new socialist party. In what was to be a decision of the greatest consequence, Friedrich Adler had turned down the suggestion.)

The loosely knit bands of ragged runaway soldiers turning up now on one street, now on another, breaking out in wild yells or in a hoarse chorus at one time, and at another shuffling along in sullen silence, seemed to usher in the actual revolution whose nightmarish image had for weeks been intruding on the upper class's wishful assurance that this just couldn't happen in their Vienna. What, ironically, scared them most, as they were watching the incipient riots from behind their windows, was the conspicuous absence from the streets of the 'workers' battalions', proudly so called by the Socialist press since the 1890s. Were those hundreds of thousands waiting for the disturbances to get out of hand, so that they could take over? And if they should would those masses retain their vaunted discipline, be obedient to the Victor Adlers and the Karl Renners? And if they would not, were the police capable of checking rebels 'determined to stop at nothing'? Wherever police showed their faces, they were hooted at and showered with derisive calls of *Mistelbachers!* (a sobriquet which, referring to the name of a backward village, had even in prewar lower-class Vienna been applied to the police force in an allusion to its predominantly rural recruitment). On 1 November, it appeared to be under orders not to provoke the demonstrators. Policemen were standing, in small squads, in the entrances of buildings, or close to their walls. No mounted police were within sight.

It was all over town that the past night's soldiers' meeting had set up the 'terror troop' whose name of Red Guard in fact had been rumoured for some days. At noon it went into action for the first time, a few hundred strong. Marching toward Parliament House, they ran into a strong column of German-National students issuing from the university with their knotty walking sticks brandished. . . . Only late in the afternoon did rumours of bloody clashes die down. Police had succeeded in keeping apart the two groups, after all. It was said that the red, white and red cockades worn by the police detachment had lowered tempers.

People of the middle class who happened to see the new cockades stared at the sight with ambivalent feelings. While the transformation might pre-empt the spreading rebellious ardour, the unwonted colours also drove home the irreversibility of the great change they had not asked for. In days to come, they would also recall how, walking through the streets of the Inner City, they saw men on ladders in front of certain hotels and coffeehouses pasting over with burlap such words as 'Emperor', 'King of Hungary', or 'Habsburg' on the familiar signs, or shopkeepers painting over the gilt letters designating the stores as purveyors to the court.

The republican rump-Austria might re-establish legal authority. But who, people were asking themselves, would enforce the law on the streets? And never free of that apprehensive question, they could not prevent their thoughts from straying to the one instrument of authority that life had taught them to view as supreme – the army. It was no longer assisting the police in their work – no longer, in fact, to be seen. But was it not still defending the country against the Italians?

For once bad news had been travelling slowly. It was true that, during the first three weeks of October, separatist passions, plain defeatism and enemy propaganda had affected the men at the front far less than their fellows to the rear. It was equally true that the Italian onslaught had met with dogged resistance for five days even from regiments made up of a rainbow of nationalities. At dawn on 29 October, however, a Czech detachment on the middle Piave, being attacked by British troops, refused to counter-attack; and the unit on its left flank, consisting of Tyroleans, ordered to close the rapidly widening gap, panicked at the sight of the Czechs withdrawing in confusion. 'Home, home!' the Tyroleans shouted, obviously foreseeing wild hordes of pillaging Czech deserters crossing their own defenceless valleys on the way to their native regions. That near-rout was the beginning of the break-up. Neither the Czech mutineers nor the unnerved Tyroleans were aware that at the very hour they refused orders a general-staff officer accompanied by a non-commissioned officer with a white flag, was crossing the enemy line to carry the emperor's request for a cease-fire to the Italians. Within forty-eight hours – while the Italians, eager to avenge Caporetto through pursuit and victory, were dragging out negotiations – resistance crumbled all along the front. Non-German soldiers simply left the trenches, or abandoned their guns and ammunition depots, and in some units hastily formed soldiers' councils stripped officers of their rank. . . . Such, then, was the situation on the south-western front – *the* front, in the day's parlance – while un-reliable news allowed the Viennese, if they so chose, to believe in a front line still holding fast despite national revolution in Prague, in Zagreb, Budapest and the capital of Galicia and despite social revolution stalking their own city.

Those two movements seemed to have coalesced in Budapest. At dusk on 31 October, the first day of Károlyi's regime, Count Tisza was murdered in the presence of his family by four army deserters. 'The hour of reckoning has come!' shouted one of them before firing his pistol. Loathed as a stubborn reactionary to the last, Tisza was also assumed, not least in Vienna, to have been the chief instigator of the war. (Nothing could be further from the truth. On emerging from the fateful meeting of the Joint Ministerial Council on 7 July 1914, he had sent a dissenting memorandum to Franz Josef, prophesying that 'war with Serbia would in all human probability bring about the intervention of Russia, and therewith world war'.[3]) The news of the murder, reaching Vienna before dawn on 1 November, did not spark off any violence against instigators of war, whether real or rumoured. Official propaganda had obfuscated the record of the outbreak of the war for so long that even the two men history would single out for that sorry distinction were no longer the butt of retributive indignation. They were also out of sight – Conrad, the warmongering general, had been deposed; and Count Berchtold, the author of the fateful ultimatum on Serbia, had long been relegated to the office of lord chamberlain. Unknown to the public, he had taken himself off to Switzerland, the Habsburg family jewels in his suitcase, at about the time when Count Tisza's assailants were forcing the door of his villa in Budapest.

Alarmed by the news of the assassination, Vienna's garrison commander detailed a company to each of the four residences of the imperial family. Those four companies constituted the entire force at his command. The rest had melted away.

> They have taken along whatever victuals were in the barracks . . . [and] civilians are busy looting the deserted army camps on the outskirts of the city [Brandl noted]. While most soldiers hailing from rural districts have left town, its streets are also empty of those with family ties in Vienna. There must be many who don't know where to turn, and what might happen to them tomorrow.

And then the police official closed his entry for 1 November by persuading himself that 'the men in the front line are still holding their ground'.

The following morning the *Neue Freie Presse* dispelled that illusion. 'The army is in the process of breaking up,' Benedikt wrote, before proceeding to plead for *some* sort of co-operation between the new states to prevent utter chaos. The Károlyi, regime had by this time instructed all Hungarian soldiers to leave their posts and start on their way towards their homeland.

> Soldiers everywhere are lacking all supplies. Escaped prisoners-of-war are threatening the country with large-scale deprivations and arson. . . . But when Graz and Klagenfurt and Vienna are being sacked, Prague and Cracow will not remain untouched. The preservation of law and order in Austria and Hungary is a problem of worldwide importance. . . . Or will the Allies rejoice in spreading lawlessness and terror? Incendiary social move-

ments have grown up in their countries, too. . . . And the nation-states within Austria [*sic*] must surely wish for their new independence to remain untainted by criminal destruction of life and property. . . .

No similar wishful thinking animated the State Council of the new Austria (which had meanwhile moved from the Landhaus to the parliament building, and taken over the chambers of the defunct Upper House). In a proclamation posted on 2 November the State Council paid no heed whatever to the states outside its own country's (tentative) borders. Addressing 'the German *Volk* in Austria', that proclamation read as follows.

The country is imperilled.

The army is disintegrating. Order has ceased. The non-German men have started on the road to their homes. So, alas, also have the German soldiers. Worn out by the long war, they obviously do not stop to consider the consequences of their disorderly disbanding – famine, destruction, mass unemployment, and bottomless misery. The guards of P.O.W. camps are deserting their posts, leaving Italians, Russians and Serbs free to inundate the countryside.

Those perils must be stemmed at once. . . . No new bloodshed must be suffered by our much-tried people. Unless the flood is halted without hesitation, the lives of thousands of men, women and children may be doomed.

To all ablebodied men who feel in their hearts the task of building up our new German state, of regaining the blessings of peace . . . and securing the liberties of our nation, the call goes out to report voluntarily to German-speaking army units. They will form detachments for the defence of all property – above all such provisions as still exist – for the protection of the lives of all citizens, and for the safeguarding of our liberties.

Citizens of the new Austrian fatherland, face the extent of the danger, and protect yourselves by heeding this appeal. Put yourselves at the service of your nation's sacred interests. The people's government is relying upon you.

Their sensibility numbed by the hyperbole of wartime announcements, the Viennese by and large were not fully trusting the dismal picture drawn by a State Council of whose actual powers they had but a hazy notion. Only some days later would grapevine news, rather than printed reports, induce the public to visualize the self-disbanded soldiers throwing away equipment, abandoning guns and waggons, pouring into the villages of Carinthia and the Tyrol, and storming east-bound and north-bound trains, forcing their engineers to proceed at full speed. For many weeks, indeed months, gruesome stories would be told and retold of soldiers crouching on the roofs of railway cars and being decapitated as the train entered some tunnel or passed under some road bridge. Accounts of the pillaging and the raping in which soldiers who were making their way on foot along the choked highways engaged would cause even sceptics to shudder. But the horror at those reported atrocities still lay in the future during the first days in November.

Coffeehouses were not deserted in those confused days. In the barely lit recesses of the *literati*'s cafés, young intellectuals congregated to discuss with fervour the day's political and social problems and those to come. Some of them opted for personal commitment. The Prague-born journalist, Egon Erwin Kisch, fresh from army service, had been quick to join the Red Guard (and for some days was to be its commander); and the poet Franz Werfel was seen one day haranguing a crowd in front of one of Vienna's big banks. (During interrogation at police headquarters, some days later, he apparently made a fool of himself.) Needless to say, it was inspiration rather than knowledge, let alone political information, that pushed revolutionists of that kind into action; and neither leftist socialist dissenters nor the political prisoners who had been released had much use for their antics.

Theatres had not stopped playing. Restaurants had not closed down, and inflammatory rumours of peace-time meals served in some of them were making the rounds. *Heurigen* places kept open for those who still managed to reach them. There was no end at their tables to stories of high policy decisions 'divulged' by citizens who swore they had been told about them by men involved in making them. Often curiosity was outweighing fear. A morbid kind of curiosity seemed to direct conversations toward Schönbrunn. The old Viennese fascination with the stage lent poignancy to the drama one knew was being played out at the court of the Habsburgs.

While the labouring population had written off the young man in Schönbrunn, his helplessness recommended him to the compassion of Vienna's middle classes. Whatever they had reproached him with in the past months seemed to retreat before the image of his dilemma. Except for appointments he had made, audiences he had granted, crown councils he had presided over, medals he had awarded, or titles he had bestowed, reliable news of his doings was hard to come by. Despite the absence of working-class demonstrations close to Schönbrunn Palace, the memory of the massacre of the Tsar and his family was never far from the minds of middle-class people. The press had remained silent on the whereabouts of Karl's small children, but it was known that the imperial couple had left them behind in Gödöllö Lodge on 27 October; and until their duly announced arrival in Schönbrunn two days later there had been talk of their being held hostage in the smouldering country of the Hungarians.

This morning's cabinet meeting [Josef Redlich (now Minister of Finance) jotted down on 1 November], I reported on the dismal situation at the treasury.... Banhans [the Minister of Railways] spoke for the cabinet's resignation ... Lammasch suggested that it be postponed for a few days because of the imminent armistice. Andrássy has, for that reason, put off his resignation.... I moved that we go into conference with him, with the Minister of War, and the German-Austrian State Council. The motion was passed, and the subsequent meeting lasted from 5.30 to 8.30 p.m.

Ahead of it, Karl Seitz and Victor Adler had been at Schönbrunn, following the emperor's invitation. He related to them [and three other members of the State Council] the Italians' armistice terms. Hard as they are, he tends to accept them, but does not wish to agree to let

Allied troops enter the Tyrol, as these would attack Bavaria. Adler told the emperor that he and his friends 'could not free those who started the war from the responsibility of ending it'.

After the emperor had withdrawn, the State-Council representatives agreed that they would definitely not advise him on the terms of the unavoidable surrender. Upon Karl's joining them again, Victor Adler, who had suffered a heart attack on the outset of the meeting, told him that 'an armistice [had] to be concluded forthwith. However, the German-Austrian nation will not shoulder the burden of the crimes of the Austro-Hungarian Monarchy. . . . That old Austria is dying, but the German-Austrian nation wants to live without being cursed by the world for what old Austria did. Those who started the war must also end it.' Whereupon Karl remarked, 'I no more began this war than you did. . . .' The fact that the old Socialist leader had spoken to the emperor with such freedom became widely known in the following days. Middle-class people, whatever their individual feelings about the Habsburg court and its recent record, could not fend off a measure of pity for the humiliated heir of Habsburg power, 'poor Karl', as he was now sometimes referred to in those circles.

In the night of 2–3 November the rumour of a new peril was seizing Vienna. The guards of the p.o.w. camp at Sigmundsherberg, less than ten miles to the north-west, had all of them absconded, and the Italian prisoners, having looted a nearby depot of rifles, were on the march toward the capital. They had not been treated well, and the Viennese knew this. As it became obvious in the course of 3 November, the self-liberated captives, weakened by a year's hunger rations, had descended on farmsteads to feast on their provisions, and appeared to have no intention of sacking Vienna. Nevertheless, many upper-class people took their valuables to the vaults of their banks. They did not know what they feared most – the escaped prisoners, the homecoming natives, the 'foreign' ex-soldiers, or the Bolsheviks; and the worst nightmares were picturing combined actions of the four.

A cabinet meeting discussed for hours security measures

for Schönbrunn and the advantages and disadvantages of the emperor's departure for Switzerland. Among the many talks he himself had on that day, none is more pathetic to recall than the audience he granted to Prince Schönburg-Hartenstein, the army commander Karl had nine months before offered the powers of a virtual dictator, only to withdraw the offer within the day. Now that old soldier had been called to Vienna.

The emperor was still negotiating with the 'State Councillors' who wish to pin the responsibility for the armistice on him, [the prince wrote in his journal]. Talking to [the chief of the general staff] I suggested that His Majesty take himself to the most endangered sector of the front in the Southern Tyrol to prevent the Italians crossing the Brenner Pass. . . . But while we were talking, information reached us that even some of the German-speaking units there had refused orders. At last the emperor received me. I found my Supreme Commander unbroken, although the pallor of his face betrayed ill health. He began listing the provisions of the armistice, which amount to Austria's destruction. Referring to the State Council, he said that he had bound himself to nothing. Then he said [Schönburg-Hartenstein wrote in a family letter of the same day] that he had summoned me to have me influence the nobility. They should assemble around the throne and help him. . . .

The prince was dumbfounded. The nobility was loyal any way, he wrote, and announced his decision to return without delay to his headquarters (which meanwhile had been moved farther to the rear), 'to restore order, if given the means to do so. However, to face mutineering troops is no easy task. Those who are still marching in formation are keeping discipline, but it's the deserters, malingerers, marauders who represent the great danger. Maybe, nay, probably, my role as an army commander will end soon, as the various State Councillors are taking over. Those gentlemen surely will want no truck with a prince. . . .'[4] By that time the high-born governors of Galicia and Bohemia had yielded to the national revolutions with barely a gesture of protest; in Hungary the magnates, stunned by Károlyi's radicalism, had withdrawn to their country estates; and in Bohemia, many noblemen had for some time been trying to make common cause with Czech nationalism.

Those men of great families who did service at court as chamberlains, or guard officers, were still going through the motions of the four-hundred-year-old Spanish ceremonial.

In the A.D.C.s chambers I saw the charming Countess Bellegarde, [Redlich noted upon one of his calls at Schönbrunn Palace]. She was moving across the parquet with all the gracefulness of a rococo marquise. A number of immaculately attired guard officers were on duty. The breath of an age passing was in the air, a whiff of decay mixed with the fragrance of an utterly refined, albeit tired culture. Are those who will soon spread their legs in these rooms going to understand that *Kultur* and be able to develop it?

Asking himself that question, Redlich was characteristic of the wealthy upper bourgeoisie he came from. In those days of farewell the Habsburg court was being mourned by him as barely more than a prop appealing to his taste for refinement. Amidst all the misery, the uncertainties and the apprehensions through which he was living, there was room for that peculiar and peculiarly Viennese sense of bereavement.

❧ 8 ❧
Exit the Emperor

Neither at the Landhaus meeting of 21 October nor in the
second session of the Provisional National Assembly a week
later had there been any unambiguous demand for the emperor's abdication. However stridently street demonstrators
demanded the establishment of a republic, even the Socialist
politicians had only gingerly tackled the question of the form
of government. 'Quite deliberately the problem has not been
discussed. . . .' Karl Renner wrote in the *Arbeiter Zeitung* of
31 October. 'For the dynasty, the court, and the civil list
belong to the institutions that were common to all nationalities [of Austria-Hungary]. We who are organizing our own
German-Austrian state . . . have nothing to do with those
institutions.' Not that the Social-Democrats doubted for a
moment the uselessness of a sovereign for the new state. But
constituting numerically the smallest of the three political
factions in the Assembly, they were careful not to rush the
decision.

On Sunday 3 November, the cardinal-archbishop of
Vienna closed his sermon with these words.

As Catholics we support the monarchical form of government – not that the Catholic Church on principle looks
with disfavour upon any other form of government, but
simply because we see no reason for breaking faith with
our emperor. . . . In these days marked by the spirit of
despair that a lost war engenders it must not be left to the
street, or for that matter to politicians whose mandates are
scarcely valid any longer, to determine the future form of

government. At the right time and after careful deliber-
ation, the entire nation must vote on how it wishes to
arrange its future.

Cardinal Piffl also said, 'If the newly formed nation-states do
not wish to sink to the level of third-rate powers, they will
have to unite sooner or later.' Did he really hope, that late in
the day, for what some politicians were now speaking of as
a 'Danube Federation'? And if he didn't, how could he fail to
see that an emperor at the head of rump-Austria would be
nothing short of an absurdity? That new Austria, as proclaimed at the Landhaus, comprised some six million people
only (not counting the Bohemian and Moravian Germans it
was claiming). Yet his declared monarchism was not merely
emotive. It was meant to build a dam against the 'Red flood'
that he and many others saw approaching, and which he and
they refused to distinguish from the republican thrust of the
Social-Democrats.

Even more than by their militant republicanism, the
Christian-Social politicians were troubled by the Socialists'
predilection for union with Germany and their obvious
desire thus to strengthen the power of her Social Democratic
party, as well as their own. 'We, too, know', the *Reichspost*
commented on 31 October, 'that German-Austria must keep
the door open to the *Anschluss* idea. . . . But we also know
that that prospect terrifies our industry.' In fact, by 3 October
the influential Association of Industrialists had reached the
conclusion that their members' Bohemian plants located in
German-speaking districts would be better off in a Czechoslovak state than in a German-Austria belonging to the
Reich.

On 4 November the Christian-Social journal declared
roundly, 'Today we are celebrating our emperor's name day,
as we have always done. Only those who have never been
truly loyal, only the wavering, the weak and the turncoats
wish to forget him. But they, too, are unable to do so. His
care is catching up with them. Even in their flight they are
not escaping his love. His heart is stronger than their pessimism. . . .' Redlich, who the following day made a note of the
high mass celebrated at St Stephen's, with Cardinal Piffl

officiating, remarked on the 'oppressive mood of the congregation. The *Te Deum* and the words ... of the Habsburg anthem sung at the conclusion of the service, on the one hand: and everybody's awareness of the [national] revolutions victorious throughout the realm, on the other – how pathetically incongruous they were!' Karl's cabinet ministers and the court dignitaries were in the front pews. Contrary to protocol, they had not donned their dress uniforms and had slipped in through the side doors of the cathedral. No demonstrations, such as the police had predicted, took place in St Stephens's Square during or after the service. Later, it was spoken of as a requiem for the dynasty, both by its detractors and by those who mourned its passing. According to Brandl's diary, 'The Emperor, accompanied by Her Majesty, went shooting in the Lainz preserve [close to Schönbrunn] in the afternoon' of his name day.

The disturbances of the past week, no less than the wild rumours, had preoccupied the Viennese to such a degree that they were all but unable to assess fully the military disaster. Persistent accounts of resistance that isolated units offered the Allied attackers, and of heroic exploits, had kept the public from recognizing the cease-fire offer of 29 October as the surrender it had been. The provisions of the armistice signed on 4 November were not published until 6 November.

By then the break-up of the Habsburg state was for all practical purposes completed. Yet the Viennese, appalled by the terms of the imperial army's surrender, spoke of them as having been imposed. By the armistice, all Austro-Hungarian troops (called thus in its documents even though 'Austria-Hungary' no longer existed) had to be demobilized forthwith and to evacuate foreign territories everywhere; and the Allied armies were given access to all sections of the monarchy and its railways. That was not, however, the end of humiliating news. Through a mixture of Italian cunning and Austrian confusion the armistice did not come into force until twenty-four hours after its signing, and the Italians, the bulk of them emerging from behind the British and French units that had spearheaded the offensive, captured some 300,000 soldiers. The 'victory' of the Italians, as their unilateral interpretation of the armistice, incensed the Viennese.

They mustered little regret when they learned some days later that a group of released Italian p.o.w.s had been beaten up by a mob in the railroad station of Innsbruck. But for all the indignation at the trickery of the Italian army command, wealthier people would soon realize that the capture of those hundreds of thousands was not only bound to ease the precarious food situation, but also cut the numbers of potential free-booters and rebels among the homecoming soldiers.

They began arriving at Vienna's western and southern termini from 6 November. Although *gendarmes* had been posted at certain railroad stations on the approach to Vienna to disarm the returning men before they reached the city, a good many of them had managed to retain their rifles. In altercations verging on violence in some cases, they brushed aside the demand, spelled out in large posters, for handing weapons over to the Vienna police, who seemed to have had orders not to make any arrests. Some squads of the hastily recruited People's Defence Force (*Volkswehr*) who had come to the railroad stations, were looked upon with little confidence, if not outright dismay, by policemen. Hunger-ridden conscripts from training camps and barracks, rather than front line veterans, had been the first to enlist upon the State Council's appeal. To believe early critics of the *Volkswehr*, many men of the 'green cadres' had made their way to Vienna to join up, and released political prisoners had known how to infiltrate the new force. Its officers, whether impecunious career men or ideologically motivated reservists, were at the mercy of the units' soldiers' councils which elected or deposed them with scant formality.

The most bizarre element of the military establishment of the new state in its earliest days consisted of Rumanian-speaking natives of Transylvania who were denied transit with weapons by the Hungarian government; informed of the threat the army of the Rumanian kingdom posed to their province, those men had refused to hand over their arms. They had been held together and provisioned through the efforts of a certain reserve captain who was also a popular Transylvanian peasant politician. Captain Maniu approached the newly created Under-Secretary of Army Affairs, the Socialist Julius Deutsch, putting his own force at the disposal of Vienna's security arrangements. The offer was accepted, and Rumanian-speaking soldiers, some 20,000 of them, started guarding public buildings, railway lines and bridges.

With a swiftness that stunned the Viennese the disintegration of the south-western army was duplicated in the other theatres of war and in 'pacified' enemy territory. German-speaking men, in units or alone, started reaching Vienna from Poland and the Ukraine, Southern Hungary and Serbia, Albania and Rumania. Each of the five railway stations and the squares those grimy buildings fronted, were swamped by veterans who, wretched or truculent in appearance, tried to regain their bearings in a world whose sights and sounds were vastly different from the nostalgic daydreams of the past. Exhausted railroad personnel, *Volkswehr* detachments, constables, curious juveniles, prostitutes and clusters of aggressive-looking tramps were bustling amid the returning soldiers, the *Heimkehrer* (men coming home) of those days' curiously sentimental coinage. Women lingered on the fringes of the crowds, and now and then stopped a soldier to ask desperate questions about the whereabouts of their own husbands and fathers. The neighbourhoods' side streets had turned into markets for military equipment or such loot as soldiers had garnered. Some squads, having managed to load horses on box cars, were selling those animals for a song, and requisitoned machine guns were purchased for the current price of a bottle of wine.

Rifles retained by returned soldiers served to arm self-appointed patrols (or commissions, as they were calling themselves), who lost no time breaking into private homes in search of food and valuables, or tampering with the iron shutters of shops, producing a clatter that frightened people within earshot into taking it for the sound of machine gun fire. The pillagers, often intoxicated, met with no resistance on the part of their intimidated victims. Sometimes a bargain was struck to get rid of a 'commission'. The police seldom interfered. Uncertain of the chain of command, they were wary of things to come. They had seen the handbill originating (as it turned out later) from a group of radical university students and hailing the 'world revolution which, having commenced in Russia, is on the march to victory among us'.

During the night of 4–5 November a group of erstwhile soldiers, harangued by some ex-prisoners from Russia and a number of bohemian *literati,* had shouted the Communist Party of German-Austria into existence in the basement of a popular tavern. Along with the Habsburgs, the army officers, the exploiters of old, and the war profiteers, that meeting condemned the Socialist politicians who were betraying the workers by co-operation with the middle-class parties. Deriding the anxieties that Vienna's undernourished work-men's families might feel at the prospect of 'real revolution' the speakers urged their audience to cut all class ties with the 'faint-hearted mock-socialists of yesterday, today's trimmers', and fill the ranks of the Red Guard to protect the proletariat.

The Social-Democratic executive did not under-rate the attraction of such wild exhortations and the emotions they might be stoking in men freed overnight from the bonds of military obedience. Radical slogans had been in the air for close to a year, and while their effect in the workshops had been small even during the great strike, the soldiers in the training camps and barracks had from mid-summer on been seen as easy prey for Communist agitators. It was then that Julius Deutsch had persuaded some of the soldiers to keep him *au courant* with the mood of the troops on the home front.

His was an extraordinary record. A worker's son who had gained a law degree, he had done his military service before the war, and in its course been promoted to the rank of first lieutenant in the Reserves. An ardent Socialist, he was early in 1918 recalled from front line duty by the War Ministry and installed as a liaison officer with the trade unions. (In certain postwar polemics of Christian-Social politicians, that unorthodox move of the Minister, which had aimed at smoothing work in the war plants, was to assume the traits of a Socialist conspiracy reaching high places.) At any rate, Deutsch's informers did come in handy as recruiters for the new *Volkswehr.*

As [it] was being born [Otto Bauer recalls] it was not a party troop. It was a motley crew of poor and ignorant men brutalized by the war. The assurance of regular pay was drawing them into the new force. Had we left it to its own devices, the *Volkswehr* would have transformed into bands of mercenaries using their weapons to plunder the country; stooges of their own naiveté which made them assume that a few hundred armed men and one machine gun in Traisen or Ternitz [small Lower-Austrian towns] would suffice to change Europe's social order. If the new force were to pose not a grave peril, it had to be put under a strong command sure of its aims. . . . One way to achieve that goal might have been to strengthen the power of the officers. But in those days when hatred of the officers' corps . . . was as general as it was fierce, such an attempt would hardly have succeeded, and if it had, it . . . would have turned the armed force of the nascent republic over to counter-revolutionaries or even monarchists. . . . In those days of the breakdown of traditional authority, the authority of the Social-Democratic party was stronger than it had ever been. Only [our] party could keep the bands of armed proletarians in order by imbuing them with its ideology . . . and prevent them from succumbing to the great temptation of misusing their guns.[1]

That was not quite what the non-Socialist members of the State Council had had in mind when, in conjunction with their Socialist colleagues, they signed the ringing appeal to all disbanded soldiers. But those politicians could not help noticing the disinclination of soldiers who had returned to the rural areas to flock to the *Volkwehr*. Nor could they themselves expect any influence to be exerted on its ranks by the few middle-class men of reserve-officer's rank who, driven by mere lack of funds, joined the new force. 'Nothing is to be seen, nothing to be heard, of any activity of Christian-Social or German-National party leaders,' Brandl wrote in his journal. 'It is as though the earth had swallowed them all. The Reds are triumphant!' Brandl did not care to separate in his mind the labouring masses and their leaders from the Bolsheviks and their Red Guard. At best, men of his kind viewed the former as waiting in the wings. The middle classes had no conception of the Socialist leadership's efforts to neutralize the Red Guard. And how could they guess the actual motive of those endeavours once Deutsch had assured the Red Guard that it would be welcome in the *Volkswehr*?

That was not the first encounter between the Red Guard and the Socialist politicians who had risen overnight to high office. On 1 November, All Saints' Day, one of its self-styled commanders, a Corporal Haller, had forced his way into the office of Karl Seitz, the State Council's 'First President,' and had demanded Red Guard representation in that body. Some three hundred of Haller's men were lending emphasis to his stormy request by intoning the *Marseillaise* in front of the building. Seitz, originally a schoolteacher, was a soft-spoken man. He also had – quite an asset even in those turbulent days – an impressively patrician appearance. Haller's troop was not yet organized, he was told, and only an organized group of citizens could hope to get representatives into the country's governing council; why did not Haller 'as a first step register the Red Guard as an association in conformity with existing regulations'? The corporal agreed that the suggestion made sense. As he led his men back to their barracks, he declared Seitz's advice to have amounted to a turning point on their way to power. Their later admittance to the *Volkswehr* appeared to them as a momentous event.

However, in the course of the following week, a chilling rumour was gaining credence among the Red Guard men. Julius Deutsch was said to be infiltrating Social-Democratic spies into their own ranks. And, unable to identify those clandestine agents, the Red Guard, now housed in the Stift barracks close to the Inner City, grew restless. With the hour of decision at hand, they were champing at the bit.

What was the emperor waiting for? Why was he not going to the proverbially faithful Tyrol? Why did not the elder arch-dukes and the great noblemen spirit him out of Vienna? It was lower-middle-class folk who asked those questions, and who may well have wanted to wash their hands of whatever might befall the occupant of Schönbrunn Palace. To be sure, Christian-Social voters might still derive some solace from the proclaimed belief of their publicists in the permanence of what always had been. On 8 November the *Reichspost*, reacting to an outburst from the *Arbeiter Zeitung* which had chided a certain judge for passing sentence, as he always had, 'in the name of His Majesty the Emperor', stated bluntly, 'Imperial rule is a fact. The provisional government of German-Austria is acting on the strength of the imperial manifesto [of 16 October] .... We have an emperor. We have an imperial dynasty. We live under imperial rule.'

Pronouncements of that kind were not likely to impress upper-bourgeois circles. At the same time they did not really fear for the safety of the emperor. They were certain that the Socialist party leaders were determined to keep their voters in line. While drawing-room conversations derided the plain labour politicians in their new roles as statesmen; while high-echelon bureaucrats gleefully expected them to stumble over the intricacies of administrative business; and while businessmen railed at the utopian experiments they foresaw, none of them could bring himself to believe that the Socialist politicians regarded the court as more than a sideshow. For Vienna's bourgeoisie, to its own embarrassment, was itself moving toward a similar way of looking at Schönbrunn.

It had been a lonely place since 2 November. At noon on that day, the Hungarian battalion that happened to be on duty with the permanent household guard marched off in compliance with Budapest's orders to all Hungarian soldiers to return home. Of the Upper-Austrian battalion that the following morning was entrained for Schönbrunn, no more than fourteen enlisted men had arrived with their officers at their destination. By that time, a company of cadets had arrived from the military academy of their own volition to take the place of the Hungarian deserters (boys aged fifteen and sixteen years whose appearance mocked their brave determination). Once the guardsmen, too, had decamped, leaving behind their colourful tunics and plumed helmets, there were no sentries in the doorways of the palace or at the doors of its halls. Except for a handful of officers, a score of aides, some ladies-in-waiting and the servants, the imperial family was alone in the vast building.

Rumours of its imminent storming had not left the chief of police unmoved. He had reinforced pickets at the locked park gates. Towards midnight on 2 November he had thrown protocol to the wind, called the emperor to the telephone, and, warning him that a mammoth demonstration of workers was to be reckoned with in the morning (a Sunday), had implored him to get away from Schönbrunn with his family at once – only to ring up again at dawn to report that the danger had somewhat receded. Nor was that early Sunday call the last telephone conversation the police chief, Johannes Schober, forced on Karl. He on his part does not seem to have lost his composure even while, during the following days, the last trappings of imperial power were falling away.

The Foreign Office of the Austro-Hungarian monarchy had dispatched one of its senior officials to Switzerland to meet representatives of the Allies and ask the victors to 'let His Majesty be of service in the orderly liquidation of the past. ...' On 7 November – forty-eight hours after Karl's name day had been celebrated at St Stephen's – the Allies' reply rebuffed that pathetic plea: 'the nations of the erstwhile Austro-Hungarian monarchy having decided on its dissolution, they themselves were precluded from negotiating further with the government of His Imperial and Royal Majesty.' By the time that message arrived no such government existed any longer even in name. Andrássy had resigned on All Saints' Day.

A meritorious general continued to sit in his office as the commander of the Vienna garrison, which in truth had ceased to exist. It would seem that that old soldier discarded for the sake of domestic peace the repeated offer of one of the field marshals to 'rescue' Vienna with some regiments he had managed to keep together on their withdrawal through Carinthia. At any rate, the garrison commander did not once go to Schönbrunn.

On Friday 8 November, Redlich was received in audience.

The emperor began by saying that we [the cabinet] must remain in office, for if we left he too had to leave – had to abdicate. I impressed on him the necessity to remain calm.

Dynasties go under, I said, only when they give themselves up. . . . Then he touched on the impossible notion of an independent German-Austria, which in reference to its cartographic shape he kept calling a 'pennant'. . . . I found the emperor talkative without being unduly excited. He looked healthier than he had some days ago. What he was saying was quite intelligent. Yet I could not rid myself of the impression of a peculiar emptiness in him, and of the unreality of his thinking. Only the voice, as he was talking away in his 'Viennese', produced a semblance of liveliness, the shadow of personality. I enlarged on my hopes for a federation of the free nations of Austria-Hungary . . . with him as the federal president. I do not think that those ideas are of much interest to the young gentleman. . . . At night I called on Lammasch, and from him heard the news of Kaiser Wilhelm's abdication.

Redlich over-rated the lethargy of the young gentleman. At the very moment when all of the twenty-odd kings and reigning grand dukes of Germany followed the Kaiser's example and relinquished their power, resilience, that most precious of Habsburg heirlooms, asserted itself in Karl. Before daybreak on Sunday (10 November) he composed a letter to the cardinal-archbishop of Vienna, asking him to bring his influence to bear on the Christian-Socials in the Provisional National Assembly, which was to vote on Monday on the form of German-Austria's government. In other words, the young gentleman who had scoffed at the oddly shaped 'impossible' rump-Austria in his talk with Redlich wanted to be retained as its sovereign. (In the light of the exiled emperor's futile attempts, in March and October 1921, to regain Hungary's crown, his last-minute effort to hang on to the throne in Vienna must be seen as a bid for keeping a foothold, no matter how small, in the dissolving realm.)

Cardinal Piffl read Karl's message brought by his press aide and without delay had himself driven to Parliament House through the rain-swept streets. Monsignor Hauser, the chairman of the Christian-Social party, was taken aback by the unexpected visit. The mood of the public, he said, was

not in the emperor's favour, but 'I promise Your Eminence to
keep the Christian-Social party by the imperial flag. And if
all [of its parliamentarians] should turn their backs on it, I
won't.'[2] Piffl returned to his mansion where Karl's messenger
had been waiting, and made a suggestion of his own. By
yielding to the 'democratic current of the day', His Majesty
would make it easier for the Christian-Socials to support the
dynasty's case. An imperial proclamation putting the
decision on the future form of government into the hands of
the people itself would give a good argument to Monsignor
Hauser, and might still frustrate the crucial vote. Surely the
cardinal could not put out of his mind the shattering news
from Bavaria, that stronghold of the Catholics of the *Reich*.
On Friday – a day before the Kaiser's abdication – a workers'
and soldiers' council had been set up in Munich, and a
popular peasant leader had made common cause with Kurt
Eisner, an eccentric leftist, in deposing Bavaria's king and
proclaiming the Bavarian republic.

When Piffl's message was delivered at Schönbrunn, the
imperial ministers had begun discussing Karl's situation.
Seitz and Renner, who at times were asked to join the
deliberations, left no doubt about the determination of the
State Council's majority to have the form of government
voted upon the following day. 'We tried to provide for
alternatives,' Redlich recorded. 'We [ministers] feared that
the republic might be proclaimed in the streets, or the Red
Guard storm Schönbrunn Palace and force the emperor to
abdicate. . . .'

Renouncing his throne was out of the question for Karl,
and little though Vienna's people knew of the actual agenda
of all the Schönbrunn conferences, rumours of his dogged
refusal were seeping through to the public. They had a
curious effect on the middle class, who could not suppress
some respect for the young man. Not for him to sneak out
from under his purple, as had the Kaiser in fleeing to Holland
under the cover of darkness.

On Monday at 10.30 p.m. Lammasch and Herr von Gayer,
his Minister of the Interior (originally a police official
charged with security measures at imperial residences), came
with the draft of a manifesto for Karl to sign, which his

cabinet had hammered out in conjunction with the State
Council. That document salved the conscience of the
former, and came close to doing all of the latter's bidding. In
the crucial passage, Karl was to declare that he renounced
'all participation in the affairs of the [German-Austrian]
state, and recognized in advance the decision [it] would
arrive at on the future form of government'. The long hours
of the past night's meeting were telling on the two ministers.
Lammasch, trying to comment on the spirit of the manifesto,
while tears were streaming down his cheeks, was unable to
finish the first sentence. When Karl seemed hesitant to distinguish between withdrawing from power and renouncing
the crown, Gayer in great agitation warned him that, unless
the manifesto was published the same day, 'masses of
workers will come here ... and then those few who won't
abandon Your Majesty will fall in the fighting and with them
Your Majesty himself and the All-Highest family.' The
emperor took his press aide aside and asked him to repeat the
message of the cardinal-archbishop. Then he called in the
empress. She no more than cast a glance at the manifesto
before she burst out, 'A sovereign may find himself yielding
to brute force. But abdicate he must never – never!' It is well
to recall that it was a princess whose grandfather had been
shot down by revolutionaries who proceeded to exclaim, 'So
be it. Even if all of us should perish on this spot, the dynasty
would live on, there would still be Habsburgs!' Only after
her husband had led Zita into the adjoining study, and both
had convinced themselves that the document before them
did not represent a formal abdication, did the empress calm
down.

Raised voices were penetrating the study, and after
repeated knocks on the door, some of the emperor's aides
entered and, without being asked, reported on the restive-
ness of the two cabinet members who were being pressured
by telephone calls from their colleagues. Gayer, who had
remained standing on the threshold, broke down in tears,
begging His Majesty for an instant decision. Finally, the
press aide, a youngish man favoured by Karl, said to his
master, 'The manifesto leaves all constitutional roads open to
Your Majesty and the imperial House.... Madness is loose

today, and a madhouse is no place for a sovereign.' Whereupon Karl Habsburg took up a pencil and signed the type-
written manifesto that had been presented to him.[3] Printed
within a couple of hours, it was posted forthwith all over
Vienna.

The Christian-Social politicians had assembled in their
clubroom early in the morning. They were rather proud of
the fact that it was one of their own, the astute monsignor
Seipel (who held a cabinet post under Lammasch) who had
devised the telling formula of the manifesto which was to
spare Karl outright abdication. But while all of them were
hoping fervently for his signature now, they began examin-
ing the tactics the signed manifesto would enable them to set
in motion. Their Socialist fellow deputies did not cease
sending messages into the meeting to impress upon it the
mounting dangers in the streets, and in front of the clubroom's windows German-Nationals were walking up and
down, carrying black, red and gold flags and shouting abuse
at the Habsburgs as the betrayers of the German nation.
What, in addition, unnerved the Christian-Social politicians
was the alarming news from the provinces (*Länder*).
Although some reports of it had reached each of the men
over the past four or five days, they evaluated their import
fully only under the strain of their meeting. The peasants of
Upper Austria, terrorized by returned soldiers and p.o.w.
escapees, were demanding a government able to restore
order; a majority of the Tyrolean diet had expressed its
preference for a republic; in Vorarlberg a separatist movement which aimed at a union with Switzerland was gaining
adherents; and hastily printed leaflets appealing to the
ancient attachment of the rural populace to the throne, and
mailed to the local party organizations by Christian-Social
headquarters, were being returned to Vienna in bulk. It was
true that the intimidated leaders could count, next to the
well-off conservative men who had come to them in the past
fifteen years or so, upon the lower middle class of Vienna –
Lueger's original constituency, whose loathing of the *Sozis*
could be assumed to have transferred itself to a republican
government so frantically advocated by *them*. However,
voting in accord with the mood of those oldest of Christian-

Socials might well expose all of them to the vengeful hostility of the proletarian masses. It might also brand the party itself as reactionary, and thwart its participation in a public life certain to be marked by the slogans of progressive policies. The unhappy politicians knew they would refrain from putting the effectiveness of the manifesto to the test. Silently, they filed out of the clubroom to walk over to the chamber of the erstwhile Upper House. At 3.15 p.m. the Provisional National Assembly, three Christian-Socials abstaining (Monsignor Hauser was not among them) passed the act for the republican form of government.

One move was still incumbent on Lammasch and his moribund cabinet. They had themselves driven to Schönbrunn to tender their resignation. The orders of merit, or Privy Councillor's titles, habitually bestowed on resigning ministers, had not been forgotten there. 'Tears stood in the eyes of every single one of us,' Redlich recorded. 'The scene was inflicting an almost physical pain on me. . . .' It was left to Gayer to apprise the imperial couple of the imminent occupation of Schönbrunn by the police. Karl, deeply shocked, said that one of his aides was on the way to the State Council to ask it to arrange for his departure abroad. 'Gayer succeeded in convincing the young monarch that railroad conditions connected with the demobilization were making such a trip impossible for the time being. The emperor said he would not spend another night in Schönbrunn Palace, which was no longer his, and would move to his own hunting lodge of Eckartsau. He would go to Switzerland later. . . .'

By the time people stopped to glance at the posters announcing what they were quick to refer to as Karl's abdication, they had been thrown into additional confusion by rumours of a Red Guard putsch. It was to take several days to establish the facts. What happened was this. A Red Guard detachment, storming into his office, had demanded that Deutsch issue an order for the occupation of Schönbrunn Palace by the Red Guard. After refusing to comply, the under secretary drew the men's attention to the command headquarters of the Vienna garrison as the true seat of the reactionaries. The Red Guard soldiers, led by an enthusiastic

Egon Erwin Kisch, hastened to the command building, where in fact a number of staff officers of the Habsburg army were still going through the motions of doing duty. The attackers, with not a little bravado, placed two machine guns in the doorway of the building, and proceeded to invade its offices and molest the elderly gentlemen. None of them was harmed. Later in the day Deutsch appeared on the scene and, commending the Red Guard for its zeal, prevailed upon Kisch to lead his troop back to its barracks. His replacement, the same night, as the top commander of the Red Guard by a former editor of the *Arbeiter Zeitung* who had done duty as a reserve officer at the front, was to be the only consequence of the farcical enterprise.

It was 7 p.m. before seven motorcars arrived at Schönbrunn. As the imperial family and its retinue got into the vehicles in the inner courtyard, the cadets of the military academy, drawn up in impeccable order, presented arms. The automobiles, eschewing the main gate, took a tortuous route to slip out of the park's precincts. It was a foggy night. The workers' masses feared by the police chief had not come. Nor were any curious people within sight in the vicinity of Schönbrunn or along the road the family travelled. As police headquarters put it in a report to the State Council two days later, 'To the bulk of the population, the form of government is a matter of indifference.'

Victor Adler, seized by a coronary attack on Sunday morning, had died some hours before the National Assembly was called to order the following day. Vienna's working men and women had been utterly devoted to the selfless man. Yet they did not give themselves up to mourning his death. They had reason for celebrating. Late in the afternoon, while the form of government resolution was being posted throughout the city – next to, or overlapping, the emperor's manifesto – red flags were appearing on the tenements of the workers' districts. Over the past two or three days the party executive, certain of victory, had been working out the logistics of the mass demonstration projected for 12 November; a march along the western section of Ringstrasse to Parliament House. The State Council was scheduled to proclaim the republic from the steps of the building. As darkness was falling on 11 November, the 'rent barracks' were alive with preparations for the great day.

In the same hours the windows of the Inner City shops and public places were being boarded up. Many apartment tenants had found a locksmith to have bolts and chains put on their entrance doors. Coming on top of the news of the Red Guard *coup de main*, the red flags on display in the suburbs seemed to undermine the workers' well-publicized plan for a strictly orderly march on the Inner City. It may be safely assumed that its inhabitants that night were fervently hoping for the drizzle that had set in to turn into a rainstorm.

Ever since 1905, when Vienna's workers for the first time paraded in closed ranks past the parliament building – encouraged by news of the revolution in Russia, they were demonstrating for universal suffrage – the Social-Democratic party had regularly dissuaded the police from interfering with marches of organized labour and their *Ordner* (marshals). Vienna's middle classes did not expect that old agreement to be broken. In fact, the chief of police had been informed by the organizers of the procession that '*Ordner* will safeguard discipline' and '*Volkswehr* units will be posted in front of Parliament House'. (Had the middle class known of the power of command the Socialist party thus assumed over the *Volkswehr* as a matter of course they would have been still more disquieted.) According to the report the police chief was to render on Tuesday night, 'the Secretary of the Interior [on Monday] gave orders ... that no constabulary must be on duty on Ringstrasse'. However, at about 9.30 a.m. on Tuesday (the workers, undeterred by the rain, had by then assembled in their various districts) Karl Seitz suggested that 'police should seal off the side streets of Ringstrasse in the vicinity of Parliament House' to prevent an influx of unorganized crowds ... and also 'keep the building itself cordoned off till 2 p.m.' At that hour a selected group of workmen from Seitz's own constituency would occupy the ramps that led up on both sides to the landing of the wide steps descending from the portal. 'That change in security measures ... was approved by the Secretary of the Interior. Still, the police kept their entire force in readiness, and concentrated a large part of it at the police stations close to Parliament House.'

Inside it, a strange meeting was in progress that morning. A week-old resolution of the *Reichsrat's* Lower Chamber asked for its re-assembly on 12 November, and sorely truncated as it was by the force of events, it had re-assembled. Besides a handful of Poles and Rumanians, who had come out of habit or curiosity, all German deputies were present, including those from regions claimed by the Czechoslovak state, by Italy, or by the new South-Slav kingdom. Silence reigned over the hall which had been the scene of so much unrestrained shouting for so many years. The House had to be dissolved – this much the deputies knew, as they were eyeing one another, or gazing at the rows and rows of empty seats. Their sense of formality, which had always been present in Austrian affairs side by side with easy-going muddle, did not allow the men to let the old country's parliament simply vanish. None but the emperor could dissolve it, according to the constitution, and Emperor Karl had 'renounced all participation in the business of government'. The dilemma was defying solution for close to an hour. Finally, a German-speaking Bohemian moved that the House be dismissed *sine die*. The motion was passed unanimously. That done, the German deputies rushed to their clubrooms to prepare for the session of German-Austria's Assembly in the chamber of the erstwhile Upper House, whose members had dispensed with a final meeting.

Meanwhile, the workers had started to leave their places of assembly, shepherded by their shop stewards first, and then by the *Ordner*. Here and there in the formations placards were carried, although the letters were even then nearly washed out, and a number of red flags were held aloft, soon to grow limp. The marchers, their miserable clothing more and more drenched by the rain, were not presenting a very festive picture.

As they entered the various lower-middle-class neighbourhoods to be crossed on the way to the Inner City, clusters of men in attire hardly better than their own were seen standing on the pavements and waving black, red and gold pennants; catching sight of the counter-demonstrators, some

workers would call out, 'Up with the socialist republic!' and
'*Hoch, hoch, hoch!*' came the response of their fellow-
marchers. 'Up with the German republic!' some of the men
posted on the pavement would call out and promptly elicit
a chorus of echoes from those about them. There was a sort
of ritual rhythm to those exchanges, which were regularly
taken up again after lengthy intervals. The knots of German-
National counter-demonstrators, vastly outnumbered by the
marching Socialists, stayed at their stationary positions. The
marchers left them unchallenged. Perhaps it was the incessant
rain that dampened the fighting spirit. Perhaps it was the
fact, bemusing the workers, that the groups on the pavements
were hailing the very union with Germany, the *Anschluss,*
which their own leaders had been advocating for weeks.
Besides, the demonstrators, forewarned of provocations,
were determined to uphold the air of decorum fitting the role
of their party on the great day. 'Up with our republic!' some
of the workers were shouting now and then as, increasingly
out of step with one another, they walked on, their footsteps
muffled by the mud that had collected on the cobblestones.

At certain intersections, special *Ordner* halted the columns
before channelling them for realignment into the main
streets leading to Ringstrasse. Considerable delays resulted
in the process. The shouts died down, and the men and
women engaged in some discussion among themselves,
besides cursing the rain. Who would proclaim the republic?
Would it be Seitz, elected chairman of the party upon Victor
Adler's death? Or Karl Renner, the chancellor of the new
Austria? Or perchance Friedrich Adler? Next to nothing had
been heard about him since his release from prison. . . . On
the fringes of the throngs, cyclists were moving with deliber-
ate slowness – some of them wearing red armbands, while
others, young fellows in quasi-military garb, had decorated
the spokes of their vehicles' wheels with strips of red paper.
Were these Red Guard men? They carried no weapons,
though. No *Volkswehr* soldiers were to be seen anywhere,
and no police.

The rain stopped at about half-past eleven. By that time
quite a few youths, who somehow had reached Ringstrasse
ahead of the marchers, had climbed the iron fence of the

public gardens facing Parliament House, the gates locked. Others perched on the leafless branches of the horse chestnuts lining the boulevard on both sides. Later in the morning, a number of young men would even mount the pedestal of the larger-than-lifesize statue of Athena midway between Ringstrasse's western pavement and the Grecian building. Upon its completion in 1883 someone had suggested that Pallas Athena, the goddess of wisdom, having found no place inside the home of legislation, had to be accommodated outside it. That quip had amused the Viennese ever since.

Long before the legislators were to meet, the 'stream of human lava' (as one journalist called the demonstrating workers) had poured into Ringstrasse. The convergence of the columns coming from different directions had been handled well by the *Ordner*. Once they had reached Ringstrasse, however, those lucky enough to march by Parliament House were slowing their pace to a near-standstill. Soon the ever-growing throng was overflowing the square-like approach to the *Burgtheater*, on the one side, and the avenue that led to the Palace of Justice, on the other. Within an hour, the multitudes had occupied streets farther off, as well. Unable to move, they nevertheless did not push on. Even though they could look forward to no more than a vicarious participation in the historic event they had come to witness, they did not appear frustrated or restless. Vendors of small red, white and red paper flags were circulating in the crowds without doing much business. Were the workers disinclined to buy those pennants? Later, it was said so in certain quarters.

At 3 p.m. a hush fell over the packed boulevard: the Assembly had gone into session. Dinghofer, presiding, was flanked by Seitz and Monsignor Hauser. Renner took the floor.

The Republic of German-Austria is a part of the German republic ... [he began, only to be interrupted by an outburst of enthusiastic approval in the visitors' gallery]. That was not an easy decision to take, [he went on when the hand-clapping and shouts had abated]. The State Council negotiated for weeks with the neighbouring

nations. For all the courtesy shown us, we did not succeed
in removing the obstacle raised [to some kind of feder-
ation] by the Czechoslovak state – its demand to have
dominance over an essential part of our nation. . . . We
now declare solemnly that we shall never surrender any
part of our *Volk*, never give up any part of our land. . . .

Again the chamber reverberated with shouts of consent. The
deputies had jumped to their feet. No doubt they were aware
of the blatant discrepancy between Renner's ringing words
and the helplessness of the rump-Austria his government had
authority over (if it had), in the face of Czech, South-Slav
and Italian encroachments. Ominous news from the borders
had reached them, and they also knew only too well that
Masaryk, months earlier, had convinced London and Paris of
the indivisibility of Bohemia and Moravia despite the three
million Germans within their borders. Were the representatives of the German-Austrian nation still pinning their hopes
on Wilson and his doctrine of national self-determination?
Or had their hopes turned to the German republic as a shield
against the greed of the nationalities of yesterday which the
fortunes of war had turned into victors? But was not the
German republic all but at the mercy of the workers' and
soldiers' councils that had sprung into existence?

There was some bad conscience in the Christian-Socials'
choice of their spokesman. The day before, Wilhelm Miklas
had been one of the three deputies to cast their vote for the
monarchical form of government. Now, speaking after
Renner, he returned to his party's original wish to have a
referendum at some later date to decide on the form of
government. 'However, we have no desire to jeopardize the
unity of German-Austria's representative body,' that upright
provincial schoolmaster said. 'We Christian Socialists, true to
the tenets of our Catholic faith, will submit loyally to the
authority of the new state as organized either by the House
now or by the whole population later. . . .'

The rest of Miklas's speech, as that of the German-
National spokesman, was swallowed up by the commotion of
the members leaving their seats. At 3.45 p.m. Dinghofer
adjourned the session. The train of deputies making their

way through the lobby lacked solemnity from the beginning. Some of them were actually running towards the doors, followed by reporters. The gentlemen of the State Council had difficulty in reaching the exit.

Meanwhile a press of people had occupied the twin ramps of the building. Red flags and a large canvas sign bearing the inscription 'Up with the socialist republic' were held aloft by that curiously silent group. It was close on four o'clock when the dignitaries stepped out of the portal. Dinghofer proceeded to proclaim the resolution that the Assembly had adopted. No sooner had he, in his closing words, ordered the red, white and red flags of the new republic to be hoisted than some Red-Guard men got hold of them, tore the white stripe out of the flags, tied their red parts together and began running them up. Reports as to whether those red flags reached the tip of the poles – or how long it took to replace them – are not conclusive. It would seem that the solemn chorus intoned, according to programme, by a workers' glee club distracted the attention from the struggle round the flag poles. At any rate the multitude listened in silence while Renner and Seitz addressed them, and then the crowd began to break up.

Meanwhile the men on the ramps had started to elbow their way toward the great portal – only to have it shut in their faces. But almost at once some armed Red-Guard men tried to force the locked portal, demanding to be admitted, and the crash of rifle butts smashing windows was heard. 'Suddenly a shot was fired. It pierced the panes of one of the side doors, and crossed the anteroom of the pillared lobby. The many men who were still there and those in the lobby itself ran for cover, and the lights were turned off. A second and a third shot followed, and then actual salvos. . . . The shooting lasted six or eight minutes.' The reporter of the *Neue Freie Presse*, who gave that account on 13 November, wrote nothing of the rat-tat-tat that, upon the first shot, had provoked some of the Red Guard into firing their rifles. Or so its two delegates, who were allowed into the building once the shooting was over, asserted in great agitation as soon as they faced Seitz and the Under Secretary of Army Affairs. That shot, that first shot, they insisted, had been aimed at no one, fired into the air. . . . The truth of the matter was that a clerk of the house administration, hearing the detonation, had hastily lowered the metal sliding shutters of his office window, producing a succession of sharp sounds which battlefield veterans could in fact mistake for machine gun fire.

Whether it was that alleged machine gun fire from inside the building, rather than the random shooting outside it, that threw firstly the people on the ramps and then the multitudes below into panic, would be long disputed. The headlong retreat of the crowds, now ruthlessly pushing forward, now trying to take cover, the futile shouts of the unnerved *Ordner*, and their equally futile attempts to link arms and stem the mad rush, and the cries of stumbling women, were not for years to be lifted from the consciousness of the demonstrators themselves and of those who by word of mouth were to learn of the disastrous aftermath of the republic's proclamation. As was learned the following day, of the thirty-two persons delivered to hospitals, three had been injured by rifle shots. (Two were to die, one of them a twelve-year-old boy.) But the tales in circulation in the late afternoon of 12 November spoke of scores of people shot or trampled to death. The details of what had gone on inside the parliament building, while its doors were blocked by Red Guard soldiers with fixed bayonets, did not become public knowledge till late at night; only then dispelling the widespread rumour of a Communist putsch attempt whose ringleaders were holding Seitz, or the entire State Council, hostage.

Actually, Seitz and Deutsch were negotiating with the two men who stuck to their story of the Red Guard having been fired upon by a machine gun, and could not be deflected from their demand that they be permitted to search the building. But no sooner had Seitz, after nearly an hour of heated talk, granted their wish than they declared they would be satisfied with his affirming, 'on his word of honour', that no machine guns were on the premises. That Seitz did, and the two men left his office. Notified by them of the satisfactory outcome of the negotiations, the besiegers cleared the ramps, and after sheathing their bayonets marched off in military formation.

The upper-class concept of a word of honour introduced at the climax of what bourgeois people were quick to call a 'socialist family quarrel' might have amused them. But the record, as it emerged, of outrages committed in various other spots of the Inner City seemed to point to a master plot, whose existence was not conducive to humour. Even while the demonstrating workers had been standing expectantly in their places, a Red Guard detachment had ambushed a group of German-National students close to the university and, with drawn revolvers, forced them to hand over the two black, red and gold flags they had carried. According to the police report, 'the flags were hurled into the mud and stamped to tatters'. And shortly before the first shot was fired in front of Parliament House, 'two officers of the Red Guard appeared at the door of the Town Hall ... and demanded peremptorily that the red, white and red flag on top of the building be hauled down, as its colours constituted a provocation'. To keep emotions under control, the [Christian-Social] mayor ordered a red flag to be flown side by side with the national colours. And then, at 4 p.m., there had occurred the storming of the *Neue Freie Presse*.

Some 150 heavily armed men forced their way into its building and occupied the offices and printing plant. A group of Communist *literati* who had hurried over from Parliament House, escaping the panic about it, proceeded to elect an editor-in-chief; and the compositors were compelled, Red Guard soldiers at their elbows, to set a special edition up in type.

Workers and soldiers of Vienna, [it read]. By seizing the *Neue Freie Presse* the German-Austrian Communist Party, supported by the Red Guard and a large part of the *Volkswehr* ... has manifested the demand for the instant establishment of the Socialist Republic of German-Austria. That demonstration has served its purpose by showing that the will of the labouring population is carried out by the Communist Party. Workers and soldiers of Vienna, we have proved that it is up to you alone to assume all

political and economic power at once. Organize and set up
workers' and soldiers' councils, which will enable you to
establish, as your brethren in the *Reich* are doing, a
socialist republic of workers', soldiers' and peasants' councils. Long live German-Austria's socialist republic!

Another text, promising continued Communist control of the
Neue Freie Presse, and also denying any Red Guard participation in the shooting outside the parliament building, had
apparently been printed earlier. At any rate, the self-styled
new masters of the paper were unable to distribute either of
the special editions in quantity. Although the Red Guard had
placed four machine guns in position, a large detachment of
police arriving at 8 p.m. made short shrift of the fellows
manning them, entered the building, and bundled the occupiers off with little fuss. By that time they also had received
stern orders from the *Volkswehr* command to vacate the
premises without any delay.

It was significant of the dislike for the young *Volkswehr* on
the part of the police that their official report did not
mention those orders. And, curiously, their own bloodless
action, as publicized, served to scandalize Vienna's bourgeois,
who compared that effective intervention with the conspicuous absence of police from the scenes on the parliament
ramps earlier on that day. Where indeed had they been?
'When the first signs of unrest became noticeable,' Schober's
memorandum read, 'some sizable detachments [of police]
were sent to the vicinity of Parliament House. In the end,
eight hundred men, a part of them equipped with rifles, plus
military police and some units of [former] marines now
under police command were on the spot, ready to intervene
if that should prove necessary.' Thus it would seem that
Schober had cast aside his earlier understanding with Seitz.
It also appears that the commander of the forces on the spot
had not deemed it necessary to interfere with the wild
shooting of the Red Guard and its virtual siege of the
building. Their restraint, whatever may have been its
reasons, had at any rate prevented a bloodbath. But that was
not the way the middle classes looked at the incident which
they insisted on calling an abortive Communist putsch.

On 13 November, the *Arbeiter Zeitung* went out of its way to dispel public alarm by declaring that only a negligible minority of the Red Guard soldiers were members of the Communist party. The Red Guard on the whole, the editorial went on, let alone the Social-Democratic party, must not be made the target of suspicion! On the same day, the Department of Army Affairs also changed the name of the Red Guard, to list it henceforth as Battalion 41 of the Vienna *Volkswehr*. But common parlance did not drop the old designation.

❧ 9 ❧

The Umsturz

The world has never seen the like. For seven hundred years the Habsburgs were great European princes. In certain periods, they rose to dominate the world. Only a hundred years ago [at the Congress of Vienna] their splendour was shining forth from the Hofburg, the seat of the world's leading power. ... Today, the crowns of Austria, of Bohemia, of Hungary, of Croatia are no more than historical relics. ... These events denote changes of such magnitude in people's thinking, one must compare them to natural phenomena. It is as though mountains were being submerged and valleys rising.

Thus the *Neue Freie Presse* had concluded its editorial of 11 November. The people's thinking was summed up less dramatically four days later in a police report from one of Vienna's middle-class neighbourhoods.

The overwhelming majority of the population favours the republican form of government [it read]. Dynastic sentiments have disappeared on account of the war's unhappy outcome. There is general indignation at the [former] army commanders, particularly those on the Italian front, who are being blamed for having brought about the present distress of 'German-Austria' by their careless and wasteful management of food reserves and equipment. ... The present shortages of food and fuel imbue people with a veritable dread of the immediate future. They are railing at the Czechs because of the total embargo they have imposed, and demand that ration cards be taken away from Vienna's Czechs in retaliation and also because their local associations are assumed to take care of their own.

The fear of the morrow was permeating the summary that Schober's own office drafted on 20 November.

A deep disillusion [had taken hold of the Viennese] inasmuch as most of them, upon the collapse of the army and the signing of the armistice, had taken comfort in the sanguine thought that at least their material conditions would be improving speedily. Given their disappointment, political events arouse very little interest. Only the news of Czechoslovak [measures to enforce their] claims to Bohemia's and Moravia's German areas, and the separatist movements in the Tyrol and in Vorarlberg enter people's apprehensive conversation. So do goings-on . . . in Germany.

In the first two weeks of November the cataclysmic happenings in their own country had made the Viennese by and large incapable of taking in the day-to-day course of Germany's upheavals. The Kaiser's abdication had dismayed no one in Vienna; even its small pan-German journal preferred to hail the German *Volk* and its 'undefeated army' rather than bemoan his disappearance. The Majority Social-Democrats who held the top government positions in Berlin were reasonable men in the eyes of their fellow-Socialists in Vienna; and while its upper classes winced at the emergence of a one-time saddlemaker as Germany's top man, they appreciated his manifest detestation of violence. However, Friedrich Ebert's Berlin government was being harassed by the Independent Socialists, the radical faction that in the spring of 1916 had broken away from the party (and whose pacifist leaders had spent most of their time since in the *Kaiser*'s prisons). Independents also dominated the 'Council of Soldiers' in Munich and the bizarre government that Eisner had established. When his haphazard actions, along with the fuzzy rhetoric, became known in Vienna, people of Christian-Social persuasion were quick to speak of the 'Bolshevik Jew regime' in Munich, even though there was in those days no trace of Communism in the Bavarian administration. In the last days of November, Eisner scandalized the educated Viennese bourgeois by publishing certain files of the Bavarian foreign office purporting to prove that it had been misled by the *Reich* government in 1914, and implying that Bavaria was innocent of any war guilt. Was she aiming at a separate peace with the Allies, it was asked. The threat of a dismemberment of Germany could not but sour the prospect of a union with her.

'Freezing temperatures have lowered people's spirit to the point of downright despair,' Schober's office stated on 20 November. 'Neither coal nor kerosene is available for households. ... It is widely said that rationing tickets will be discontinued, as it has become impossible to redeem them and war regulations are no longer in force anyway.' Like countless other rumours, that one, too, was without foundation. The bureaucratic machinery kept working on all levels. The co-existence of the new authorities with the old civil service did not result in chaos. The State Council had in no uncertain words reminded the populace of the continued validity of all laws and ordinances.

Attacks on government property or any looting of such constitute the most heinous crime against our commonwealth, [a warning posted on 15 November declared]. Any perpetrator caught red-handed must be turned over to a military or *gendarmerie* post. In conformity with the Articles of War, which are still in force, such crimes are punishable by death.... Individuals who prior to 20 November hand over [government-owned] goods they have stolen, come by in the course of pillaging, or concealed for others, shall be exempt from persecution.

None of the plunderers appear to have availed themselves of that promise of clemency. But neither are any summary trials on record. Military commanders had no stomach for executing offenders out of hand. The soldiers' councils could not be expected to approve what would have amounted to drumhead justice.

The first of those councils had been formed during

October, on the Russian pattern, in barracks and training
camps rather than in the trenches. As soon as the *Volkswehr*
began taking the place of the self-disbanded army units in
Vienna's barracks, Deutsch had encouraged orderly elections
of councils, ostensibly as committees charged with investigating grievances of individual soldiers. Actually, he had
hoped that the soldiers' councils, their revolutionary
language notwithstanding, would keep up a measure of
discipline in the motley force.

That discipline had not been put to the test yet. During
the ill-fated mass march of 12 November the *Volkswehr* had
been kept in the barracks; and the Red Guard men who
turned up in front of Parliament House – or, for that matter,
occupied the *Neue Freie Presse* – had acted against orders.
But middle-class people were not at all certain how
Volkswehr units, had they been called out, would have
behaved in the turmoil. So far from regarding the soldiers'
councils as watchdogs over *Volkswehr* battalions, all middle-
class strata considered the councils as agents of radicalism.
Moreover, in certain of the battalions avowed Communists
were known to challenge the soldiers' councils and their
Social-Democratic party allegiance in wild discussions. Most
ominously, the *Volkswehr* itself was evidently not content
with the role allotted to it. The Socialist leaders did little to
destroy the emerging image of the *Volkswehr* as the armed
force of their party. Its units could be seen marching through
the city with the band playing the *Marseillaise* and red flags
flying; and that paraded self-assurance did more to keep the
fears of a second revolution alive than did stories of
Volkswehr soldiers among the gangs that stopped trams and
ordered passengers to walk home, or 'requisitioned' some
of the few motor cars still on the streets. The red flags on top
of some of the barracks also reduced the credit due to the
Volkswehr for such undoubted accomplishments as the
successful protection of Vienna's arsenal, or the courage
shown in preventing disbanded Czech and Hungarian
soldiers from looting as they were crossing Austrian territory.
The picture that Vienna's middle classes were forming of the
new army was not too different from that which Otto Bauer
himself was to draw five years later. 'The *Volkswehr* had

taken the place of the imperial army [he wrote] and that republican body was filled with the proletarian, the socialist spirit. The power of using the armed forces had passed from the emperor to the nation. Within it, that power also had passed from the propertied classes to the proletariat.'¹ How far would it go in deploying that power? That was the question asked over and over again by people who at the same time tended, wilfully sometimes, to blur the lines between the *Volkswehr* and its soldiers' councils, between the entire *Volkswehr* and the Red Guard and between the three of those and the councils of workers in the industrial plants.

Workers' councils had been set up first in the great January strike. Although an *ad hoc* committee of them had negotiated the end of the strike and driven a hard bargain with the Socialist leaders, in the months since then the councils had on the whole supported the policies of the party and carried its messages into the workshops. The establishment of the Communist party, however, had put the councils under pressure: the Communists, small though their number was, demanded representation in them. Rebuffed, they took the demand to the workers themselves. Haranguing them, Communist 'functionaries', as often as not outsiders, called the councils 'mere lackeys of the sclerotic party machine', which in turn they accused of 'betraying the revolution'. Sometimes, members of the Red Guard would turn up at meetings and call for 'action, immediate action'. To be sure, the Red Guard according to a police report, 'seems to have lost much of the [workers'] sympathies because of the part it is supposed to have had in the shooting [of 12 November]'. Indeed, police headquarters went so far as to suggest that 'worsening business conditions and the increase in unemployment ... also seem to have reduced the workers' confidence that a Socialist regime would be the one to cope best with the present difficulties.'

The difficulties were enormous. The armistice had not lifted the *Hungerblockade*. 'The supply of flour, milk and bread has not improved. ... Similarly, the situation in fruit and vegetable markets has not changed for the better. Various sorts of beets are offered in abundance, and those must

make up for the dearth of everything else. . . .' Even before
the proclamation of the republic the State Council had
applied to Wilson for help, and American aid was being
spoken of endlessly all over Vienna. Not until 24 November
did Washington reply: foodstuffs would be forthcoming,
provided the Austrian government maintained order. The
government understood the victor's alarm at the conditions
in Bavaria, and their determination to keep the Austrian
proletariat, if need be by famine, from emulating the disorders rampant in Munich. Surely Otto Bauer was not alone
in realizing that Wilson's note requested the end of social
revolution in Austria.

Vienna had always relied for its coal on mines in what now
was Czechoslovakia. Negotiations with its government about
deliveries had been opened shortly after 12 November, only
to drag on, exacerbated by the territorial question. Of the
one train-load of coal released finally on 5 December,
nothing was put on the market. With the onset of freezing
weather, 'self-help' became a matter of routine. In the morning of any day, thousands of men and women could be seen
setting out for the woods beyond the city limits. Just as in
late autumn they had dug up potatoes in open country,
heedless of property ownership, now they cut down medium-
sized trees, chopped them up on the spot, and lugged the
wood home. The *gendarmerie* scarcely ever tried to stop
them. In one wooded area the owner was forced by such
scavengers to sign a 'permit'. None of Vienna's newspapers
bemoaned the three-or four-foot stumps left standing as
though to mark the vandalized Vienna Woods so dear to
sentimentalists of the city. Rather, bourgeois journalists were
lamenting the changed face of Vienna itself.

A deep gloom hovers over Vienna during the present
winter evenings, [wrote the *Neue Freie Presse* of 6
December]. The entrance doors to blocks of flats are being
locked at eight o'clock. Only the merest shimmer of light
can be seen behind some of the windows. The city lies in
darkness. The streets, particularly those of the outlying
districts, are as good as deserted. . . . If it should become
impossible to have substantial amounts of coal brought to

Vienna, a total breakdown of gas and electricity production is to be expected.

The *Neue Freie Presse* had rarely referred to living conditions in the outlying districts. Now their desolation was invading the Inner City. And so were the most pitiable of the inhabitants of Vienna.

For a good many months children had turned up in the Inner City to beg. Their numbers were now rapidly increasing. The police averted their eyes from the urchins, many of whom were wrapped in some piece of military clothing much too large for their emaciated bodies. Even less did police officers feel like moving on disabled veterans. The dissolution of the army had reduced the personnel of overcrowded hospitals and rest homes. It had also loosened their discipline. Patients were known to complain aggressively about unheated wards, the paucity of food and the lack of tobacco. Although army hospitals were under the authority of the Liquidating War Ministry of the defunct imperial government, the soldiers' councils of certain *Volkswehr* battalions took it upon themselves to investigate conditions. The doctors maintained that they interfered with the policy of discharging patients who could walk, thus contributing to the restlessness among inmates. Soon, some of them made it a habit to leave their wards for some hours on days without snow and reach the Inner City as best they could. Never accosting passers-by, the invalids could not be accused of begging. They merely accepted coins or cigarettes such as some passers-by would hand them. Along Kärtnerstrasse and Graben, once the locale of the *Corso*, one-legged veterans hobbled along on crutches – a reminder of the shortage of artificial limbs which had long been whispered about – and from time to time stopped to lean their maimed bodies against a lamp-post or the wall of some building. Although the Viennese had known of mutilated soldiers returning from the front and they had even heard that there were soldiers returned from battlefields with parts of their faces blown off, newspaper stories telling of the wonders that plastic surgery wrought had not prepared them for such grotesque mutilations as they now caught sight of. Foreign newspapermen, who had begun to arrive, were reminded of the streets of Near-Eastern cities as they watched the cripples who seemed to display their disfigured bodies. Perhaps the most shattering sight of all was provided by ex-combatants trembling, or shaking, all over – called *Zitterer* in a new Viennese coinage. Their jerky movements of head or arms, frequently accompanied by a facial tic, carried an element of angry impatience, which seemed to reproach the able-bodied survivors of the war for their good luck or the cunning that might have kept them out of harm's way. All of those wounded wore pinned to their faded greatcoats a row of service medals, which under the impact of the men's awkward motions produced an insistent tinkling. In front of one of the *de luxe* hotels on Ringstrasse one legless man could be seen daily, what was left of his body fastened to a little low cart and covered by an army blanket to which he, or whoever had wheeled him into his place, had attached the Gold Medal of Valour, the highest decoration the Habsburg army could bestow on a common soldier. A tin cup was standing next to the hero on the pavement.

In four years of war, the awareness of its horrors had been reducing the intensity of compassion for war's victims. Being confronted with the most pathetic of them nevertheless came as a shock to Inner City folk. That shock, however, did not keep them, as well as lower-middle-class people, from giving some credence to tale. that had habitual mendicants pose as blind or disabled combatants. The *Zitterer* in particular came under that suspicion.

A week after the proclamation of the republic an ex-foreign minister of the late Monarchy met Josef Redlich at the luncheon table of a certain countess. Count Burián, taking Redlich aside after the meal, told him that over the past years he had often pointed out to his fellow-Magyars 'how untenable their hegemony over Hungary's [other] nationalities was. And while some of the gentlemen agreed with me in private conversation, any attempt to reverse the course [of Magyar policies] would have been hopeless. Nor was it different with the attitude of the Germans [in the Austrian half of the Habsburg state] toward the Czechs or the

Slovenes . . .' Burián was far from being the only important
person of the old regime to discuss the recent past and
unburden himself of the memory of missed opportunities of
averting the disaster. Such post-mortems, in fact, prevailed
in upper-class discussions whenever they rose above the
day's discomforts and the grim uncertainty of the future. 'If
only. . . .' were the key words of such rambling conversations.

On the other hand it was, according to Redlich, 'very
curious indeed how swiftly those old "top gentlemen" [were]
accommodating themselves to the new conditions'. Some
days later he attended a dinner party that the old manipu-
lator, Sieghart, had arranged for a group of pensioned-off
cabinet members and privy councillors. One of the former
was talking most critically about the republic. He said that
its government had merely put new labels on the old bottles.
Prince [Alois] Liechtenstein made a point of his being, only a
spectator'. It would appear that that nobleman, a leader of the
Christian-Socials for the past ten years, was as much stressing his disapproval of *their* acquiescence in the establishment of the republic as his own unwillingness to face its
existence. He was more outspoken than most men of the
privileged classes, whose narrow interests he for one had
surmounted to serve the interests of the masses, as he had
seen them.

Drastic demonstrations of feelings had been loathsome to
the aristocracy for a long time. A proclivity to temporize,
indeed let things ride, regularly had weakened high-born
men even in elevated office – a trait, incidentally, that had
not displeased middle-class observers of that charmed circle.
In the autumn of 1918 no Jacobites were emerging from it.
There was scarcely any contact between Vienna's princes
and counts and the Eckartsau 'court'. (The closest they ever
came to manifesting their loyalty to Karl as a group was their
reaction to his death in exile in April 1922: that being the
racing season in Vienna, their ladies appeared clad in mourning at the Freudenau track.)

To be sure, their families had plenty to worry about upon
the collapse of the Habsburg state. Few of them had made
contingency preparations. When Count Berchtold departed
for Switzerland on 1 November, only a handful of his peers

had followed suit. Some at that time had been staying at one or other of their hunting lodges for the deer-shooting season; and they remained there. Of those who had remained in their Vienna mansions, many owned property mainly in what had become Czechoslovakia; and once it was obvious that Masaryk's government was not intent upon changing the social order, and the workers remained calm on the whole, these members of the aristocracy moved to their Bohemian or Moravian estates. Aristocrats whose land was within the Austrian republic were far more disquieted. A drastic land reform was under discussion. Besides, the Alpine peasants were growing restless. They had not forgotten the machinations through which feudal families had enlarged their holdings over the past two generations, and the owners of the great estates knew this. They also knew that the provincial governors, imperial appointees, had turned over their powers to the provincial assemblies, and surmised that feudal interests could no longer count on the old *de facto* protection. Poaching had become out of hand; agricultural labourers were asking for higher wages; strikes had occurred. The peasants, burdened as they had been by army requisitioning of cattle and grain in the closing year of the war, and furious about the privations they had subsequently experienced, could well be imagined to turn on the timberlands of the nobles and their beloved preserves. Generally, once wood for the fireplaces of their Vienna mansions was lacking and their tiled stoves could not be heated any longer, the big landowners one after another moved to their country estates. Promptly, rumours sprang up of homeless ex-soldiers ready to move into the vacated buildings. Those stories soon stopped, and together with the deserted mansions, their owners were less and less mentioned. The *Arbeiter Zeitung* might still write with cutting derision of the 'feudalists' and their idle way of living. Its readers were inclined to dismiss them as people no longer of any consequence.

In one instance only did the Viennese pass strictures on the grandees of the *ancien regime*. No sooner had Karl withdrawn to Eckartsau than Hungary's Upper Chamber dispatched two of its most prominent members to the lodge, along with the cardinal primate. Eager to find a *modus vivendi* with the republican mood growing apace in their country, those titled emissaries requested the king's abdication. Karl responded by relinquishing his 'part in the business of the state'. That declaration as such aroused scant interest in Vienna. But the anxiety of Hungary's magnates to shake off the anointed king elicited many a sardonic smile in Vienna. The events of 12 November and afterwards had not turned their minds altogether away from the Hungarians as former fellow-countrymen, and their long record of trouble-making. Lueger, of blessed memory, had taken the measure of the Magyar gentlemen, Christian-Socials would say with a shrug, choosing to forget the nimbleness of *their* parliamentarians in shedding their long-mouthed fealty to the Crown. But then, any occasion for flaying the Hungarians was welcome in those weeks when they were withholding all supplies from Vienna.

The criticism of the Magyar grandees did not signify a renewal of dynastic emotions in Vienna. The upper class might now and then be sorry for Karl himself, but there was plenty of gossip about his family. 'Archduke Friedrich is a particular target of accusations', police headquarters reported. 'Besides being blamed for incompetence as supreme army commander [a post he had held till early 1917] he is taken to task for his inordinate greed and for the huge profits he is alleged to have reaped from his large estates and industrial enterprises [during the war].'

None of the tales was bandied about with greater abandon than the story, chuckled over for years in privileged circles, of Friedrich's involvement with a merchant's young wife, whom he had lured away from her intimidated husband. The puritanical severity with which people chose to react to that disclosure left room for such ridicule as the picture of a paunchy family man in his sixties involved in an amorous intrigue was inviting. The preoccupation with that affair was in tune with the delight the Viennese had always taken in royal bedroom scandals, whether funny, romantic, or macabre. Karl Kraus – who as early as December 1914 had in his magazine, *Die Fackel*, wondered whether the war would 'bring salvation or merely the end,' and who from 1916 had been thundering against the misuse of power and wartime corruption – told (in a mordant long piece entitled *Obituary*) of the shabby means that the archduke, once he was tired of his mistress, had employed to reduce his financial obligations. But then Kraus went on to berate Vienna's upper classes for their having always accepted 'the moral and mental shortcomings of the [dynasty's] personages as a topic of amusement'.

Kraus's eloquent satisfaction at the Habsburgs' downfall gave scant satisfaction even to those who had realized before 1914 that not everything was to the best in the Habsburg state. Not a single Viennese could find it in himself to believe in the viability of Vienna – although all resented the sobriquet '*Wasserkopf*' (hydrocephalic head) that provincials had been quick to bestow on the capital with its two million people out of the country's six million. At the same time the city's middle classes were looking with growing apprehension at the grave disorders in the German republic; and there was still much talk about rump-Austria's possible federation with yesterday's nationalities – in effect, a Habsburg empire without the Habsburgs.

Developments in Germany also gave no pleasure to the Socialist politicians in Vienna. Nearly all of them had viewed the split in the German sister party with keen dismay ever since 1916. Now, the fratricidal socialist struggle in the *Reich* was likely to sharpen tensions within the Social-Democratic executive in Vienna; and the aggressive policy of the German Spartacus League (a group of extremist dissenters led by the redoubtable Karl Liebknecht) might well strengthen the influence of the Communists in Vienna.

Hardly any news of the German army had been published in Vienna since the armistice concluded in the forest of Compiègne on 8 November. Thus it was with amazement that the Viennese learned, late that month, that the divisions evacuating French and Belgian territory, unlike their own (or rather, unlike the Habsburg divisions), were marching home in perfect order. Considering the thousands of mutineering sailors who had disrupted the German Grand Fleet in the first days of November and spawned revolutionary outbursts in a score of cities, the accounts of the high morale of the German army approaching the fatherland's border

strained credibility. On 12 December Vienna's newspapers
carried an account of the entry of nine divisions into Berlin.
The men, their steel helmets wreathed with oak leaves, had
goose-stepped behind their mounted officers, wearing their
war decorations; and at the Brandenburg Gate the republic's
chancellor had welcomed the troops as 'unvanquished
soldiers. . . .' What followed that festive homecoming was not
at first known in Vienna. No sooner had the front-line men
met the soldiers' councils in the barracks than they themselves turned impervious to orders. Similar breakdowns of
discipline were occurring in other garrison towns after the
parade-like entry of field formations. By the end of the
month enough of such reports had reached Vienna to make
most people assume that the German army, like their own,
was melting away, after all. What the Viennese could not
know was that the republican government in Berlin had
concluded a secret pact with the army command. Whereas
the Vienna Socialists, through the Department of Army
Affairs they controlled, kept the officers of the late Habsburg
army powerless in the *Volkswehr*, the Majority Socialists in
power in Berlin had allied, for the sake of order, with the
reactionary officers' corps.

On the other hand, Germany's infant government was to a
large degree dependent on, and its decisions interfered with
by, the workers' and soldiers' councils – bodies that had no
equivalent in Austria. Only in a few cases did *Volkswehr*
soldiers' councils unite, for a limited time, with the local
councils of workers. The political aims of both more often
than not yielded to the urgent problems posed by the economic situation. Also, neither was under the massive radical
pressure their counterparts in Germany experienced. When
in mid-December a congress of workers' and soldiers' councils assembled in Berlin and elected a Council of the German
Socialist Republic, Viennese of all classes agreed that radical
tendencies were gaining the upper hand in Germany. Continuous news of grave disorders and of bloodshed strengthened that impression.

While events in the *Reich* had been spoken of in Vienna as
a revolution from the day of the Kaiser's abdication, that
term had not in general entered the language of Vienna's

people in reference to what had happened in their city. The word employed was *Umsturz*. Literally, it meant the toppling-over of an object, as well as the fall it suffered in the process. As a synonym for 'revolution', some scholars had used the word as early as the mid-eighteenth century; it became more widely known after the great French upheaval. It had become popular only at the time of the Central-European revolutions of 1848. In subsequent decades the epithet *Umstürzler* was in Germany attached loosely to men of subversive ideas. There was in the expression an overtone of mockery aimed, next to the dismal failures of 1848, at the peculiar clothing that many such would-be revolutionists sported, in particular the wide-brimmed slouch hat which was suspected of being worn because of the shadow it cast on the *Umstürzler*'s face. He was a stand-by of cartoonists. In a more serious vein, conservative politicians in Germany had labelled the Social-Democratic party the *Umsturzpartei* at the time of Bismarck's anti-Socialist legislation; and the coinage had remained in currency among right-wing publicists for a good many years. It had never been adopted in Vienna. The term *Umsturz* itself had been practically unknown there before the autumn of 1918.

It first came into usage among the middle classes. Perhaps they felt that the term reeked less of bloodshed, and reminded them less of chaotic Russia, than did 'revolution'. But soon working people, too, began speaking of the *Umsturz*, even though their politicians as a rule referred to the Austrian, or simply to 'our', revolution.

The constitution of 1867 had created an awkward appellation for the Austrian half of the Dual Monarchy. It was not officially referred to as Austria, but as 'the kingdoms and *Länder* represented in the *Reichsrat*'. Their diets were confined in their legislation to comparatively minor matters, and all bills they passed were subject to the sanction of the Crown and its government. Rump-Austria's Provisional National Assembly took that unitary tendency one step further. The first law it promulgated did not even mention the provincial legislatives, and on 12 December it came close to abolishing the diets by vaguely referring to plans for future popular representation on the provincial level. Meantime, the *Umsturz* spirit had encouraged the provincial politicians to exercise the right of self-determination. Representative bodies had been formed under such names as People's Council, National Council, or Committee for Public Safety. Assuming powers beyond those of the old diets, they posited their right to join, or not to join, the new state. Styria's Provisional Assembly proclaimed its allegiance and 'recognized the National Assembly in Vienna as the supreme authority of the state for the time being'. The Tyrolean 'National Congress' had declared the Tyrol's union with Germany even before 12 November, and did not bother to vote on the *Land's* relationship to the government in Vienna. Neither did Lower Austria. In Carinthia, the establishment of an independent Carinthian republic was being deliberated; and a certain lake resort in that *Land* one day proclaimed its transformation into a sovereign republic, which would send its own delegates to the peace conference.

Such bizarre resolutions caused hardly a ripple in Vienna. The chancellor, Karl Renner, informed the National Assembly, amid cheers, of the various 'solemn declarations of joining' that he had received. He and his Socialist colleagues had been concerned about the attitude the provinces might assume toward the government. For outside the industrial centres of Lower Austria and Styria Socialists formed comparatively small minorities in the *Länder*. The bourgeois press failed to reach the root of the matter. No one in Vienna wanted to see Vienna threatened with losing its role as the seat of central power.

Moreover, Vienna's middle classes were fairly quick to recognize the self-assertiveness of the provinces as a potential counterbalance to the momentum of the Socialists who seemed to engulf them. For the Christian-Social politicians in Vienna appeared less and less able to stem the 'Red flood'. It was in the rural areas that their party had retained its pristine power, and it was towards them that Vienna's middle classes began turning their eyes. Notwithstanding the anti-Semitism endemic in the *Länder*, even Jewish upper bourgeois had only qualified misgivings about the potential of that force.

Originally the peasant boys among the returned soldiers had been as rebellious as those of working-class origin. But while rural ex-soldiers had approved of the establishment of the republic, the policies it began to practise in their valleys alienated their kinsfolk, and soon the veterans themselves. When the imperial army had forced farmers to sell at pegged prices, they had taken their helplessness more or less for granted; what the new government (or as they put it, 'Vienna') was doing seemed a different matter to them. The government's appeals to the 'republican spirit of self-sacrifice' sounded hollow in the face of the harsh methods employed in many places to secure supplies for the urban population. *Volkswehr* squads made themselves at home in several hamlets to enforce sales at fixed prices, and their zeal and the *Sozi* language they were using made their efforts doubly distasteful. Neither did the *Zentralen,* who had survived the *Umsturz,* hesitate to obtain deliveries through persistent persuasion which often amounted to coercion. Also, provincial workers' councils took it upon themselves to frustrate sales to free-market dealers. Not content with sabotaging such galling activities as best they could, the farmers began organizing peasants' councils. Complaints they took to the district committee were bound to clash with the councils of workers which, although numerically inferior, did not easily agree to compromise. Relations between the two bodies were growing more openly hostile. In the valleys of the Tyrol, Styria and Carinthia the disbanding troops of the Habsburg army had sold rifles and even machine-guns.

On 12 December regular forces of the kingdom of Serbs, Croats and Slovenes (the later Yugoslavia) invaded Carinthian territory; and while the *Heimwehren* (Home Defence Forces) that the peasantry was forming were devised to hold off those attacks till the Vienna government could mobilize resistance, the *Heimwehren* also made no secret of their animus against the proletariat. Those first stirrings of counter-revolution were not recognized as such among the lower middle class in Vienna, whose press was stressing the peasants' patriotic spirit rather than their anti-Socialist feelings. The *Reichspost* was making little of the ideas spread by the rural clergy, who told the peasant that his grain and livestock were seized to enable the government to feed hundreds of thousands of unemployed in Vienna, acquiescing in their going idle; that the war regulations which oppressed him were kept in force by an alliance of Jewish profiteers in the *Zentralen* with the Jewish Socialists in high posts; or that the ultimate aim of the revolution was the nationalization of his property and the destruction of his church.[2] As it was, Vienna's lower middle class did not reproach the government for extending relief to ex-soldiers unable to find work; rather, it was hoped that this assistance, pitifully small though it was, would keep them from joining the Communist party.

> Law enforcement remained insufficient for weeks, [Heinrich Funder writes in his memoirs]. Unauthorized patrols kept roaming the city and, without interference, searching private flats, looking for provisions and whatever else might catch their fancy. . . . Self-styled security detachments squatted in Schönbrunn Palace and in the Hofburg . . . and while the populace was starving, being reduced to a diet of gruel three times a week, those men were guzzling the wine they had come upon in the cellars, and devouring the rationed reserves of the maintenance staff of the imperial buildings. [Funder continues with particular indignation] some middle-class people, too, regarded imperial property as no more than flotsam at that time. Large bundles of monogrammed table linen somehow found their way into the closets of burgher families from the chests of the court. . . . Carloads of woollen blankets, besides costly harnesses, were taken from the imperial stables on the basis of some 'permit' signed in the Department of Agriculture, and in the course of a rather informal auction of the horses some of them were acquired by certain [former] dignitaries to be shipped to their country places. The [Assembly] deputy from a certain Styrian district told me with obviously innocent glee that one of the emperor's hunting rifles had been presented to him without the emporor's knowledge. . . .[3]

In the second week of December, a group of disabled servicemen broke into the suburban *Schloss* of the hated dried-

vegetables archduke, who had taken himself and his wife to
Spain; and as no one attempted to remove the squatters, and
horror tales about the destruction wrought in that place
made the rounds, well-to-do people could not help fearing
for their own houses or apartments. Painful as anxieties were
on that score, they did not constitute the only cause for the
alarm in bourgeois circles. When Inner-City people were
walking, at any hour of day or night, through narrow
Bankgasse (a stone's throw from the Hofburg) and passing
the building of the Austro-Hungarian Bank, the clatter of its
printing presses could be heard constantly. Some Christian-
Social politicians suggested that the Socialists were intent on
creating a runaway inflation to destroy middle-class savings.
As it was, the increased money circulation and the consequent rise in the cost of living had been playing havoc with
savings since mid-war. The progressing devaluation of war
bonds appalled the lower-middle-class strata. If wealthy
people, their misgivings mounting, nevertheless had
purchased war bonds up to the late summer of 1918, among
small savers that kind of investment dated back to the earlier
years of the war. Career officers of the Habsburg army had
been forbidden by law to marry unless they or their pros-
pective brides possessed a certain amount of funds. Referred
to as the *Kaution* – it was graduated according to rank, with
the youngest officers having to put up the largest sum – those
funds could be invested only according to strict regulations.
Conversion into war bonds had been recommended persuas-
ively early in the war.

Even as the country had been dissolving before their eyes,
upper-middle-class citizens had on the whole failed to
appreciate the extent of the monetary disaster. Cut off from
international markets, Austria's wartime economy had not
done full justice to the devaluation of her currency abroad.
Even though its purchasing power had been slipping, drasti-
cally so since late in 1917, the exchange rates on foreign
bourses had remained beyond the domestic value of the
Krone. It took another dramatic plunge some two months
after the *Umsturz*, when industrialists began importing raw
materials, to drive home the extent of the lowered value of
the currency. By that time it had become clear to observant

men that the 'successor states' (the term had, incidentally,
not been thought up in Vienna) must be eager to issue money
of their own. What means they might use to render the old
Krone worthless within their borders was a matter of anxious
guessing. 'Yesterday Mr Philpott, the former British consul
[in Vienna] called on me,' Redlich noted on 25 January. 'I
drew for him a picture of the financial situation. I stressed
the necessity of a common regulation of the public debt and
of all [other] matters pertaining to the currency. He said
that in Prague he had gained the impression that the Czechs
wished to ruin Vienna. . . .'

A good many of the industrialists residing in Vienna had
large interests in Bohemia, Moravia and Slovakia. Some of
them began making preparations for acquiring Czechoslovak
citizenship. While men long established in business were
thus trying to accommodate themselves to the new order in
Central Europe, they also awoke to the fact that certain
outsiders had risen to inordinate importance – men less
burdened than they themselves were by time-honoured con-
ventions (or, as their patrician expression had it, tradition).
Although the lower classes tended to talk of all businessmen
as war profiteers, upper-middle-class folk made a point of
reserving that appellation for middlemen who, coming from
nowhere, had made a fortune during the war and were
beginning to infiltrate legitimate enterprises. Stories of their
unorthodox methods, their ostentatious living, and their lack
of Viennese culture were beloved in the offices and the
homes of the bankers and mine or factory owners who had
been rich prior to 1914. Jews among the upstarts were talked
about with greatest scorn among Jewish people of pre-war
wealth.

A particular butt of widespread gossip was one Siegmund
Bosel. He had, as it were, put the black market at the
disposal of certain government departments in the latter
years of the war. That shrewd operator had known how to
get hold of large quantities of hoarded textiles that all the
government decrees and all the supervision had not succeeded in acquiring. The undeniable services he had
rendered the government (at a price) had involved a measure
of corruption. His mysterious connections had given birth to a

malevolent saga of its own. Yet it would seem that Bosel, quite Viennese on that score, had been seeking status, as well as profits.

He still was.[4] During the first weeks after the *Umsturz*, the republic's Department of the Interior did not bridle at the continuing contacts established to the great middleman-financier, who enabled it to hand out the basic necessaries to thousands of refugees. It was through that department that Vienna's chief of police, Johannes Schober, had met Bosel. Now Schober conceived the plan of using the inventive man to better the lot of his own policemen. Although their pay had been raised, they could not possibly keep their families out of want. 'Despite the shortages that existed [also] ... beyond our borders, Bosel succeeded in bringing hundreds of carloads of food and textiles to Vienna, and those goods were distributed to the police and their families. He could arrange for those transports only because he had managed to gain the confidence of the Inter-Allied Military Mission', which had been set up in the capital.

The bounty descending on the police did not for long remain a secret. Rumours of hidden government stores were renewed. Apparently Schober considered the irritation of working men and women a smaller danger than the flagging morale noticeable among his men. A number of them had been veering towards socialist ideas even before the *Umsturz,* and now were encouraged by propagandists. According to Brandl, it was none other than Bosel who in several private talks finally 'pulled the poisoned fangs' of the headman of that group in the force. Some years later, Schober's extraordinary relations with Bosel would be decried in various quarters, including the Socialists'. Yet their party organization had dealings of its own with him in the winter of 1918–19.

What had happened was this. Schober was trying to induce the *Hammer* bakery works to produce, for his 4,000 policemen, bread more palatable than the 'sawdust loaves' reaching the market. The board of the large plant, which was run by the Social-Democratic party, turned Schober down, pointing out that they could not infringe regulations. At the same time they insinuated that a differently constituted board might act differently. At Schober's request, Bosel acquired the majority of the shares of the company (which had for some years operated with heavy losses). Thus it came about that bread such as the populace could not possibly hope to see appeared on the tables of Vienna's law enforcers in quantities way beyond the notorious ration. Harassed as they were in their often gruelling duties, they could feel that at least in their homes they were coming close to those 'normal conditions' that were wistfully spoken of all over Vienna.

❧ 10 ❧

The 'Leftover Country'

The membership of the Communist party had been almost static throughout November. Yet it kept distributing handbills in the workshops and organizing meetings in suburban taverns. Audiences varied in size. Ex-soldiers who had found no work yet were the most regular attendants, along with a sprinkling of *Volkswehr* soldiers; and as the government seemed to take its time reforming the invalids' wretched pensions, those unfortunate ex-combatants were more frequently appearing. Except for one Karl Toman – a pre-war union functionary who had been active among prisoners in Russia – the speakers were virtually unknown to the bulk of the proletariat. Most of them were young intellectuals, who did not always hold the attention of their impatient listeners. *Der Weckruf*, now untrammelled by censorship, was stepping up its distribution. 'All power to workers' and soldiers' councils!' was the watchword of that weekly, which in every issue was attacking the Socialist leaders – the *Bonzen* (party bosses) – for their 'intrinsically counter-revolutionary leanings' and the 'tendency to compromise with the reactionaries, forsaking the masses'.

The Communists gained some more strength early in December, when the left-wingers, so called, of the Social-Democratic party cut their ties with it. That group – its origins went back to the early months of the war – declared bluntly that the 'Communist party alone is devoted to the class struggle in this country, and it alone upholds the pristine socialist ideas'. But none of the men in the seceding group proved capable of weaning large numbers of Socialist party members fron its organization. On the other hand, the left-wingers, joining the Communist party, did not remove the jealousies and dissensions that had beset it from the start. The *Arbeiter Zeitung* was playing down the importance of the left-wing exodus; and it was not least that seeming unconcern which prevented Communist predictions of an imminent 'revolution to complete the *Umsturz*' from scaring the middle classes. What was frightening them towards the new year was the waxing power of the soldiers' councils and the lawlessness that the *Volkswehr* encouraged.

While in autumn the disbanding of the Habsburg army had put transportation by rail out of the reach of the population, *Hamster* trips now were being made to the countryside by railway. (That picturesque designation of people collecting provisions had been taken from the rodent's habit of storing food in the two pocketlike folds in its mouth.) Thousands of men and women ventured farther and farther afield not only on Sundays. The railwaymen were said to overlook working-class passengers without valid tickets. In the same spirit, *Volkswehr* patrols would post themselves at the terminals in Vienna to confront returning lower-middle-class *Hamsterer*, search their valises and knapsacks, and seize the contents out of hand. The confiscators hardly ever proceeded to distribute the loot, as they prided themselves on doing, to invalids or war widows. Criticism of such illegal actions remained muted nevertheless, and were even glorified by a growing number of working people. In January, *Volkswehr* patrols, usually under the command of some soldiers' council member, resumed searches in food stores and in flats of well-to-do families or their villas in garden suburbs. Police headquarters pleaded in vain with the central committee of the soldiers' councils of Vienna to make soldiers abstain from such raids, and notify the War Usury Office of caches of hoarded provisions. (The War Usury Office was set up late in 1917 under the authority of the police, and was empowered to check the stocks of merchants.) The *Volkswehr* raiders seemed to derive much satisfaction from investigating upper-class homes, taunting the 'exploiters' in the process. Accounts of those expeditions were developing into a sinister saga.

Through a notice in the tabloid *Der Abend*, people had become aware of the declaration published at the time of the swearing-in of the *Volkswehr*. 'Any oath will be honoured [Kisch had written] only as long as we deem it compatible with our convictions.' True, the overwhelming majority of the soldiers had indicated that it was not subscribing to that qualification of the loyalty oath. But could that majority be trusted in another crisis?

The police had looked askance at the armed force of the republic from the beginning. The *Umsturz* had not loosened the emotional ties of a Schober or a Brandl to the old regime. Instinctively, they kept identifying the peacefulness of the imperial city (the *Kaiserstadt*), with the order they were duty-bound to maintain in republican Vienna. They flattered themselves that the police were above political strife, and indeed laboured to convince the Socialist leaders of their own lack of bias. The rank and file of the force, however, had always disliked the *Sozis* as potential disturbers of public order. They now came to fear their leaders as the protectors of the *Volkswehr*, which was taking it upon itself to encroach on the authority of the police. Repeated warnings against clashes with *Volkswehr* soldiers, received at headquarters and passed on to the force, were driving it to frustration. The number of Vienna's *Volkswehr* men had risen to 16,000, as against some 4,000 uniformed policemen.

At about the time of the first *Volkswehr* recruitments, the police on their part had set up an auxiliary force, which went by the medieval-sounding name of *Stadtschutzwache*, or City Protection Guard. 'Some ten thousand men have come forward,' Brandl had noted in his journal. 'We will have to sift them properly later on. For the time being, the main thing is to get them off the streets.' In general, those who enrolled were older than the *Volkswehr* soldiers, and there were not many frontline veterans among them. After the purge foreseen by Brandl, they did not acquit themselves badly; probably they too were given some of the Bosel bounty. Lightly armed, they assumed many of the duties until then performed by the Transylvanians, who had departed for their homeland. They were also detailed to guard food markets, where altercations between stallholders and customers who accused them of overcharging or withholding merchandise, were a daily occurrence. Whenever the controversies threatened to erupt into violence, the *Stadtschutzwache* called in regular police. Sometimes a *Volkswehr* detachment joined them on its own, or its council's, volition. In one instance, some *Volkswehr* soldiers turned up at a butcher's shop and, elbowing through the boisterous would-be buyers, grabbed cuts of horse meat from the counter under the eyes of the auxiliary policemen. Time and time again Schober begged the Defence Department to keep the republic's army from interfering with police work. But Deutsch himself was aware of the limitations of his power in dealing with the soldiers' councils, and was anxious not to antagonize them. Besides, violence in butchers' markets was far from being the main concern of the government – or, for that matter, the police chief. Communist activities began to engage much of his attention. But when he suggested that he might clamp down on agitators who were mingling with soldiers at their barracks, he was reminded of the right of free assembly and, as for the Communists, was told that only force could be met by force.

In addition to the constables and the *Stadtschutzwache*, a large number of plain-clothes men were in the service of the police. They infiltrated meetings and observed their participants; they watched the coffeehouses at whose tables young intellectuals gathered for millenial or tactical discussions; and they kept an eye on known or suspected troublemakers. They were also on good terms with the *concierges* of apartment houses, the disgruntled *Hausmeister* of Viennese folklore, in their diminutive, darkish ground-floor dwellings, who needed little encouragement to report a tenant receiving a large number of callers, or another who was spending nights away from his flat. Also, a torrent of anonymous denunciations descended on police stations day after day – although it was usually found that these reports came from people embroiled in a petty conflict with a neighbour, from jilted women, people in the throes of hysteria, or others who simply derived a strange gratification from blackening a fellow-citizen's name. Undeterred by the volume of such communications, the police were keeping under close surveillance, people they suspected of subversive intent. Those unable to claim Austrian citizenship were expelled out of hand; if they managed to get back to Vienna one way or another, they were deported across the Czech or Hungarian border. Certain Socialist politicians were making representations about 'capricious police harassment'.

In the same weeks developments in the German republic had a curious impact on readers of the bourgeois press in Vienna. Comparing the growing violence in German cities with conditions at home, they told themselves that it was the split in her labouring masses that was pushing Germany toward civil war. Thus they came close to congratulating themselves on the absence of a similar rupture within their own Socialist party, and were slow to do full justice to the changing mood of the Austrian workers.

Actually, the estrangement of the unemployed from men holding jobs had been gaining a political edge since Germany's Spartacus League broke with the Independent Socialists in the last days of December and adopted the name of German Communist Party. Communist publications in Vienna were bombarding their readers with furious denunciations of the Social-Democratic leaders. 'The despicable clique at the head of the working masses,' one of those publications declared, 'men who [throughout the war] succeeded in saving their skins, lined their pockets, filled their bellies, and did the bidding of the imperial government, are now the workers' representatives in the top offices of the democratic republic. . . .' Whatever the emotional effect of such scurrilous outbursts may have been on deeply dissatisfied ex-soldiers or despairing invalids, it did not seem likely to make a significant dent in the ranks of Labour. If a member of the middle class chanced to see that kind of strident Communist propaganda, he may well have shrugged it off: the abuse that members of the late *Reichsrat's* Lower Chamber had hurled at one another for so many years in their nationalistic struggles, had lowered the sensitivity of the Viennese to intemperate political language.

On 5 January, the Spartacus League had risen in Berlin, and after ten days of ferocious fighting in the streets the government managed to shoot into surrender the Spartacists and such Independents as had thrown in their lot with the League. In support of the army battalions loyal to the government, it had called in some hand-picked members of the so-called *Freikorps* (para-military formations that army officers, under the eyes of like-minded civil servants, had built up outside the city from the debris of disbanded regiments).

Recruitment for them had all but escaped the notice of the Viennese, whose newspapers had reported on the budding *Freikorps* with barely any reference to their ties with the Berlin government. The public in Vienna had been aware of its efforts to counteract the radical temper of the soldiers' and workers' councils; one had not, however, conceived of the lengths the government would go in its alliance with the officers' corps. The bloody intervention of the *Freikorps* caused an enormous impression in Vienna. Middle-class folk, after the first shock, were talking under their breath about the resistance of the Berlin government as something their own could not possibly have undertaken, with no armed forces besides the red *Volkswehr* as its disposal. But the victory of the governing Majority Socialists in Berlin also satisfied some of Vienna's Social-Democratic politicians to the point of their averting their eyes from the counter-revolutionary *Freikorps* which had assured the sanguinary triumph. That satisfaction was not shared by all workers. During the Berlin upheaval, admiration for the Spartacists' courage had been fairly widespread, and a great many had been heard wondering whether a 'truly proletarian' action would not have to be set in motion in Vienna too, 'should the elections [scheduled for 15 February] return a bourgeois majority' to the Constituent National Assembly. That at least was what a police report asserted, adding that 'the Socialist leaders [were] losing their hold over the masses'.

In the course of the liquidation of the Spartacus rising, Karl Liebknecht and Rosa Luxemburg had been captured and savagely murdered; and though accurate information was still lacking (Luxemburg's body had not then been found) their fate stunned Vienna's workers. Still, when the Communists, by distributing handbills, asked them to assemble on Sunday 18 January in front of the Town Hall 'in memory of our martyrs', a mere 2,000 people arrived. To the relief of the police dispatched there in impressive numbers, the demonstrators listened in perfect silence to passionate orations, and after the speakers had done, marched to Parliament House. For a while they stood there in the cold. Shouts of 'Down with the bill' were heard – a reference to the armed-forces bill which had been introduced in the National Assembly by the State Council six weeks after the *Umsturz*. It had caused heated discussions within the soldiers' councils, as well as the *Volkswehr* at large. The organ of Battalion 41, *Der Rote Soldat,* suggested that the 'militaristic and reactionary bill' had been drafted with the intention of holding down the labouring population and 'scotching the revolution so gloriously started'. The bulk of the soldiers do not seem to have believed in such a sinister scheme. But all were pleasantly conscious of the intimidating impact the anti-bill propaganda was having on the middle classes.

But once the reactionary forces had shown their hand in Berlin, workmen by and large were gripped by apprehension. To be sure, no *Freikorps* existed in Austria, and none could be imagined to come into being. There was no longer an officers' corps such as had created those formations in Germany and had drummed loyalty to the government into the remnants of the army. Professional officers whom the *Volkswehr* had accepted were under the tight control of the soldiers' councils; and those who had been rejected and left to their own devices to eke out a living, could hardly be thought of as plotting counter-revolution. But while conspiracies against the republic were as good as beyond imagination, tales of insidious hostility towards it were rife among working people.

For one thing, the bureaucracy was pictured as a 'den of reactionary forces'. Certainly civil servants of the lower and middle echelons were not imbued with the republican spirit the *Arbeiter Zeitung* was extolling; certainly they were bewildered by the new regulations they had to cope with and the novel procedures recommended to them by the new political heads of their departments. Moreover, the lack of deference shown the bureaucrats irritated them. That traditional respect used to flatter their self-importance and partly make up for their poor salary. Even the lowliest government clerk had been entitled to add the letters '*k.k.*' (*kaiserlich-königlicher,* that is, 'imperial-royal') to the office title he would attach to his signature. Those magical letters had of course been done away with in the *Umsturz.* The counter-revolutionary leanings imputed to the bureaucracy consisted of no more than a nostalgia for the social order of the *ancien régime* and their privileged niche within it. They were thus resentful of the *Sozis* and 'their' republic, but were far from sabotaging its day-to-day administration.

So were the judges, even though Socialist publicists tended to call them convinced reactionaries. Trained for the bench and government-appointed, Austrian judges were, in effect, civil servants. They shared the conservative stance of the latter, and their sense of social superiority. Wartime corruption had not touched the judges even though the soaring cost of living was playing havoc with their resources. Having come face to face with wartime misery in the courtroom, they were of two minds about the blessings of the old order – while the new filled them with scepticism, as the republic, for all the new oratory about social justice, seemed unable to make headway against the cynical misuse of economic power. Facing conditions almost beyond comprehension, many judges may well have been tempted to blame the *Umsturz* for them, and look askance at the Socialists who had engineered it. At the same time, their ingrained loyalty to the old state had become meaningless on its dissolution. It was said that radical German nationalism was making inroads into the judiciary.

German nationalism at its most aggressive was rampant in a large segment of the university's student body. The defeat of the 'greater fatherland' had not weakened the shrill enthusiasm for German greatness among Vienna's pan-German students. No sooner had the news of the crushing of the Spartacus rebellion reached them than they gathered for a rally – less to celebrate the victory of the Berlin govern-

ment, which in truth they despised, than to hail the participation of *Freikorps* in the bloody battles. *Deutschland,
Deutschland über alles* was sung, and flags of imperial
Germany were brought into the meeting. To Vienna's Socialists, whatever their individual feelings toward the van-
quished Spartacists, the students' victory meeting was
primarily a proof of the spreading reactionary spirit at the
seat of higher learning. Actually, that spirit had been one of
the facts of Viennese life for a long time. Rather than the
proletariat, it had disquieted enlightened middle-class
people, including many faculty members.

Workers' sons had hardly ever been university students, or
even studied at a *Gymnasium*. They would not have been
discriminated against at either, and tuition fees were
nominal at government-supported institutions. But the sons of
working-class families had to earn wages as soon as they
possibly could. Withal, an Association of Socialist University
Students had come into being. It consisted almost exclusively
of young men of middle-class background. During the war, it
had remained aloof from the various small radical groups
formed with conspiratorial secrecy at certain *Gymnasia*.
Unlike the pan-German students, nearly all of whom were
provincials, their Socialist fellow-students were in general at
home in Vienna. Many of them were Jewish, some were sons
of Galicians who had settled in Vienna. Thus anti-Semitism,
the touchstone of the pan-German *Weltanschauung* since
the 1880s, nurtured the hostility of the pan-German student
corporations towards the Socialist Association. If the clerical-
minded Catholic corporations had not adopted those racist
tenets, their ingrained enmity toward Jewish students –
future competitors in the professions – had gained a militant
edge of its own.

The Social-Democratic politicians had never faced the
Jewish question squarely. (One of those, not Jewish himself,
used to dismiss anti-Semitism as the 'socialism of the morons'.)
Nor did they do so now as anti-Semitism of one kind or
another was intensifying the pressure brought to bear on
Socialist students. In pre-war days the various corporations
used to promenade on Saturday mornings on the twin driveways and in front of the university building, wearing the

rakish cap and sash both of which by their coloured stripes distinguished each corporation. Provoking individual encounters, which were meant to lead to subsequent sabre duels, were part of the performance which was known as the *Bummel*. Since 1914 it had taken place only on special occasions. There were attempts to revive it at the beginning of 1919, even though most university lectures had been suspended because of the shortage of fuel. The *Bummel* was much less formal, and altercations tended to erupt in bloody scuffles involving whole groups. The police, which in the name of the university's autonomy had for decades been barred from entering not only the building but its driveways as well, did not interfere even when the affrays spilled over on to the pavement of Ringstrasse. After some Socialist students arrived one day and were beaten up, the *Arbeiter Zeitung* began harping on the 'counter-revolutionary provocation' enacted every week. It was in Graz, the capital of Styria, that pan-German students went beyond mere provocation.

Communist agitators had become particularly active in that city and the heavy-industry centres nearby, coinciding with the increase in unemployment. On 21 February some hundreds of idle ex-soldiers took to the streets demanding a large increase in the veterans' severance pay. Heinrich Brodnig, a local Communist returned from Russia, forced his way into the presence of the commander of the *Volkswehr* and, overriding its council's more moderate plan, asked the commander to agree to his proposals within forty-eight hours. Before twenty-four had elapsed the demand was met half-way, but Brodnig refused to compromise, and redoubled his threats. Now the authorities mustered what strength they could, including the Students' Self-Defence Force of Graz University, an association of pan-German students originally established to help ward off incursions of Slovene bands on Styria's southern border. In the early morning of 22 February, a Saturday, the centre of the city was sealed off and declared out of bounds for demonstrations. Whereupon Brodnig called an open-air meeting in one of the suburbs.

No one ever knew how the Socialist workmen reached Graz's main square that afternoon despite the cordon. At any rate, they remained peaceful – until they caught sight of the rifle-carrying students. Angry shouts asking for their disarmament rose from the demonstrators. Apparently, there was no one in authority to consider the demand even as the crowd, grown larger, had begun pressing on in the direction of the students. Suddenly they opened fire – on no one's command, it would seem, and without any warning. Even though their volley killed four men and thirteen others were wounded, the enraged multitude did not break up. It surged forward against the killers, who promptly took refuge in the nearby town hall. Only when the now riotous people threatened to force its locked door did police compel the beleaguered students to hand over their rifles. Still the crowd could not be dispersed until the Workers' Auxiliary Corps had appeared and persuaded them to leave. That volunteer body had proved its loyalty to the Social-Democratic party on earlier occasions. So had the *Volkswehr* battalions in Graz.

The trigger-happy students – who maintained that they had only done their patriotic duty alongside the other forces of public order – were generally condemned as hotheads by Vienna's middle classes. Workers denounced the alleged acquiescence of the government in 'counter-revolutionary' measures; heeding a call for help from Graz, it had dispatched a *gendarmerie* detachment equipped with machine-guns. But once the soldiers' councils of the Styrian *Volkswehr* units had put the blame for the bloody incident squarely on the Communists' shoulders, the wrath of the Socialist working class began to abate. Their leaders could not have been altogether displeased by the swiftness with which the police in Graz arrested the Communist ringleaders. Communist-inspired wild actions had, after all, come close to compromising Vienna's entire proletariat even before the ill-fated day in the capital of Styria.

Demonstrations of varying size and violence had occurred in Vienna since mid-January. The bourgeois press, intent on playing down the political demands that could be heard regularly in the course of those disorders, referred to them as *Hungerkrawalle,* or food riots. Only the *Reichspost* spoke of

'Bolshevik instigators'. The middle-class population came to deride the 'kid-glove' methods employed to contain the demonstrators. Rather than dispersing the potential rioters by breaking up their formation, police would escort them, impose a semblance of order on the march by more or less stern admonitions, and for the rest station small detachments in front of food stores. Mounted police were as a rule kept at a distance. It was a nerve-racking business for the force – or, for that matter, for Johannes Schober, whose superior, the Secretary of the Interior, was adamant in his orders to avoid any bloodshed. He knew, and told Schober so on at least one occasion, that sanguinary clashes with hungry proletarians were bound to hand the Communists a powerful tool.

On 2 February an unusually boisterous crowd of some 5,000 penetrated the Inner City and provoked an incident whose climax somewhat changed the kid-glove image. The police, having heard of an impending demonstration in front of Parliament House, had thrown a strong cordon around it. Light snow was falling when people began pouring on to Ringstrasse in small groups. At first they restricted themselves to the kind of violent mischief that had become routine since the *Umsturz*: they stopped the trams on the boulevard, or threw rocks at the few motor cars passing by, or shouted full-throated abuse at the *Mistelbacher*. Once the throng of demonstrators had grown more solid, however, the front ranks, having noticed that police were not making arrests, started pressing against the cordon. Suddenly a flat-topped lorry, for which a pathway had opened in the multitude, headed at full speed for the dented line. At that moment, the mounted police commander, revolver drawn, spurred his horse and galloped straight up to the vehicle – and so flabbergasted was the driver that he jerked to a halt and offered no resistance to policemen rushing forward to seize him. Others, similarly emboldened, dragged the half-score or so men from the lorry. In the following days, the courageous horseman, one Inspector Pramer, became the hero of middle-class conversation. It was suggested that the motorized attackers had been carrying rifles or carbines. No information about their identity was put out.

Gossip singled out the Prater *Marineure* as the culprits.

Those four hundred or so sailors and marines, lodged in a wartime army training camp on the Prater grounds, were known to have retained their carbines while making their way to Vienna upon the transfer of the Habsburg fleet to the South-Slav state. Called up as security auxiliaries on 12 November, they had proved to be of questionable value on that turbulent day, and ever since had been left idle. Waiting for their severance pay – the claim seems to have run into difficulty – they had acquired the reputation of an unruly lot. The police made no attempt to disarm them, even though contacts between them and certain Communist leaders appeared to have developed. At least one of the *Marineure* seems to have turned informer. Be that as it may, their alleged key role in the demonstration of 2 February served to add to the morbid fascination with which the middle classes were searching for budding Communist terror.

What they did not realize was that the proletariat in general, disillusioned with the lean results the *Umsturz* had had with regard to living conditions, was not in need of Communist support to press demands for improvement and the kind of legislation that would guarantee it. Within the *Volkswehr*, it was not only the Red Guard that saw Socialist dominance imperilled by a resurgence of reactionaries. 'We'll be consigned to the barracks on 16 February [election day],' the commander of one particular battalion told its assembled men. 'Should we ... [Social-Democrats] be defeated, we'll throw open our doors, and then blood will flow in the streets of Vienna ... and we'll rub out the Christian-Social and the other bourgeois bloodhounds.'[1]

While such wild talk was heard in some of the barracks, the Socialist politicians learned that Communist headquarters not only had recommended abstention from voting to its members, but was also dissuading them from disturbing election day. The Communists had bigger fish to fry: Lenin had invited them to send a delegate to the International Communist Congress he was to open in Moscow. While the man chosen, Karl Steinhardt, was known only too well to the Socialist leaders, it is fair to assume that ordinary workers knew little of him and his tortuous record. Whatever the well-informed middle class, on the other hand, may have

learned of his mission to the Moscow congress (he was to be
instrumental in the formation of the Comintern) is not likely
to have distracted its attention from the impending elections.
A Communist coup engineered by Moscow was not within
middle-class imagination.

'Yesterday the elections to the National Assembly took
place,' Redlich recorded on 17 February. 'Despite the gains
of the Social Democrats, the outcome leaves everything as it
was. No one expects the Social-Democratic party under the
leadership of a Renner, a Seitz . . . and an Otto Bauer to aim
in earnest at the establishment of *La Sociale* [*sic*]. And the
present problems simply exclude a "socialist" solution.'
Redlich, well known to scholars both in England and the
United States, had been called upon by many of the Allied
officials and newspapermen serving in, or passing through,
Vienna. He was convinced that the Allies would not tolerate a
Communist, or quasi-Communist, regime in Vienna, and did
not doubt that the Socialist leaders understood this. Evidently, Redlich did not waste any thought on considering
outbursts whose revolutionary momentum might brush aside
decisions of the great powers. Nor could he fail to be
impressed by the 'solemn calm' that, as the official gazette,
the *Wiener Zeitung*, put it, had marked the elections
throughout the republic. Upper bourgeois dismissed as a
figment of Socialist apprehensions a rumour asserting that
many Communists, defying their party's directive to abstain,
had voted Christian-Social in order to weaken the Social-
Democratic party in the new legislature. As it was, the party
had not only retained its old constituency, but also gained
numerous supporters in circles scarcely ever thought of
before as leaning toward *Sozi* ideas – professionals.
municipal white-collar workers and even small tradesmen. A
good many of Vienna's Jews (who used to form a stronghold
of the German-Liberal party) had voted Socialist, as well.
Some of the wealthy among them were rumoured to have
cast their votes for the party of their late adversary, Lueger.

The Socialists emerged with seventy-two mandates as
against fifty-three won by the Christian-Socials. No less than
twelve small parties had put representatives into the
Assembly, six of them a single deputy only. No more than

twelve mandates went to the German-Nationals, who had formed the strongest bloc in the country's Provisional Assembly. (They were soon to merge with some of the minor 'national' factions and form the Greater German People's Party.) As considerations of their philosophies kept either of the two great parties from combining with any of the small factions to secure a majority in parliament, a Socialist-Christian-Social coalition government came into being.

Of the 225 seats in the new House, as decided on by a law passed in December, 85 had not been filled by election: the Czechoslovak army was in firm control of the German-speaking regions Masaryk's republic had declared as its own; and whereas the State Council had issued a regulation whereby the eight German-speaking deputies of the Italian-occupied Southern Tyrol, elected in 1911, were to be appointed to the new assembly, no similar provision had been made with regard to the 'temporarily occupied parts of German-Austria' in Bohemian and Moravian territories. Even though the December law had apportioned those districts to different *Länder*, the Viennese had known even then that this was barely more than a defiant gesture. Socialist voters might still believe in the prospect of a union with Germany, and look at their new parliament as a plateau on the road to the German *Reichstag* in Weimar. Lower-middle-class folk had been cheered by the surprisingly lively pre-election activities of the Christian-Social apparatus.

Vienna's upper bourgeois could not rid themselves of the irrational notion that the new assembly in Parliament House was the truncated *Reichsrat* of old. They found themselves drawn, in their emotions, to the disinherited in their midst – those higher civil servants who had relinquished, or been relieved of, their jobs in the administration of former *Länder* which had become sovereign states, and who were flocking to Vienna, expecting employment or pensions; or the host of career officers who, unable or unwilling to apply for a commission in the armed forces of the successor countries, had no chance of being accepted by the *Volkswehr*. Stories of former captains or majors keeping themselves afloat by minor work for the new breed of currency speculators, or peddling toys or such like in the few night clubs in operation, were being told in bourgeois drawing rooms with indignant compassion. The esteem in which professional army officers used to be held in those circles in pre-war Vienna had been qualified by a good deal of condescension; in fact, a popular humorous weekly, *Die Muskete*, had specialized in making sport of them. The pointed post-*Umsturz* sympathies for men dispossessed and demeaned by the new order constituted a protest against it, a protest also against the dismemberment of the Habsburg state.

Rather than the Monarchy, it was its existence as a unitary country that the *haute bourgeoisie* was mourning. Karl Renner, in a widely quoted *mot* referring to 'this republic without republicans', missed the point as far as he intended to censure the upper middle class : even big business, much as it resented the new self-importance of workers in its plants, would have offered wholehearted co-operation to a republican 'Danube federation'. As citizens of what Clemenceau, at his most mordant, had referred to as the 'leftover country' (*ce que reste*) they could not throw off a feeling of disorientation amounting to claustrophobia. Their city, where government offices used to regulate the affairs of a great power, and where its banks used to finance the industry of fifty million people, and which itself had been the *ville lumière* of Europe's East – had not their city surrendered its very *raison d'être*? Unsure of their own status in the degraded Vienna, amid a population that seemed no longer to acknowledge its hallowed social structure, the upper classes were tempted to stand aloof from the concerns of the republic. On the day after the elections, Josef Redlich noted in his journal with obvious self-satisfaction, 'I abstained from voting.' In fact, a large segment of the upper classes chose that political no man's land.

Another section had voted for a new 'liberal' party headed by none other than Count Czernin. 'Europe's public opinion becomes attentive whenever Count Czernin takes the floor,' the *Neue Freie Presse* declared in reporting a speech he had delivered, 'addressing a so-to-speak [*sic*] intellectually and politically closed [group of] society, an audience of serious-minded and serene men eager to get a ... view of the past amid the over-excited, deafening turmoil of

these days.' Czernin – the Bohemian aristocrat accused by
some people during the Sixtus scandal of having betrayed his
sovereign for the sake of the German alliance, while others
had pitied him as the scapegoat for the emperor's blunder –
had been talking, as the great journal had it, 'for the first time
as a private citizen, as a citizen of the German-Austrian state.
... His audience left deeply impressed, and filled with a
desire to hear him talk frequently in the future.'

Eight days after the elections Lieutenant-Colonel E. L.
Strutt, Royal Scots, arrived in Vienna on his way to
Eckartsau Lodge to take command of its security measures.

> I determined to proceed to the Hotel Bristol, where I used
> to stay in former times [he wrote in his diary on 25
> February]. Went for a short walk on the Ring [-strasse]
> where the first person I bumped into was Kary Czernin.
> We stared at one another and then burst out laughing and
> shook hands warmly. He asked me to lunch, adding that
> they had nothing to eat. Accordingly I secured a loaf and
> some tins of bully beef and jam and we proceeded to
> Kary's enormous apartment. ... Found Maritschy
> [Countess Czernin] looking charming as ever but thin and
> worn. I forgot myself and embraced her in front of
> Kary. ...[2]

The renewal of old friendships between Viennese and British
society people came naturally to both. The Viennese had not
in general hated the British during the war and the German
propaganda slogan 'May God punish England' had never
really become popular in Vienna. Besides, only a handful of
the British military was stationed in Vienna.

More surprising was the readiness of some upper-class
hostesses to open their drawing rooms to the officers of Italy's
large Military Mission. They would bring tinned goods or
Egyptian cigarettes as presents and, barely less welcome, a
whiff of the carefree living of the privileged circles and their
hangers-on in pre-war Europe. In later months an ugly story
was heard about one of the handsome Italians having in-
fected a number of society ladies with a venereal disease. But
that may well have been malicious gossip on the part of
people infuriated by the reception accorded Italians in upper-

class salons, while they strutted along the streets of the Inner City, causing down-at-heel passers-by to edge off the curb.

On 21 February, Kurt Eisner, the prime minister of Bavaria, was shot to death in clear daylight by a titled ex-officer in one of the liveliest streets of Munich; and barely an hour later an unemployed butcher walked into the chamber of the Diet, and in full view of its members shot and gravely wounded the foremost adversary of the murdered premier (a Majority Socialist) who had just finished eulogizing Eisner. The hastily formed government of Independents was unable to impose even a semblance of order. Even as Munich's streets resounded with gun shots and newspaper offices were put to the torch by mobs bent on avenging Eisner's murder, the central government in Berlin, its armed forces insufficient, found no way of intervening. Stories of the anarchic situation in Bavaria abounded in Vienna's press. None of them excited the middle classes more than the news of the arrest of a score of noblemen who were then held hostage.

The Social-Democratic executive in Vienna were disturbed more greatly by news which was emerging from the confusing reports toward the end of the month. Two Russian-born Communists had arrived in Munich and, besides swamping the city with inflammatory leaflets, had begun re-organizing the local Spartacus apparatus. The Socialist leaders in Vienna had realized earlier that the near-silence with which they treated Austria's Communist party had not stopped the slow but steady drain their membership suffered. The vituperation they were exposed to in print and in oratory as 'lackeys of capitalism' now started mingling with bold forecasts of the establishment of an 'Austrian republic of councils'. The executive decided to bring the Austrian Communists under a measure of control by yielding to their demand for representation in the workers' councils. At their conference of 5 March, Friedrich Adler came out with the declaration that 'it [was] both the purpose and the task of the workers' councils to express the will of the entire working population'. New elections for the councils were to be completed by 15 April, and Adler was nominated as

chairman of the board of the consolidated council. By thus
opening its ranks to the Communists the Socialists not only
hoped to take some of the wind out of the former's sails; they
also wished to intimidate the middle-class parties in parliament, and make them amenable to the drastic social legislation they themselves were drafting.

The impending reform of the workers' councils was not,
however, discussed at any length in bourgeois newspapers.
The *Neue Freie Presse* was devoting much space to the
affairs of Hungary, where Károlyi's government of liberal
bourgeois and moderate Socialists had grown less and less
popular as Czechoslovak, Rumanian and South-Slav troops
were seizing more and more of the country's territory. The
resulting economic dislocations and the virtual collapse of
the railway system had eliminated Hungary even as a
potential source of supplies for Vienna. From late January its
press had been publishing news of mounting dissatisfaction
in the Hungarian countryside, whose big landowners were
frustrating Károlyi's design to break up the large estates for
the benefit of small peasants and agricultural labour; and in
Budapest demonstrations inspired by the demands of the
workers' and soldiers' councils, were said to surpass by far
Vienna's in turbulence. The name of Béla Kun, the young
extremist who upon his return from Russian captivity had
founded a Communist party in Hungary in November – and
late in February had been taken into custody, together with
some seventy other radicals – was seldom mentioned by the
Neue Freie Presse or the *Arbeiter Zeitung*.

Meanwhile, the latter had resumed its attacks on 'Herr
Karl Habsburg'. The 'necessity of his abdication' was reiterated almost daily. *Der Abend* had never ceased to publish
stories as colourful as they were indignant of his 'holding
court' in Eckartsau Lodge. It was alleged to be provisioned
inordinately well by the government. On 19 March, a
Volkswehr patrol intercepted a waggon destined for Karl's
residence, laden with quantities of potatoes and a sack of
coffee. After appropriating the cargo, the armed men forced
the coachman to accept an obscene letter addressed to 'Herr
Habsburg'. Four days earlier Karl had created a minor sensation by informing the press he had bestowed the Order of

the Golden Fleece on three noblemen; no doubt he wished to prove that this privilege was still his.

It became rapidly clear to the Socialist leaders that the 'Eckartsau question' had to be settled – not least to silence Communist criticism. (Strange to say, the Christian-Social cabinet members, in agreeing with their Socialist colleagues, were influenced far more by their party's rural members than by Vienna's politicians.) The chancellor went ahead: he confronted Karl with the choice of either abdicating to live on as a simple citizen of the republic, or removing himself from its territory for good. For the better part of the following week he refused to do either. Only after nightfall of 23 March did he and his family leave Eckartsau Lodge. Lt-Col Strutt had extracted from Renner the promise that the court train as used in the past would be put at the travellers' disposal. A British military-police squad provided security at the tiny railway station where they entrained for Switzerland, which had granted asylum to Karl.

The departure of Franz Josef's heir should have become the paramount topic of conversation all over Vienna. But, as it happened, an event that occasioned far greater agitation had preceded his exodus by barely forty-eight hours.

❧ 11 ❧

Between Munich and Budapest

The establishment of the Hungarian Soviet Republic on 21 March struck not only neighbouring Austria as a bombshell. The Allied statesmen assembled in Paris were suddenly confronted with Russia's nefarious shadow falling on Central Europe. To the Viennese, the bloodless transfer of power in Budapest also posed an enigma. It took some days before they grasped the bizarre chain of events that had led to what was spoken of as a coup.

On 19 March Count Károlyi had been faced with a French ultimatum that demanded the withdrawal of all Hungarian forces from the front held by the Rumanians. He resigned, and the Socialist cabinet members felt unable to take over the government without the support of the Communists, whose dominance the masses of soldiers returned from Russia had accepted. In hurried negotiations carried on partly in the prison cells of the Communists, a 'united socialist party' was put together, which 'elected' a government of people's commissars, with Béla Kun in charge of foreign affairs. Within hours of his release, Kun had emerged as the virtual head of Hungary's governing body, rejected the Allied ultimatum, and started recruitments for a 'red army'.

'I understand that behind it all is the [Magyar] gentry, who hope thus to checkmate the Allies,' Josef Redlich wrote on 23 March in his journal. Apparently he was one of the few men in Vienna who, having watched the obstinacy with which the Magyar ruling classes of old refused to acquiesce in the truncation of their country, also gauged the political impotence they had imposed on themselves. To Vienna's middle classes, Kun's victory seemed to have been brought about by Communist cunning alone. The range of Communist intentions became manifest when Kun promptly proceeded to offer Russia a treaty of alliance, and in a proclamation, 'To All', entreated the international proletariat in general, and German-Austria's in particular, to follow the example of the Hungarian workers. 'There is great apprehension here lest we, too, be caught in a councils' republic soon,' Redlich concluded his brief entry. The wildest stories were circulating on the weekend of 21–2 March. Friedrich Adler, the supposed 'president-designate of a council's republic-in-the-making', was rumoured to have flown to Budapest to confer with Kun; or Julius Deutsch was said to be enlarging Battalion 41 of the *Volkswehr*; or some suspicious work was in progress on Vienna's airport.

Actually, the deeply worried Socialist leaders, including the Socialist cabinet members, had assembled within hours of Kun's accession to power. 'The issue was clear [to us] from the first moment on,' Otto Bauer writes in his memoir of those years. He does not indicate whether the meeting was aware at that juncture of the immediate aims of Kun's government in appealing to Austria's proletariat for collaboration – namely, to lay hands on the equipment of the late imperial army stockpiled in Austria, as well as the printing works of the Austro-Hungarian Bank. 'The establishment of a government of councils in Vienna,' Bauer continues, 'would have been tantamount to concluding an alliance with Hungary,' and inasmuch as Kun left no doubt about his intention to regain the Slovak counties by force, 'a Hungarian alliance would have involved German-Austria in hostilities with Czechoslovakia'.[1] Moreover, a dictatorship of the proletariat in Vienna and the industrial centres near Wiener Neustadt would have been unacceptable to the *Länder*; they would simply have seceded. And would not the Allies have reinforced the *Hungerblockade* with all of its wartime rigours?

Those were the reasons that shortened the deliberations of the Socialist leaders, and brought about their unanimous

resolution that 'everything must be done to prevent the
formation of a regime of councils in German-Austria'.
Middle-class people who heard of that resolution did not
trust it. The leaflets with which the Communist party,
acting with breath-taking speed, swamped Vienna's working-
class districts alarmed middle-class Viennese during the
evening of 21 March. That handbill called on the proletariat for a mass demonstration in front of the town hall on the
following day, a Sunday.

By the time the rally got under way, the *Arbeiter Zeitung*
was on sale in the streets. It carried the text of a message to
Hungary's proletarians that the Austrian workers' councils
had dispatched to the Budapest councils of workers. Expressing 'heartfelt sympathy' with their revolution, that letter,
signed by Friedrich Adler, assured them that the 'working
people of German-Austria would joyfully follow suit. However, there is no food in our country. Even our skimpy bread
ration depends on the [Allied] supply trains. We know that
the Russian Soviet Republic would leave no stone unturned
to extend help to us. But we would starve before such help
could reach us. . . . All our good wishes are with you, and we
ardently hope that the cause of socialism will triumph. . . .'

The equivocal message did not dampen the enthusiasm of
the crowd of between fifteen thousand and eighteen
thousand which assembled on Townhall Square on Sunday
morning. As if in reply to the workers' councils – which were
still composed of Socialist party members only – the speakers
exhorted the crowd to prove by deeds their solidarity
with the Hungarians. 'We must not rest,' one of the orators
exclaimed, 'until the councils' republic has become a reality
in our country, too.' The listeners cheered but did not march
off to break windows, or light bonfires in front of Parliament
House, as police headquarters had been fearing they might.
The following morning, the *Reichspost* emphasized the
presence, in force, of the Red Guard at the rally.

The Christian-Social journal also was quick to point out the
great number of Jews in the new Budapest government.
Their prevalence in it greatly embarrassed the Jewish bourgeoisie. A new wave of anti-Semitism had been sweeping the
lower middle classes in the past two months, as thousands of

Jews were arriving from Rumania and Galicia (now part of resurrected Poland) whose triumphant nationalism had turned against them. To them Vienna still appeared as a natural haven, and neither its wretched living conditions nor the strife in its streets deterred them.

Towards the end of the month an altogether different group of refugees began trickling into Vienna – fugitives from the socialization that the Kun government was rapidly putting into practice. Together with capitalists dispossessed by the nationalization of industry and banking, and the bourgeois politicians of Károlyi's defunct government and some of their moderate Socialist colleagues, many of Hungary's princes and counts made their way to Vienna. They had become intimidated by, or disgusted with, the government-appointed managers of their estates, who were unable to prevent agricultural workers from settling down in great numbers. Those aristocrats moved into the great hotels on Ringstrasse, or the *de luxe* hostelry of Frau Sacher; and soon the tabloid press was publishing colourful stories about their meetings in some of the *chambres séparées* at Sacher's and their feasting on gourmet meals and French champagne, with a gypsy band in attendance. The Viennese in general were as much amused as indignant at the reported antics of the irrepressible Magyar nobles. But persistent rumours that had the aristocratic refugees in collusion with certain government or police officials began to circulate among the workers of the Wiener Neustadt area, where Communist propagandists were harping on the sinister plans of those 'sworn enemies of world revolution'. With the appearance of an increasing number of Hungarian Communist emissaries, the Socialist leaders laboured to stress their decision to stay aloof from the Hungarian regime. Yet on 1 April the *Arbeiter Zeitung* published a resolution of the central committee of the workers' councils, expressing their 'deep regret at not being able to join the admirable action of the Hungarian fellow-workers'.

'It was within the framework of the workers' councils that the struggle against Communism was being fought,'[2] Otto Bauer wrote four years later. But in March of 1919 the emotions of the working class went beyond the issue of the

pending elections to the councils. Even while the Socialist
functionaries dispatched to Wiener Neustadt managed to
keep the number of defections within bounds, its railway
workers, brushing aside the directives of their union, went on
strike; and within hours it was clear that their demands were
not confined to higher wages. 'The capitalist system has
become intolerable to the masses,' the *Arbeiter Zeitung*
declared in its editorial of 28 March. 'They are striving
impatiently for a new order regulating their work, for self-
government in their workshops.' It may well be that the
Socialist journal merely tried to steal the Communists'
thunder. But many middle-class people, taken aback by the
new language of the *Arbeiter Zeitung*, tended to brand the
Sozis as pacemakers of Bolshevism. The strike was spreading,
and soon brought the country's entire railway system to a
virtual standstill. More ominously still, white-collar
personnel had begun to join the walk-out, and Vienna's food
reserves were dwindling. The eloquent anger of the *Reichspost* about both the 'irresponsibility' of the railwaymen and
the 'equivocations' of the Socialist press encouraged attacks
on the government, which was 'failing to bundle off Kun's
emissaries and without an hour's delay send them back
where they came from. . . .'

A cold spell had descended on Vienna; and the coal trains
which started arriving again from Czechoslovakia once the
government had made liberal concessions to end the strike,
were highly welcome. But when those deliveries continued
to come only at irregular intervals to Vienna, there was
instant talk of the 'currency problem' that seemed to be
causing the delays. A government regulation – as it happened issued on the eve of the railway strike – had stipu-
lated that henceforth only bank notes bearing the official
stamp 'German-Austria' would be considered legal tender.
To educated citizens it had become obvious earlier that the
country could not possibly bear the burden of all the late
Habsburg state's bank notes in circulation abroad; nor were
such men surprised by the new rise in the cost of living that
followed the currency regulation. The Viennese by and
large, however, were dumbfounded. The inexorably sinking
value of the *Krone* in Zurich ever since the *Umsturz* had

been a matter of anguished comment even among simple folk, who used to have no conception whatever of the meaning of foreign-bourse quotations for their well-being. As those bourses began to attach a lower value to bank notes stamped in Vienna than to those stamped in Prague or Zagreb, that anguish gave way to a keen embitterment.

It was the South-Slav kingdom that as the first of the successor states had created a currency of its own by stamping the bank notes circulating within its borders. The Viennese nevertheless blamed Czechoslovakia, which had been the next. Wartime indignation at Czech treason still lingered on in middle-class Vienna. It was compounded by the *de facto* incorporation of the German-speaking areas of Bohemia and Moravia in violation of the principle of national self-determination. By that time quite a few well-educated Viennese had persuaded themselves that Wilson's Fourteen Points and their moralist language had lured the Habsburg state into self-destruction, and that in truth the Allies had all along intended to create *die Tschechei* as a bulwark against the Germany of postwar Europe. (That was the name by which the Viennese referred to Czechoslovakia that winter. It would seem that they could not bring themselves to think of the backward Slovaks as a nation.) The *Tschechei*'s reported life of plenty aroused rancorous envy. Even workmen wondered at the unjust world order which their politicians appeared to be accepting.

At the same time, the idea of union with Germany was becoming less and less tempting. The collaboration of Germany's ruling Majority Socialists with the reactionary army command, as well as the brutality of the *Freikorps*, bewildered Austria's proletarians, however much they might have disapproved of the Spartacist uprising. That 'betrayal of the working class' on the part of Germany's right-wing labour leaders was useful to the Communist agitators who were inveighing against the 'traitorous Socialist party leaders in Vienna and their bourgeois cronies in parliament'.

But the Hungarian propagandists concentrated more on promises than criticism. Crossing the frontier not far from Wiener Neustadt, and partly proceeding to Graz and Vienna, they told their audiences about ex-soldiers in their own

country who, lacking accommodation, had been moved into
the mansions of the rich, or about the identical earnings fixed
for plant managers and workers, or about the impending
solution of the unemployment problem through mass
recruitments for the country's Red Army. That last piece of
information could not but affect the *Volkswehr*. As early as
January the Allies had requested a reduction in its strength,
and wild stories about the forthcoming 'decimation' were rife
in the barracks. None of the tales of Kun's emissaries made a
deeper impression on the unemployed than the rosy picture
they drew of the Hungarian reserves of foodstuffs. Out of
these the Austrian workers would be fed once they had
joined their Hungarian brothers; so the embargo the Allies
had threatened if a councils' republic was proclaimed in
Vienna would have little effect. Within less than a week,
those 'Hungarian reserves' were replaced, in the oratory of
the propagandists, by the 'bulging granaries of Slovakia,
which Béla Kun's army was certain to bring back to the
mother country.

The self-assured forecast of a Hungarian offensive with the
intent of large-scale border revisions had a speedy effect on a
group of men most unlikely to be thought of as Bolsheviks.
For some reason, the pilots' school of the Habsburg army in
Wiener Neustadt had not been disbanded, and its trainees
had remained together. The prospect of a revisionist adven-
ture, reviving hopes for the military career, electrified the
young officers. Led by a captain of Hungarian descent, a
number of the pilots put their services and 'their' airplanes at
Soviet Hungary's disposal. Soon they were flying across the
border war material the Communist party had obtained, and
returning with propaganda material and money. By the time
the public learned of the gun-running, its ringleaders had
been apprehended by the Wiener Neustadt police. However, the episode disturbed middle-class people. What
seemed a conjunction of revisionism – generally thought of
as a criterion of monarchist die-hards – with enthusiasm for
Kun's Red Army, worried them all the more as the latter had,
so to speak, established a bridgehead in Vienna. This was
how they saw the Hungarian recruiting office that had been
opened in Vienna. Fantastic rumours about the size of the

nascent Austrian Legion were bandied about; and rather than as an auxiliary corps for the Hungarian army in its march on Slovakia, that legion was feared to be the nucleus of what a later period was to term a fifth column. Not much credence was given to the idea that the government tolerated recruitment as a way of trying to get rid of the Red Guard.

On 6 April news reached Vienna of the setting up in Munich of the Bavarian Republic of Councils. And two days later the *Neue Freie Presse* reported the declared determination of that republic's self-styled leaders to work for the formation of a revolutionary 'Danubian confederation of Bavaria, Hungary and Austria'. 'Throughout this week enormous fear in Vienna of a Communist revolution', reads one line in Redlich's diary entry of 14 April.

The number of men out of work had risen from day to day over the past six weeks. They were given a pittance. No revised regulations of invalids' pensions had been issued as yet. The decaying purchasing power of the currency had made a mockery of the severance pay they were collecting in instalments. Food shops had practically ceased honouring ration tickets at pegged prices; fines imposed now and then on some of the transgressors had shrunk through inflation and no longer frightened merchants. 'Unemployed ex-soldiers and invalids crowd the Communist meetings,' a police report stated, 'and they hail the speakers' every reference to the neglect allegedly suffered through indifference on the part of the authorities.' Prophesies of world revolution touched those audiences as the promise of an order under which they would be better off than they were at present.

Upon the noisy conclusion of one such rally – it was held in the circus building on the farther side of the Danube Canal – a troop of some 5,000 participants crossed the nearby bridge to march on the War Office building which housed the republic's Department of Army Affairs. The discontinuance the day before of the distribution of emergency clothing to unemployed ex-soldiers – an action that in fact had been widely misused – added to the old grievances voiced by the demonstrators. They requested that a deputation be received to present their demands. Once they were in the presence of some of the officials still on duty in the late afternoon, the men rudely ordered them to haul down the flag of the 'bourgeois republic' on the building's roof and run up the 'socialist standard'. The demand was complied with, and for an hour or so a red flag was flying on top of the building. Middle-class people spoke of those guilty of such outrages as 'plain *Gesindel*' (mere rabble), as though using that term could exorcize one's alarm. And, as if to dispel any compassion one might feel for the misery-ridden demonstrators, they were widely accused of misguiding the mutilated soldiers they were 'trotting out' in wheelchairs.

Perhaps the anger at the way those veterans were alleged to let themselves be used was at the bottom of the dwindling compassion for the pitiable men the *Neue Freie Presse* wrote about on 6 April. 'A sign asking for consideration for war invalids has been put up in trams. . . . That admonition amounts to a rebuke, accusing tram-passengers of a lack of consideration towards invalids who barely sustain themselves on their crutches in the overcrowded cars while persons with enviable healthy limbs do not appear to think of offering them their seats. . . .' Insensitivity to the disadvantaged and the weak was noticeable not only on public transport, however. 'Never before have so many people been jostled on the street or elbowed off the curb. . . .' 'Plainly un-Viennese', the newspaper called such behaviour, and went on to remind its readers of the indignation they had voiced in the spring of 1915 when the Italians, turning against the battle-weakened Habsburg state, 'talked of man's *sacro egoismo*'. But from that reminder the writer quickly took flight into rueful nostalgia. 'If we were allowed to be five years younger upon awakening tomorrow morning, would we not be astonished and vexed by a poster recommending consideration toward the handicapped? Ah, how welcome for many, many reasons it would be anyway to find ourselves back in 1914!'

Comparing the present with pre-war days had not stopped with the end of the war. While Communist agitators hurled deprecations at the 'bourgeois republic' and asked for its overthrow, lower-middle-class folk vented their frustration more and more by blaming *die Republik,* rather than the break-up of the old country 'engineered by Herr Wilson'. Karl Kraus, sardonically retracing the train of their thinking, had them argue as follows. 'The Monarchy got us into war; the war ruined us; and out of our ruin rose the republic. Hence, it is the republic that brought about our ruin.' A ditty drawing its inspiration from that conclusion had sprung up in a tavern, and grew popular in step with the mounting disappointment at what the times of peace had turned out to be like. 'Once Vienna's wine gains its old appeal [that ditty ran], We'll counter the *Umsturz* with repeal.' In such rashes of anti-republicanism there was a measure of escapism – a trait that had grown during the past half-century as the economic importance of the lower middle class had declined.

Gossip about scandals involving archdukes had lost much of its savour for them. Black-market tales seemed to have become pointless. The advent of better weather removed the scarcity of fuel as one of the topics of grousing. What incensed the middle classes most of all was what seemed to be hesitancy on the part of the government to nip Bolshevism in the bud, and the seemingly cautious reaction of the police to 'anarchy'. They were ignorant of the tug of war between Johannes Schober (who was beseeching the government to declare a state of siege in Vienna) and the chancellor, Karl Renner (who maintained that the proletariat 'must not be persecuted'). Upper-middle-class people were talking of the 'cowardice' of Renner and his friends, and adduced the warning example of the weak-kneed Budapest Socialists who had allowed Kun to assume power.

A union functionary by the name of Vilmos Böhm had emerged as the war minister of the Hungarian soviet republic and commander-in-chief of its army. It was tempting to think of Julius Deutsch as Böhm's counterpart in an Austrian republic of councils. Little credit was given to the anti-Communist speeches he was delivering before soldiers' councils. As it was, the bourgeois press reported those speeches, if at all, in a cursory manner only. It was known that Deutsch had refused the request of the Austrian Legion that they should depart for Hungary while retaining their weapons. On the other hand, the *Arbeiter Zeitung* of 9 April carried a

glowing account of the reception given by Böhm to the first
detachment of the Legion to report for duty. All of them
were, or had been, *Volkswehr* men; and their resignation or
dismissal from Austria's armed forces was not explicit.

On 9 April the evening edition of the *Neue Freie Presse*
published on its front page some remarks of the chancellor to
one of the editors of the paper. The day before a small-
circulation paper of pan-German outlook had referred to
suggestions known to have been made to the Allied missions
by 'private persons' with regard to 'an occupation of German-
Austria by Allied troops', as well as the reduction of the
Volkswehr.

'In the Monarchy,' Renner was quoted as saying, 'any
citizen approaching a foreign legation with the request for
the country's occupation by enemy troops would have been
prosecuted for high treason in compliance with Article 58c of
the criminal code.' But the republic had instituted freedom
of the press, and the present government, rather than appeal
to the courts, preferred to 'give guidance to its citizens by
admonition and counsel'. Then the chancellor turned to the
matter of the *Volkswehr*. The Allied demand for a reduction
of its strength had been welcomed by middle-class people.
Subsequently they had been impatient with the victors for
not pressing the issue – it was said that they shelved it upon
urgings by the foreign secretary, Otto Bauer. Whereas even
hostile critics of the *Volkswehr* had to admit that its units in
Carinthia were doing their duty in the defence of that *Land*
against South-Slav encroachments, the Vienna *Volkswehr*
appeared, if not necessarily as an instrument of social revolution, yet (in the phrase of the day) as 'a state within the
state'. Its arbitrary raids enraged upper-middle-class housewives, who contended that, whatever else the 'housebreakers
in uniform' might gain through their illegal actions, they
certainly derived a spiteful pleasure from them.

The legendary *Fasching*, the Viennese carnival season
stretching from Epiphany to Ash Wednesday and marked by
scores of dances and fancy-dress balls, had not been celebrated since the outbreak of the war. No one would have so
much as thought of reviving the waltzing tradition in the
grim winter of 1918–19. Still, a number of well-off bourgeois

families arranged dances in their homes, insufficiently heated though the rooms were and lit only by malodorous acetylene lamps. The young men, freed from army service and completing their studies or having secured (as a rule through family connections) employment in business or banking, and the young women who had missed steady male companionship for so long, greatly enjoyed those affairs – unless they were interrupted by a *Volkswehr* 'commission' searching for unlawful hoards of provisions. To believe subsequent accounts of the merrymakers, the intruders, before proceeding to inspect kitchen and larder, made themselves at home at the dining room's sideboard with its plates of cold cuts and cakes and its bottles of wine. Asked for the sources of that supply, the hosts were likely to mention foreign friends, and deny any dealings with the black-market. In at least one case, the raiding *Volkswehr* soldiers had run into some young British officers and had beaten a hasty retreat.

The heads of well-to-do households have become angry at arbitrary searches by the *Volkswehr*, [Renner said in his interview]. Their anger is understandable, and the government, which had disapproved of such actions as soon as they came to its attention, directed the War Usury Office to undertake orderly searches, as is within its legal powers. At any event, it seems to have been overlooked that, as is often the case, one kind of inequity has bred another. Throughout the war and during the months of transition, many thousands of upper-class households have accumulated a supply of foodstuffs in defiance of all pertinent laws and regulations. The *Volkswehr* searches represent but a natural reaction. . . .

The attacks on the *Volkswehr* by a part of the press misjudge the legal and practical character of that institution. Of course every citizen is free to wish the *Volkswehr* were different from what it is, and of course the government does not intend to silence critics. But it goes a bit far to describe [as has been done] the legally set-up defence establishment of the country as a praetorian guard. In the days of the Monarchy, the army was indeed trained as a praetorian guard, inasmuch as it was the emperor's army, and not the army of the people and their commonwealth. And the same newspapers [that are at present denigrating the *Volkswehr*] not only accepted that state of affairs, but glorified it. Certain sections of the population deem it intolerable that our armed force is no longer a mere tool of the ruling classes, but the people's army. How unfair the detractors of the *Volkswehr* are is shown not least by the fact that, of all the countries racked by defeat, German-Austria alone established her institutions without bloodshed and without any attacks worthy of notice upon her citizens' property. To a large extent, that was owed to our *Volkswehr*.

That pronouncement failed to pacify the anxieties of the middle classes. Rumours were growing of even more *Volkswehr* men leaning towards Communism. Any actual growth in Communism was largely because of the fear that the *Volkswehr* would be reduced. But that explanation did not stop talk about 'galloping Bolshevization' of the armed force. Two days after Renner's interview a police report quoted Gruber, an influential member of the soldiers' council of Battalion 41, as having concluded a speech to its men with these words, 'We'll do what has to be done – with or without the Socialists. No blood will be shed if they stick to us. If they should oppose us, they'll find out that the *Volkswehr* is not a government force. . . . The government tried to weaken us [by the change in the battalion's command]. . . . We'll carry the revolution nevertheless into all the battalions. The final struggle is at hand!' But it was the frame of mind of the *Volkswehr* on the whole, rather than the rebellious antics of the Red Guard, that kept the middle classes in a state of uneasy suspense. Signs of mistrust on the part of the police were multiplying. Plain-clothes-men, easily recognized as such, could be seen at all hours in the vicinity of barracks, and both Communist headquarters and the Hungarian embassy building were under undisguised police surveillance.

Over the past weeks the pages of the *Neue Freie Presse* had been full of news from Budapest and Munich, and about the troubles the new governments there had to cope with;

the grave street disorders erupting time and again in Prussian, Silesian and Saxon cities had the full attention of the great journal; it was speculating regularly upon the peace terms the German republic might be presented with; it published detailed reports from the Czech-occupied German-speaking areas of Bohemia and Moravia; and it valiantly tried to inform its readers on the happenings in Russia, not least the operations of the various counter-revolutionary armies and the British-American forces dispatched there to combat the Reds. In short, the *Neue Freie Presse* was living up to its name of Vienna's window on the world. Former ambassadors were asked for their views on affairs abroad, while members of the late Upper Chamber, aged bourgeois politicians or retired bank presidents, grappled in the columns of the paper with the countless problems brought about by the dissolution of the Habsburg state. No matter how evident the shortsightedness of such 'experts' had become while in their influential positions, it did not seem to tarnish their names in the eyes of upper-middle-class people. Their taste bade them remain loyal to yesterday's prominent men at a time when their abilities were being mocked so widely and their past accomplishment denigrated. It also did not escape notice that the Allied missions in Vienna tended to seek the opinions of those men of the past; in fact, they appeared to put greater stock in *their* wisdom than in the judgment of the men serving the republic. As the decisions of the forthcoming peace conference began to agitate Vienna's upper bourgeois no less than the rest of the population, they felt an affinity with the Allies, confiding not only in their unflinching hostility to Communism, but also in their mistrust of socialism as practised in German-Austria.

Some pieces of social legislation rushed through parliament in April seemed a further step on the road to a radical policy. A law compelling industry to create new jobs raised the spectre of its nationalization. 'The masses are impatient,' Otto Bauer said in a speech to the Assembly. 'They want to see the work of socialization started, and they are entitled to see it under way as soon as possible.' Nothing shows that big business – or, for that matter, the *Neue Freie Presse* – wondered whether the Socialist leaders, by pressing legislation delayed since the immediate post-*Umsturz* period, might not primarily aim at stemming further defections from the party. A modest rise in unemployment compensation moved Josef Redlich (on the very day he noted the 'great fear of a Communist revolution') to forecast the financial collapse of the country, whose 'government is giving away millions and millions ... to the workers!'

Two of the newly enacted laws in particular affected Vienna's middle classes, even though their interests were not touched – the 'Habsburg law', as it was instantly dubbed, and the abolition of all titles of nobility. The former banished Karl Habsburg for good from Austrian territory, and made residence of other members of his family contingent upon renunciation of their privileges. Moreover, both the entailed funds of the Habsburg dynasty and the real estate it owned were declared seized, and the income from both earmarked for invalids and war widows. Talking to representatives of the press on 20 March (the day preceding the Budapest coup), the chancellor had enlarged on the proposed legislation. According to the *Wiener Zeitung*, he pointed out that the government had 'not to deal with Karl Habsburg as a person'; rather, it was his evident concept of himself as the 'head of the Arch House' and the administrator of its property that had to be 'cleared up'. The Arch House was, or had been, 'an institution'. It had been 'responsible to a large extent for the catastrophic collapse and for the destruction of much of our own national wealth. The Arch House cannot refer to its immunity under the [old Austrian] constitution, for the last emperor refused to take the oath on it.' He had indeed, wishing in the late autumn of 1916 to preserve his options for a possible reform along ethnic lines (that vague plan whose implementation would not have solved the Habsburg's state's problem anyway, considering the oath that Karl took at the Hungarian coronation). Renner went on to list the wartime malfeasances of certain of the dynasty's members, including Karl's Parma relatives, and declared that 'burghers and workers, as well as the host of unemployed career officers and civil servants who now are facing an uncertain future ask themselves whether the historical responsibility of the Arch House [for their misery] must not receive its proper deserts.' Whatever sentimental chords may have been touched among the middle classes by the wholesale seizure of the dynasty's possessions, including its superb art collections, the confiscation shocked owners of property above all, as the first brazen act of governmental expropriation. It seemed to be doubly ominous inasmuch as a property levy was known to have been suggested – guesses about its likely size had been made for some time – and the passage of the Habsburg law coincided with the issue of an ordinance freezing all bank accounts (and making safe-deposit boxes inaccessible to their owners) for the sake of the registration of assets.

As for the abolition of titles of nobility, it irritated mainly the numerous military and civil-service families which in the course of the past century had been ennobled as a matter of imperial routine. The particle *von* preceding the family name – which, in one kind of ennoblement was enriched by a fancy name added – had immensely enhanced their self-importance. Even the servile lower-class habit of addressing well-to-do commoners as *Herr von* had not prevented that petty nobility from valuing very highly the mark of status. Moreover, their sons had enjoyed privileges in the admission to certain secondary schools. The new status instantly estranged from the *Republik* even those in that group who had started to overcome their bias towards the new form of government. They were shaking their heads at the apparent lack of opposition the revolutionary legislation had met with in parliament from the Christian-Social deputies who, in speech and print, were making so much of tradition.

The financiers and industrialists who had purchased the coveted *von,* or even a baronetcy, with big charitable donations, were not really affected by the new law. They had always been aware of the malicious jokes about their lack of aristocratic refinement. Their vanity had been pleased nevertheless by the address due them – and they could continue enjoying it, for only the use of titles by the former title-holders themselves was put under sanction. It may also be surmised that the economic problems the 'stock-exchange barons' faced in those days and their fear of Communism crowded out what pique they may have felt. Thoughtful middle-class people traced the whole thing back to the wish of the Socialist leaders to cater to the levelling spirit they had fostered for decades in the masses, and assure them of a reformed social order. Working people themselves were not swept off their feet by the 'anti-nobility' law. Viennese that they were, besides being proletarians, they realized its inherent weakness, indeed its comical side.

For the very stratum of society Socialist literature had attacked for two generations – the families of princes, counts and barons that till the mid-nineteenth century had provided the sovereign with cabinet ministers, generals and many senior civil servants, and which until the Habsburg state's last day had had a virtual monopoly on the foreign service and the governorships of the *Länder* – those 'feudal' families were hardly touched at all by the abolition of their centuries-old titles. (Only the closing of the secular homes reserved for aristocratic spinsters and widows caused a painful readjustment.) Members of the high aristocracy had never used their titles within their own circle. Outside it, the mere names of those families, appearing over and over again in the history of the country, sufficed to set them apart from the common run of mortals; and their landed wealth had withstood the ravages of inflation. They thus made light of, and were likely to scoff at, the decreed egalitarianism. That kind of amusement spread beyond their class when one particular nobleman, Count Adalbert Sternberg, decided to make fools in public of the law's drafters.

The quixotic escapades of that hard-drinking Bohemian count had partly annoyed, partly entertained the Viennese over the past twenty years. Now he had visiting cards printed which read 'Adalbert of the House of Sternberg which Karl der Grosse [Charlemagne] ennobled and Karl Renner stripped of its title'. Nor was that all. People walking along a certain stretch of Ringstrasse sometimes caught sight of the mountainous, purple-faced Sternberg seated on a stool next to the stand of a hot-chestnut vendor, distributing visiting cards to passers-by and loudly ridiculing the new legislation. Tabloids published vivid accounts of his performance, and *Der Abend* called it a 'feudalist provocation'.

To nostalgic lovers of the old order, Adalbert Sternberg seemed hardly a proper spokesman for it. As a *Reichsrat* deputy in the early 1900s, he had on two different occasions severely criticized Franz Josef, and in the latter of those scrambled speeches had, in so many words, called for his abdication.

The Allied blockade was officially lifted on 3 April. Within the week the first trainload of American salt pork arrived in Vienna. Shipments of maize arrived from Yugoslavia, even though that country's military activities were being stepped up on the Carinthian border. Delivery of eggs from Poland was resumed. Italian spring vegetables were to be seen again in Inner-City stores. The bourgeois press was making much of the permission granted the city's bakers to bring white rolls to the market again – the cherished 'emperor rolls' of pre-war days.

But such sporadic signs of improvement in the food situation deluded no one into the belief that the crisis was passing. It had become painfully evident that most of the *Länder* were less and less willing to allow food supplies to be shipped to 'red Vienna' from their territories. On 16 April a notice from the government's press office was published, reading,

> Some days ago all aliens who recently fled to Vienna from the eastern parts of the former Austro-Hungarian Monarchy were ... notified that they must leave the city immediately. That order proved to be ineffective. About 1,000 such aliens are residing in Vienna's hotels and *pensions* at present, and their lavish way of living contrasts sharply with the distress of large sections of the indigenous population. ... Plans are in preparation for expelling [those aliens] or relocating them in communities where their housing and food requirements will not interfere with those of the so sorely tried Viennese.

Probably that resolute warning was meant not least to calm the enraged talk about 'moneyed foreign Jews', on the one hand, and 'high-living Hungarian counts', on the other.

The outcome of the elections to the workers' councils,

concluded on 15 April, heartened the leadership of the
Socialist party. The number of Communist delegates elected
turned out to be very small; and the councils, after a lengthy
debate, heeded Friedrich Adler's warning that 'any attempt
to set up a dictatorship of the proletariat would, under the
circumstances prevailing in German-Austria, be tantamount
to a suicide of the [November] revolution'. The workers'
councils passed that resolution on to the factory workers
through the grass roots apparatus of the Social-Democratic
party.

Success in the workshops did not blind the Socialists to the
effect of Communist agitation on the unemployed and the
invalid ex-soldiers. Unable to profit from the slight improvement in the supplies situation, those bitterly disgruntled men
and women were only provoked by talk about improving
conditions. Bakers, greengrocers and butchers were almost
regularly out of stock when visibly indigent women turned up
to have their ration tickets honoured. More and more of the
unemployed were flocking to Communist meetings, where
speakers promised them a new deal in a republic of councils.

A particularly vociferous group at those rallies consisted of
the wives of P.O.W.s still unaccounted for in Russia. The
speakers pretended to know that the prisoners, liberated,
were staying on in Russia of their own volition. Stories of
their living with native women had been circulating for some
time; and the allegedly abandoned wives, while decrying the
loose morals of the Russian Bolsheviks, were, at the same
time, drawn to their fellow-Communists in Vienna and their
forecasts of social justice. Moreover, Hungarian Communists
maintained that *their* P.O.W.s had all been shipped home
from Russia upon the establishment of Kun's regime. A
grievance of a different kind animated the families of prisoners still in Italy. They accused the late army command of a
gross dereliction of duty in allowing those tens of thousands
to fall into the hands of the Italian army after the armistice
deadline, and pointedly asked why the 'bourgeois republic'
did not call to account those former military leaders. The
dependants of P.O.W.s, who had to eke out a living on the
allowance granted them earlier and now considerably
devalued, were among the most needy of the hundreds of

thousands of poverty-stricken people. A 'National Association of Families of German-Austrian P.O.W.s' had been formed in the early days of April.

Tension in Vienna had mounted almost hourly since the beginning of the month. A Communist seizure of power was said to be imminent. Despite the absence of any information, 17 April was the accepted date for this coup. This would be Maundy Thursday, and churchgoing people suggested that it would be typical of the godless Bolsheviks to stage a bloody putsch during Holy Week. On 16 April,

> counter-measures were discussed in the chancellery, Doktor Renner presiding, [Brandl recalls in his memoirs]. I submitted the plans of the Communists. Their intention was to lead the masses after the conclusion of their scheduled rally, to Parliament House and occupy its premises. They would bring the *Volkswehr*, which sympathized with them anyway, out on the streets, would harangue . . . the workers in the factories, and through that [twofold] pressure force the government either to join in the proclamation of an 'Austrian republic of councils', or else disappear. . . . I requested that the rally be banned, the *Volkswehr* confined to barracks, and the suppression of the [Communist] enterprise left to the police. . . . Complications could be expected only if the government should call out the *Volkswehr*. It was all in vain. [It was decided that] the rally must not be banned, and the police kept out of sight altogether. . . .[3]

Later that day Schober, who had not attended the meeting, pleaded with Renner to change the decision. The efforts were futile, and the police began to make preparations of their own. At the same time Deutsch, having hastily called a plenary session of Vienna's soldiers' councils, addressed them :

> We are confronting the question as to whether a republic of councils should be proclaimed at this juncture, an alliance concluded with both Hungary and Russia, and war declared on the Allies. . . . To adopt mechanically the tactics of Russia and Hungary might well lead our proleta-

riat into a catastrophic impasse.... Vienna, with two million inhabitants in this country of six million people cannot feed its population. ... Let us face it: we live on hand-outs from the victorious powers. ... We have neither the military strength for breaking with the Allies nor the economic strength to sustain ourselves without them. It would be folly, it would be a crime to ignore those facts. ... For all the willingness of the Hungarians, they could not possibly help us. Perhaps they would send us two trainloads of supplies per day, as against the twelve we are now receiving from the Allies. Plain famine would become our lot within a few days. ... And, besides, would the country as a whole be prepared to go to war? Why, not a single one of our peasants would join us.

The text of Deutsch's oration was to be published only on 19 April by the *Neue Freie Presse*; and his critics would point out that he had failed to allude to the sinister conspiracy of the Communists. Apparently Deutsch was poignantly conscious of the growing strength of Communist agitation in the ranks of the *Volkswehr*. Thus he appealed to the men's pride. 'The proletariat can assert itself only if the *Volkswehr*, as the powerful backbone of the [November] revolution, retains its discipline ... and is ready to march with the workers through thick and thin. ... A *Volkswehr* lacking discipline would only embarrass the revolution.' After touching on the 'necessity to weed out all those who do not submit to proletarian military discipline', he closed: 'In this grave hour I am asking for your trust. Perhaps on the day of our victory you will recall my words and realize that our policies were shaped by the firm will and determination to preserve the [fruits of the] revolution and lead the proletariat to final victory.' A unanimous resolution thereupon 'expressed its full confidence in Doktor Deutsch as the representative of the workers in the Department of Defence [*sic*].'

While the meeting of the soldiers' councils was under way, Vienna's Christian-Social party was holding a meeting of its own in a suburban beer hall. The main speaker was Leopold Kunschak. One of the youngest of the intimate circle of the late Lueger, that politician, originally a workman, had remained extremely popular with all Christian-Socials even while the apparent pusillanimity of most of their party's leaders had discouraged them to the point of distraction. In the days preceding the elections to the National Assembly, Kunschak had been indefatigable, hurrying from one meeting to another to thunder, in his folksy manner, against the Bolsheviks and their 'well-known friends in our midst'. He had changed his theme only slightly in the intervening months. That evening he was holding forth against the soldiers' councils and their illegal searches, and accused those in power of closing their eyes to the outrages, or dismissing them as isolated excesses. 'But they are anything but isolated,' he exclaimed. 'There's terror wherever one looks. And, by God, that's not what we [before the *Umsturz*] imagined conditions would be in a republic!'[4]

Even as Kunschak was whipping up his audience, the beer hall had been surrounded by a band of armed men of Battalion 41. A couple of machine-guns had been brought into position, their barrels aimed at the locked doors of the building. It has never been ascertained whether or not the besiegers heard of the decision reached by the soldiers' councils. At any rate the Red Guard men departed before Kunschak's meeting adjourned. Even though their deployment seems to have puzzled rather than alarmed the police, Schober, overriding instructions of the Secretary of the Interior, ordered a state of alert for his entire force.

The following morning the cabinet assembled for one of its regular meetings in the chancellor's office. Foremost on the agenda was the matter of the families of the prisoners of war. But no doubt more pressing problems were on the minds of the cabinet members. Disturbing news had arrived from Carinthia. The number of men out of work in Vienna alone had risen to 130,000. The stock of flour in the city was equal to the requirements of one week. Police headquarters had reported rumours once again sweeping the workers' districts of 'bulging government warehouses'. The day before the police had been notified by the central committee of the Communist party that it had nothing to do with a number of demonstrations apparently planned by certain *ad hoc* associations for Maundy Thursday. But as the central committee was known to the police to be still in turmoil, the government attached no particular importance to that information.

It was 3.30 p.m. Perfect tranquillity reigned around Parliament House. There was no evidence that anything out of the ordinary was to be expected [stated the report in the Friday issue of the *Neue Freie Presse*]. No special police contingent was to be seen. Only the usual four-men squads were posted in front of the building. Somewhat more lively was the square in front of Burgtheater. Knots of people were standing about ... to watch from a safe distance what was going on around the Town Hall, where a rally of unemployed was in progress.

It had been called by a committee of unemployed unknown to the police before its handbills were distributed during the previous evening. No more than 2,000 people had followed the call. The usual speeches over, the demonstrators began to turn into the avenue running parallel to Ringstrasse.

It was coincidence that the large procession of ex-soldiers and war invalids coming from a meeting at Kadrmann's, a beer garden on the Prater grounds, reached Ringstrasse at precisely the time the other meeting was disbanding. Even while *Ordner* prevented bystanders from joining the ex-soldiers' columns, many of the participants in the meeting of the jobless fell in with the Kadrmann marchers. The others started marching in a formation of their own along the broad street, which runs parallel to Ringstrasse, towards Parliament House.

The first of the veterans to arrive lost no time in mounting the base of the Athena fountain, and while the masses pressed on, intoning the Internationale, red flags were run up by a group of demonstrators. No one interfered. In fact the small police detachment on duty withdrew when the jobless marchers approached, and the crowd was given access to the ramps of the building. It was, as one reporter was to put it, '12 November all over again'.

Meanwhile, a five-man deputation had gone to the eastern entrance of the building. Having being told that no cabinet member was inside, they elbowed their way through their fellow demonstrators to reach the western side street. The door there was locked too, and neither knocking nor ringing the bell was of any avail. The shouts of the men and women who had joined the deputation were growing ever more strident. Apparently they did not know that the crowd on the opposite side of the building was bombarding the ground-floor windows with lumps of coal grabbed from a nearby waggon. The sound of the shattered glass could not be heard above the din; the door itself was finally forced and the crowd penetrated the courtyard – only to find police carrying rifles blocking their way. The policemen were about to throw out the invaders and shut the door when a shot was fired. 'As is the rule in such deplorable occurrences,' the *Neue Freie Presse* remarked, 'reports as to who fired that first shot are contradictory. The demonstrators contend that they were shot at by the police, while the latter maintain that the shot came from amid the crowd.'

Be that as it may, at that moment mounted police came galloping from behind Parliament House, sabres drawn, but with revolvers secured in their holsters. They were greeted by a shower of coal and a succession of shots. But unlike the shots of 12 November, those fired during this demonstration did not cause a panic. Whenever a detonation was heard, people threw themselves on to the pavement, only to re-assemble and redouble their screaming and attacks. Again and again demonstrators and mounted police clashed.

The multitude seemed to be getting somewhat calmer, but just then a band of demonstrators in Ringstrasse had stopped a lorry laden with petrol drums, two of which they pulled down and rolled toward Parliament House. It so happened that a Parliament House official had lowered the iron shutter after the windows had been broken, but the narrow cushion (which Viennese place between their double casements) had remained outside the rolled-down shutter and was within reach of the mob on the pavement. The cushion was soaked with petrol and set on fire, and almost instantly the window frame burst into flames. Within seconds various window frames were ablaze – the glare of the flames being visible from afar.

It was seven o'clock. The performance in the Burgtheater had been under way for an hour. Suddenly the curtain was

lowered, the lights went up in the house, and the director of
the play stepped forward to ask the audience to leave the
theatre 'as the performance must be terminated'. His
announcement was met by catcalls, with people demanding
that the show should go on, despite the continuous wails of
the fire engines outside.

The police had gone into action, trying to clear the way for
the horse-drawn engines. The tumultuous crowd, watching
the spreading flames and obviously bent on adding to their
work of destruction, did not budge. 'After a salvo fired over
the heads of the demonstrators had proved ineffective, police
shot into the multitude ... which thereupon retreated in
flight. As people withdrew, a succession of pistol shots was
fired from in their midst. There were casualties on both
sides.'

An ever-increasing stream of demonstrators still faced the
police cordon on the driveways of the building leading to the
Ringstrasse, pressing on and hurling obscenities at the
police, who refrained from moving forward. It was difficult
for Julius Deutsch, who at long last had arrived on the
scene, to 'address the demonstrators' in the hubbub and
fading light. The *Neue Freie Presse* reported, 'He expressed
his horror at what had happened, and vowed that a ruthless
investigation would ascertain the men responsible for it. The
Volkswehr was on its way to restore order. . . .'

Three companies arrived towards eight o'clock, and at
once began to scatter the crowds. The demonstrators
welcomed the *Volkswehr*, and were mostly co-operative. 120
men of Battalion 41, turning up somewhat later, joined in the
swift action. At the same time some members of the councils
of soldiers entered the courtyard of Parliament House and
opened negotiations with the police about their departure,
which would not be interfered with if rifles and ammunition
were abandoned. The discussion lasted only a short time.
The policemen deposited their rifles in a corner of the
courtyard and their withdrawal took place without any
further disturbance. Night had descended, and all lights in
the building had been switched off. The members of the
soldiers' councils and other *Volkswehr* men soon persuaded
the last demonstrators to leave.

'Whoever was walking along Ringstrasse some time after 8.30 p.m. could still observe some movement in the neighbourhood of Parliament House. But [several hundred yards farther] the boulevard showed its normal face . . . and not the slightest trace of disorder was to be noticed around the Opera House.' Those were the closing words of the account in the 18 April issue of the *Neue Freie Presse*. Essentially accurate as later investigations proved it to be, it was incomplete in several respects. For one thing, it left unmentioned the most macabre incident that had occurred. 'Demonstrators fell upon the killed police horses,' Otto Bauer writes, 'to cut pieces of flesh from the carcasses – a welcome prize indeed, a delicacy not tasted for a very long time.'[5]

Grim news was spreading on Good Friday morning: five policemen had been shot to death, and a number of others gravely wounded, while some thirty demonstrators, a woman among them, had sustained injuries from bullets; nor had the *Volkswehr* escaped unharmed. Appalling as that record was, it was not the most pressing concern of Vienna's middle classes or of much of the working class. The rumour of an attempted Communist putsch was refusing to die.

The riots around Parliament House did not constitute any attempt to carry out a putsch . . . [the *Neue Freie Presse* declared in its leader of 18 April]. Those raving people . . . had no political goal. They clamoured for more money from the government, for a pecuniary contribution towards personal re-equipment, and for more liberal bread rationing. True, Communist motives were certainly not absent as a contributory factor. But at the root of the deeply distressing events there was no clear desire to change our form of government by force. Bread is what the unemployed want. Hence, they could not possibly try to bring about an upheaval bound to rob them of what little bread they have and create instantaneous famine in Vienna. . . . There must have been foreigners present, instigators from abroad. For it just was not in tune with the nature of the Viennese to open fire on human beings,

and put to the torch a building that is a landmark of
German art on Austrian soil. . . .

Everybody knew that Hungarian rabble-rousers had been
among the speakers both on Town Hall Square and in the
Prater beer hall. There was less certainty about what they
had been doing in the course of the riots themselves. None of
the stories current accused them of having participated in
the arson. On the other hand, heavily armed Prater *Marineure*
had been moving through the multitudes in motor cars,
enticing them to 'complete the revolution'. The most disturbing of all stories, however, dealt with the Red Guard.

In the afternoon of 17 April a number of automobiles
drove up to the barracks of Battalion 41 [according to an
official press release published by the *Arbeiter Zeitung* on
19 April] and their passengers, telling totally unfounded
horror stories, harangued the *Volkswehr* men to go out and
join the demonstrators. . . . When the agitators realized the
futility of their efforts, they upbraided the battalion . . . for
its treason. Later, soldiers' councillor Gruber of Battalion
41 drove to Parliament House and declared himself ready
to employ his force in restoring order. The police officer
[he talked to] accepted the offer, which was subsequently
implemented by 120 men of the battalion, who throughout
the action showed exemplary discipline.

That communiqué did not silence rumours; nor were the
rumours confined to the conduct of the Red Guard. Who, it
was asked, had called out the three *Volkswehr* companies?
Brandl in his memoirs has said that '*Volkswehr* men who
were loyal to the government persuaded the emergency
contingents in the barracks that it was high time for them to
restore order and prevent the police claiming all the credit.
To be sure, the police had the situation well in hand by the
time the *Volkswehr* arrived.'[6] Whether that version of its
intervention found credence immediately after Maundy
Thursday, or whether that version was even then suggested
at the time, is open to question. The widely talked-about
'jubilation' of the multitude at the appearance of the *Volkswehr* sufficed to convince middle-class people of the

sinister and portentous part it had played. Besides, horrified bourgeois talk dealt with the disarmament by the *Volkswehr* of the police detachments in the courtyard of Parliament House. It was an episode inviting embellishment. So were published accounts of 'armed criminals in *Volkswehr* clothing' having broken into several police stations during the night of 17–18 April, and compelled the men on duty to surrender their weapons. Were the police, then, abdicating their law-enforcing power?

Now it was true that many policemen, growing wary of the future, had recently béen searching for a *modus vivendi* with the *Volkswehr*, or even shown sympathy for the Socialist party. The humiliation suffered on Maundy Thursday on the whole did away with such leanings. Even the *Stadt-schutzwache*, suspected of Socialist tendencies all along, no longer wanted much to do with the *Volkswehr*. At the same time the Communists continued to accuse the *Volkswehr* of treason. In fact, many of the men and women who had hailed its intervention on 17 April turned against it now that the *Volkswehr* had followed government orders and occupied all public buildings. During protest marches past Parliament House in the week following Easter Sunday, *Volkswehr* units standing guard there were regularly exposed to an ear-splitting chorus of invectives. In one instance, the climax that the protest demonstration reached provided middle-class Viennese and Communists alike with a good deal of amusement. On that day, the *Volkswehr* detachment on duty in front of the building had brought along fire hoses, and attached them to hydrants. One particular squad, unnerved by the ugly abuse rising from the crowd that had come to a standstill, opened the hydrant – only to be doused itself by the powerful jet of water ejected by the hose which had over-turned under the sudden pressure.

On 27 April the Viennese found a placard posted all over the city. Signed by the soldiers' councils, it read as follows:

Workers, unemployed, returned soldiers and invalids: In the last days Vienna's *Volkswehr* men have proved that the revolution is in good keeping in their hands. This is why we appeal to you brothers in proletarian garb, beseeching you not to let our revolution be endangered by unscrupulous mock-radicals and reactionary elements. Every revolution has its parasites. Let us recognize them as such, and prevent them from harming our cause.... The Social-Democratic and Communist *Volkswehr* men call on you. Proletarians of Vienna, do not tolerate the provocations of irresponsible men. Support us *Volkswehr* men in keeping in check the hyenas of the revolution. We earnestly warn their leaders and instigators: the patience of the *Volkswehr* is exhausted!

The existence of Communist *Volkswehr* men, thus acknowledged, delighted people who insisted that there had been definite plans for a putsch. The Communist party published a strong denial. 'We are against a putsch, for we know that the liberation of the proletariat will have to be the work of the entire labour force willing to fight.'[7] That was not the whole truth, however. Although the actual developments had taken the central committee by surprise, plans for a putsch had been harboured by the most radical of the committee's members, who appear to have collaborated with Hungarian emissaries. To them, as indeed to the Hungarian government, a speedy change of regime in Vienna was of strategic importance: the Rumanians had started a new offensive on Hungarian territory, and Czechoslovak forces were about to establish contacts with them; and in Bavaria, a number of strong *Freikorps*, which had gone into action two weeks earlier with the support of the Berlin government, were closing in on Munich. What the Hungarians who were advising the Vienna committee wanted to see accomplished, was a paralysis of the Austrian government through the revolt of the most disadvantaged and least disciplined of proletarians, a split in the Socialist leadership, and the defection from it of Friedrich Adler, whose personal following was immense. According to an anonymous Communist publication two months later, Friedrich Adler appeared unannounced at Communist headquarters in the afternoon of Maundy Thursday, and declared that, should a councils' republic be proclaimed, he would remain passive; and that sobering declaration promptly destroyed the determination of the committee's hotheads to bring matters to a head. A memorandum preserved in Moscow's files has Adler talk on that occasion in the name of the Socialist party: it would remain neutral in the case of a Communist take-over. . . .

Early in June, and under circumstances hardly less critical than those prevailing in mid-April, a man by the name of Mühl, whom Brandl calls 'one of the main culprits of the bloody events of Maundy Thursday', addressed his fellow Prater *Marineure,* and warned them against pinning any hopes on Friedrich Adler. 'He is a sick man. He still suffers from [the trauma of] his deed [the assassination of Count Stürgkh].'[8]

❧ 12 ❧

The Fifteenth of June

On the eve of Easter Sunday, Meissel and Schadn's hotel had reopened its restaurant after several weeks of redecoration. The hotel patrons had not changed much since the day Count Stürgkh was shot to death there and neither had the décor of the second floor dining room. The few ex-ministers who could still afford it would now and then come to take their lunch and linger over coffee; and bankers and business-men would exchange their worries or discuss the sad record of the past. It was a place as quiet as it had always been. While mobs which continued to rove Ringstrasse could be heard demanding that its *de luxe* hotels, or Sacher's, should be shut down and their provisions seized, staid Meissel and Schadn appeared not to provoke such violent intentions. (Yet not many *nouveaux riches* availed themselves of the peace-able atmosphere. Although often frustrated by waiters who looked down their noses at them, the 'war millionaires' pre-ferred the more glamorous hostelries. There they were likely to rub elbows with officers of the Allied missions, and titled Hungarian refugees as well. At the Grand Hotel, whose sumptuous dining room was shunned by the latter, some of Kun's emissaries were in appearance.) In one respect Meissel and Schadn *had* undergone a change. Although not serving gourmet dishes (which it never had), its management no longer even pretended to comply with austerity regulations. Upper-class people such as its guests had ceased paying any attention to them.

If the starving tens of thousands fulminated against the

rich who seemed to scoff at regulations, they themselves abided by them only out of necessity. But their spokesmen loved to contrast the law-abiding spirit of the poor with the indifference of wealthy transgressors. Conversely, well-off people, if they ever stopped to consider their infringements of austerity regulations, tended to justify them by the violence with which the *Volkswehr* had taken the law into its own hands, trampling on property rights. The *Volkswehr* had not desisted from its arbitrary searches, and of late 'action groups' of the workers' councils of certain plants had begun to stage raids of their own. And, worst perhaps in the eyes of men of property, the government had suggested regulating those encroachments by admitting workers' delegates to the decision-making of the War Usury Office.

Some of the councils of workers were also meddling with landlords' right of disposing of vacant flats. In step with the currency's *de facto* devaluation, the rent-control law passed early in the war had made urban real estate a questionable investment. The interference with the basic right of landlords seemed to cap the injuries real-estate owners had sustained over the past three years. Not the least vexed were those small capitalists who had invested a lifetime's savings in narrow two-or three-storey buildings. They used to form a parochial élite of sorts in the suburbs of pre-industrial Vienna, as much held in awe as made sport of by the artisans and petty officials who were their tenants; and some of that social prestige had survived. The loss of local status strengthened their dislike of *die Republik* no less than the pauperization they were certain they faced. The 'creeping expropriation' also agitated real-estate owners of greater wealth, not least the owners of workers' tenements. However, such grumblings were drowned by the utter dismay felt in the middle classes by the results of the municipal elections.

No less than seventy per cent of the city's population had elected Social-Democrats in the National Assembly elections. Yet the outcome of the city elections of 5 May went beyond the worst fears. It put an end to the Christian-Socials' dominance in the town hall, taken for granted for nearly a generation. They secured only fifty seats, as against one hundred the Socialists gained. The German-Nationals could send no more than three representatives to the new chamber. The newly set-up Democratic Burghers' Party found itself reduced to one seat. Lueger's successor resigned.

The man the Socialists planned to nominate as mayor was not an extremist. (The City Council was to elect him on 22 May.) But the reform intentions his party had made no secret of ever since the *Umsturz* were far from being considered moderate by middle-class citizens. The projected city-tax legislation filled people of property with consternation. A progressive housing tax was in preparation, whose proceeds would be earmarked for an ambitious or (as critics put it) extravagant public-housing programme. The municipality would collect an excise on such bourgeois amenities as motor cars and carriage horses and even servants. (That projected tax rose steeply with the numbers of staff employed in one household. *Der Abend* gleefully calculated the annual sums the palatial Rothschild establishment would have to pay.) Most frightening was the rumour of a drafted emergency ordinance that would empower the city government to billet demobilized soldiers lacking living quarters in 'super-numerary' rooms of large flats; so unsettling was that prospect that some families hastened to take in as sub-tenants well-recommended refugees from Czechoslovakia's German-speaking districts.

Soon the new City Council began to reform the inherited administration by electing 'Governing City Councillors' to head the various departments. All of those men of course were Socialists. In the months to come, and for many years, none of them was more talked about and more fiercely detested by middle-class Viennese than the head of the treasury, a former bank branch manager by the name of Hugo Breitner. Although he was of Jewish extraction, the Jewish bourgeois railed no less against him than did anti-Semitic lower-middle-class people, who suggested that Breitner's true aim was the destruction of the Viennese way of life. Even well-informed bourgeois refused to give him credit for his insistence that the municipal utility and trans-portation enterprises pay their own way. It was dawning on them that the long-range consequences of the rigorous fiscal policies of the new city administration might strengthen

Vienna's position *vis-à-vis* the *Länder*, and fortify the political power of Labour in national issues. However, that consideration belongs to a somewhat later period. In the spring of 1919 Breitner and his policies were simply the focus of all anti-*Sozi* emotions, which were but slightly lessened by the knowledge of the Socialists' own anti-Communist struggle.

Among Christian-Social constituents, Otto Glöckel was scarcely less a *bête noire* than Breitner. Glöckel was the head of the city's department of education, a one-time teacher who had lost his job under Lueger's regime. Primary schools as well as the secondary schools in which the children of both workers and most lower-middle-class people were educated had been imbued with the dynastic spirit of the Christian-Social town hall; and the influence of the Church had been very strong. (Any applicant for a position in the municipal school system had had to declare under oath that he was not a member of the Social-Democratic party.) In the latter part of the war, many teachers, motivated by the rapidly deteriorating health of their pupils as well as their own reduced living conditions, had started to sympathize with the Socialist party, and in fact had joined it during the *Umsturz* days. Now, the Socialists started packing teaching staffs with party members. Churchgoing families foresaw with revulsion their children's likely estrangement from their own traditions. A handful of school principals had stopped the daily recital of Pater Noster and Hail Mary in class, or had the crucifix removed from the classrooms, and thereby occasioned acrimonious debates in parliament. But there was for the time being no certainty as to official policy. Even though no attempts were made then or later to abolish religious instruction as prescribed by law, the secularism directing the city's educational policies could not but offend devout Catholics, and the clergy did not fail to remind them of the papal encyclical of 1907 condemning modernism.

Vienna's social élite had not been fighting *fin-de-siècle* cultural modernism. Innovations in literature and the arts had intrigued it. The emperor's own Burgtheater had produced Ibsen's plays. If the young Kafka had been as good as unknown, Rilke had not. Kokoschka, it is true, had been ridiculed. But the group of his seniors who had broken with the Academy of Arts, a sterile government institution, had been widely admired, and their leader, Gustav Klimt, had been a darling of the sophisticated upper bourgeois. Nor had they joined in the popular derision directed at Adolf Loos's functional building which had gone up opposite the Hofburg. Rather, Vienna's élite would, in double-edged amusement, imagine old Franz Josef's helpless perplexity at the sight. What was known about Freud among laymen had been discussed less with animosity than with (sometimes facetious) scepticism. Contrary to legend, the teachers at the Medical School had not taken a clearly antagonistic stand toward his research. Music was the only field in which that cultured public refused to have anything to do with modernism. The symphonies of Gustav Mahler – who as the Opera's manager brought its productions to a new flowering – had been anything but popular in pre-war Vienna. Of Alban Berg, only a small clique had taken notice. The story of the fist fight at one of the rare performances of a Schönberg work lived on as proof of the resolve of Vienna's music lovers to 'uphold standards'.

In the spring of 1919, one particular 'cultural affair' aroused rancorous passion. The Italian government had demanded the 'restitution' of certain Italian paintings and Roman antiquities from the Habsburg collections. Tentative lists had been published; and the dismay at the likely loss of those art works intermingled with plain fury over the rape the Italians were determined to commit. Even such lower-middle-class people as had never troubled to visit the Kunsthistorisches Museum, let alone the library housing the incunabula which also were claimed, grew highly indignant. The *Neue Freie Presse* published an article by the president of the Academy of Sciences urging the nation to 'keep high the banner of art and science even in these days of despondency and want', and to protest about the 'criminal assault on our most precious cultural heritage'.

In the same issue that carried that appeal (27 April) another distinguished citizen, the First Public Prosecutor, wrote on a matter of the 'utmost urgency in this period of decaying civilization in which we are living'. As in all such periods, crimes were becoming frighteningly frequent, he warned. Their perpetrators must be 'divided into two groups'. While the state had the means to cleanse society of 'constitutionally anti-social elements', people 'who have committed a crime totally at variance with their former conduct' posed a different problem. 'Such people can be seen regularly in our courtrooms nowadays, and we cannot possibly blame their offences solely on the misery of the times. They must be accounted for by the loss of confidence many honest citizens suffered under the impact of sadly misguided government policies. Their paramount mistake had been a cynical lack of candour, which in effect cultivated untruthfulness and bred lies.'

It is unlikely that the author, castigating the wartime regime, realized that one man in Vienna had all along been fighting governmental deception and the bourgeois newspapers' collusion with it. The bold article seemed to echo much of what Karl Kraus had written. He might have devised the heading under which the Prosecutor's piece was printed, Mendacity – One of the Causes of the Rot'. It even touched on the corruption of language, which Kraus had been chastising for twenty years as the helpmate of official deceit.

Because the enemy was assumed to have his ears everywhere, facts were suppressed. But facts were also distorted. As people realized what was going on, they treated those prevarications ... with waxing mistrust. That consistent falseness reached its climax in the hypocrisy with which wholly inadequate food rations were laid down by law even while the high living of privileged circles was open for all to see.

It was then that many people unlearned how to distinguish between right and wrong.

Whoever feels that the tricks and briberies [through which those circles secure their way of life] cannot possibly be prevented under the present circumstances must not grow indignant over the wave of burglaries we experience. Such indignation would be only another exercise in mendacity. . . . What harsh truth underlies the defence heard over and over again in court, 'I became a thief because others were thieving, too'. ... Big thieves who, having gained a place in the sun through wrongdoing or even crime, yet had gone scot-free, looked at law-abiding citizens as mere fools. And the legitimate guardian of the citizens' sense of right and wrong, the state, itself made a mockery of decency and fairness. No sooner had the criminal activities of some great profiteer come to light than some ministry ... got busy protecting the supposedly irreplaceable individual for political, monetary, or food-supply reasons. ... That was the point at which citizens who had made great sacrifices as a matter of course only to find themselves lacking the necessities started to despair of justice. And that [state of mind] is the depressing cause of the present increase in crimes. How ominous is that atti-tude ...! In order to regain public trust, the men in authority must make it their business now to present the public with the untarnished truth. They must also eschew demagogic slogans, which may flatter the self-importance of street demonstrators, but are unable to accomplish anything.

That closing aside may have brought bitter smiles to readers' faces: the demagogues might yet accomplish something! Street violence had been scarcely quiescent since Maundy Thursday. Hardly a day had passed by without the plate glass of some coffeehouse being broken, or public transpor-tation disrupted, by gangs of supposed ex-soldiers. One late afternoon, a group of marchers protesting against the sump-tuous meals assumed to be served in the great hotels on Ringstrasse, was thrown into a paroxysm of rage whenever some Allied officers showed their faces at the windows. When one of them happened to drop a cigarette butt down on the pavement, the crowd accused him of bombarding them with broken glass; and only a gigantic bearded marine mounting the top of a stalled tram dissuaded his fellow-demonstrators from hurling themselves against the locked doors of the Hotel Bristol. The most puzzling incident occurred in one of the narrow side streets of Kärntner-strasse: a mob of noisy people rushed the small *Volkswehr*

squad posted there, wrenched the rifles from the flabbergasted soldiers, smashed the weapons into pieces, and amid
shouts of jubilation festooned lamp-posts with the débris.
Why had those followers of the proletariat chosen to attack
its own *Volkswehr?* horrified Socialists asked each other.
Only in the first days of June did the Socialist leadership – or
the government, for that matter – comprehend that the Communist party, doubting its chances of winning over the
labour masses or the workers' councils, had decided to use
its undisciplined fringes to spread confusion.

Educated people surely saw some merit in the First
Prosecutor's theory. Still, Vienna's bourgeoisie in general
preferred to refer loosely to the 'shattering historical
developments' as having fostered the breakdown of public
morality – the long war, the disappearance of the old country
with its hallowed institutions and the vengefulness of the
victors which blocked the recovery of the new.

In the first week of May it became known in Vienna that the
Allies had made it clear to Germany that they expected her
not to interfere with Austria's independence. Middle-class
Vienna met that prohibition with louder criticism than was
warranted by its true feelings toward union with the strife-
ridden German republic. When the peace delegation, headed
by Renner, entrained for Saint-Germain-en-Laye on 12 May,
no more than a few hundred people had come to the railway
station to wish him well; and voices imploring the chancellor to 'bring home a good treaty' drowned the cries urging
Anschluss. The day before, the *Neue Freie Presse* had
reported that, 'to believe the Paris news agency, the French
minister in Vienna has succeeded in convincing its political
circles [*sic*] of the necessity of abandoning the idea of
Anschluss.' The bourgeois press had been vacillating for at
least the past two months, though it had refrained from
drawing attention to the lukewarm response given the
project by the German policy makers. Only the *Reichspost*
had warned the peace delegation against pressing the issue.
The *Arbeiter Zeitung* had continued to treat it as a matter of
life and death. But working people by then looked upon
union with Germany (as Karl Renner was to put it in 1945) as
'but a way of escaping mass unemployment and starvation'.

As it happened, a matter of sensational dimensions, the 'rape of the Tyrol', was superseding the *Anschluss* discussion by the time of the departure of the peace delegation.

In the days of the Brest-Litovsk negotiations the Bolshevik government had made public the secret treaties the original Allies had concluded with the Italian kingdom in 1915. That so-called London pact had, among other baits held out, promised the Italians a part of the Tyrol along strategic, rather than ethnical, lines. The euphoria following the signing of the Brest-Litovsk treaty had made the Viennese all but forget this threat; and ever since the armistice they had been persuading themselves that Woodrow Wilson, the drafter of the doctrine of national self-determination (and whose country had not been a signatory to the pact) would never allow the overwhelmingly German-speaking southern part of the Tyrol to be turned over to the Italians. On 1 May news reached Vienna that he had committed the United States to implementing the London pact *in toto*, in concert with its signatories. His seemingly sudden reversal raised a storm of protest in the journals of all shades of political opinion. It mirrored public opinion. The Tyrol and its peasants held a special place in Viennese lore. A ringing song immortalizing their sadly abortive revolt against Napoleonic occupation had been something of a second anthem. Neither the lack of co-operation on the part of the Tyrol's bourgeois politicians since the *Umsturz,* nor their truculent sympathy with extremists advocating a clear break with Red Vienna, softened the shock over the truncation of the age-old province. In fact, the 'South-Tyrol question', as both parliament and the press called the Allied decision, filled the Viennese with that Austrian, as against local, patriotism at whose sluggish growth among them the *Länder* had been scoffing.

The South-Tyrol question barely took second place to the festering problem of the Sudeten Germans (to give them the name under which Czechoslovakia's three and a half million Germans became important in the world scene twenty years later). As early as 13 December the Austrian government had asked for a plebiscite in the disputed areas where the Czechs had taken over the administration. The local people had heard little on the barrage of notes with which the Prague government justified its historical claims and also warned the Allies of creeping Bolshevism in Vienna. Rumours of arms smuggled to the irredentist Sudeten Germans by some unnamed organization in Vienna had met with little belief. On the other hand, the ruthlessness of the Czechoslovak authorities in suppressing protest demonstrations in 'their' German cities had been reported regularly in Vienna's papers and commented upon with acrimony.

Although a number of Sudeten-German politicians, men who now resided in Vienna, had journeyed to Saint-Germain with Renner as 'experts in border questions and the affairs of occupied and endangered territory', it is fair to say that the Viennese by and large were hoping by then for no more than some sort of autonomy for their co-nationals within Masaryk's republic. On 20 May they learned that when credentials were exchanged, Renner had also been handed those of the Czechs, along with those of the countries the Habsburg Monarchy had been at war with. No compromise could be expected from a Czechoslovakia which, as an Associated Nation, had joined the powers prepared to sit in judgment over the 'leftover country'. A few days later Renner was advised that it would be recognized as the Republic of Austria. That enforced new name caused no great excitement in Vienna: the name of German-Austria had not widely entered common parlance. Not until the draft treaty was published on 2 June did the meaning of the new designation become obvious: the Allies had decided to consider Austria as a new country only in the sense that her old frontiers and her form of government had been changed. The outburst of indignation – to be traced in Vienna's papers from the *Neue Freie Presse* to the *Arbeiter Zeitung* – cannot possibly have surprised foreign observers on the spot. As early as 10 January the chief of the United States Mission in Vienna had written to his government, 'In very human fashion [people] tend to put all blame for the faults and errors on their former rulers, and to look on themselves as victims who are no more to blame for the war than the other nationalities [of the Dual Monarchy] that took part.'[1]

'It would be the height of immorality,' Moritz Benedikt

wrote on 3 June, 'if the nations that were waiting to see
which way the wind would blow in order to join the stronger
contestant in the end – it would be the height of immorality
if those nations were freed from all responsibilities.' After
taking up the terms of the draft treaty one after another and
enlarging on each with passionate scorn, he turned – true to
the spirit of the old ethnic pecking order – to the inequity
the Sudeten Germans were to suffer. 'An autonomous region
within the Czech state is to be created south of the
Carpathian mountains. The Slovaks [who inhabit that
region] are given self-administration under a great-power
guarantee ... [while] the Germans in Bohemia, Moravia
and [the former small Habsburg province of] Silesia, who
constitute a people of the highest culture ... are turned over
to the Czechs with no more than a pious assurance of equal
civil rights.'

Throughout the past winter and early spring, reaction in
Vienna to coercive Czech methods had been contained by the
awareness of its dependency on Czech coal deliveries. When
the Sudeten-German workers proclaimed a general strike,
and about forty of them lost their lives in clashes with local
police or army units, Otto Bauer leaned over backwards
to reduce the risk of armed conflict with the Czechs. Whatever her brutal excesses, Czechoslovakia was the only
effective adversary of Communist Hungary in Central
Europe. In May, reacting to her attack on Slovakia, Prague's
troops took the offensive, and soon were approaching
Budapest. And on or about 19 May a special emissary of
Kun's (or, as gossip had it, of Lenin himself) showed up in
Vienna to reorganize the Austrian Communist party, on
whose activities the Hungarian government appeared to be
pinning its hopes.

In one particular case, the sympathies that large sections of
Vienna's population continued to feel for the persecuted
Sudeten Germans took a peculiar turn. In March the Czech
authorities had compelled all civil servants and railway
personnel, including the Germans among them, to take a
loyalty oath under pain of dismissal. Some eight hundred
low-echelon men had been discharged anyway. Arriving in
Vienna with their families, they did not give the lie to a story

about their having refused to swear allegiance to the Czech state. Destitute refugees, they were clamouring for government support or jobs. In their meetings, one of the spokesmen loved to contrast their plight in Vienna, German soil, after all, with the affluence to which hordes of alien refugees were supposed to have risen within its walls since 1914. That point did not fail to arouse, among lower-middle-class people and in the pan-German intelligentsia alike, emotions whose strength was out of proportion to the size of that group of Sudeten Germans.

Meanwhile banking and business circles had with dismay become alert to a 'giant plot hatched in Prague': Czechoslovakia was laying claim to all Austrian property within her borders, justifying that demand by the sequestration on the part of the Allies early in the war of the holdings of all Habsburg subjects on their own territories. Considering the very large investments of Vienna-based enterprises in Bohemia, Moravia, Silesia and Slovakia, the projected wholesale confiscation was in fact, as the *Neue Freie Presse* called it, the 'ultimate assault on the economy of German-Austria'. Sincere patriotic indignation was not incompatible with the great fear seizing businessmen and bankers. In the end their expropriation by the *Tschechei* was thwarted thanks to the efforts of the president of one of Vienna's great banks who, well connected in the City of London, had been attached as an expert to the peace delegation.

The publication of the draft treaty coincided with a deeply disappointing event in the conflict in Carinthia. Its resistance to South-Slav incursions had been heartening the Viennese since early in the year. It was, after all, the only instance of a popular rising against arbitrary truncations of the republic.

A demarcation line had been agreed on in January under the auspices of the Allies. The struggle against its repeated violations had been sporadic until mid-April. But when the South-Slav formations began to advance on Klagenfurt, the capital of the *Land*, the Carinthian volunteers, supported by the local *Volkswehr* battalions, staged a counter-offensive and, supported by troops and arms from Vienna, halted the invaders on 2 May. Promptly, fantasies were spun in Vienna about similar 'freedom fights' that might erupt in the Tyrol, or even in some Bohemian districts. People engaging in such speculations did not at once realize that the success was due to the disinclination of the South-Slav government to strengthen its army units in Carinthia, its own kingdom's flank being endangered by the Italians. It became clear within days that the Italians, their enmity toward the South-Slavs notwithstanding, would not tolerate further Austrian triumphs. Thus the Vienna government, under Italian pressure, on 2 June ordered the *Volkswehr* formations to desist from advancing, and stopped all shipments of war material. The Carinthian volunteers refused to abide by the terms of a new armistice hurriedly concluded in Vienna; and the 'betrayal of the freedom fighters' by the foreign secretary, Otto Bauer, became a matter of harsh criticism among his numerous detractors. (The protracted operations of the freedom fighters, bringing strong South-Slav forces into battle, was to result in Klagenfurt's occupation, but also to lead to the great powers' decision to have the conflict solved through referenda in the disputed districts.)

At the height of the Carinthian fighting the Vorarlberg diet carried out a plebiscite in its *Land*; and its population declared for union with Switzerland by a four-to-one majority. Vorarlberg, the westernmost, smallest and least populated of the *Länder*, had never been much in the thoughts of the Viennese. In general it was regarded as an adjunct to the Tyrol (as in fact it once had been). The outcome of the illegal referendum was denounced by the Viennese of all classes as proof of the desire of the Vorarlbergers to escape the country's post-war hardships. The Socialist leaders saw in the victory of the separatists above all a manifestation against the *Anschluss* they themselves were still hoping to make a reality.

> The particularism of the *Länder* [Otto Bauer wrote four years later]; the tradition-laden Austrianism of both the patriciate and the petty bourgeoisie of Vienna; fear of Spartacism throughout the middle classes; the special interests of big industry and banking; the hopes for restoration in the monarchist nobility, the monarchist high

clergy and the monarchist [former] officers' corps – all those forces combined to work against our policy of *Anschluss*.[2]

The fear of counter-revolution was troubling Socialist politicians in May 1919. In the first days of the month, the *Freikorps* had burst into Munich and put an end to the chaos that had dominated the city for ten days. The atrocities that followed the conquest were vastly more savage than the terror to which the quixotic government of the republic of councils had resorted. *Its* misdeeds, notably the cold-blooded murder of some twenty upper-class citizens held hostage, had been reported with horror by all sections of the press in Vienna. The ferocious 'combing actions' of the *Freikorps*, reliable news of which may have been hard to come by, seemed to be given less prominence. It was not only Communists who accused reactionaries of sympathizing with Munich's brutal new masters to the point of sharing their proclaimed determination to 'crush underfoot all November criminals'. At that point in time Hungarian counter-revolutionaries in Vienna happened to stage a bizarre *coup de main* in the very heart of the city.

During the night of 2–3 May a small group of their army officers broke into the Hungarian embassy and kidnapped Kun's two ambassadors. They also appropriated several millions in bank notes, besides a trunk filled with jewellery, and managed to carry both out of the building on Bankgasse. Within less than twenty-four hours, the police identified the masterminds of the bold raid, two Hungarian counts and a prince. Summoned to police headquarters, they made no excuses for the 'confiscation': the money and valuables had been 'seized in the name of the future Hungarian government'. Even before their interrogation the whereabouts of the abducted diplomats had been discovered and become known all over Vienna. The place of their detention, the Franciscan monastery, added to the sense of piquancy with which the story was retold and embroidered. 'The occupation [*sic*] of the embassy,' the *Neue Freie Presse* declared, '. . . shows that the officers deem the collapse of the Hungarian government of councils a *fait accompli*. . . .'

Brandl in his memoirs gives an account of his interview with the titled raiders.[3] The release of the kidnapped diplomats was quickly agreed. 'Your well-meaning enterprise has failed,' Brandl told the Hungarians. 'But you had better realize that, with the Communist government in firm control [in Budapest] I have no choice but to take the position that you have burgled a foreign embassy. I'm asking you to hand the money over to me.' The gentlemen demurred. 'How could we think of handing it over to the Bolsheviks who're busy wrecking our fatherland? . . . Besides, we don't know where the money is.' 'You needn't know where it is,' Brandl retorted, 'as long as you make arrangements for its being in my hands within the next twenty-four hours. In return, I promise you, on my word of honour, that the embassy will never see the money again.' But wouldn't they, one of the noblemen asked, by bringing the money to Brandl, admit to their being the perpetrators, or at least accessories before the fact? 'Anonymous delivery will do,' Brandl declared, adding, 'Surely you understand that, for the sake of the good name of our police, I've got to have some success.' A compromise was worked out: half of the confiscated money would be surrendered to Brandl without delay; the other half, according to the Hungarians, had already been transferred to the new 'government-in-being' in their country.

Police statements continued to advise the press of the 'continuing investigation' of the break-in. But no one in Vienna doubted that an agreement had been reached between the high-born burglars and the police. Amusement tinged that assumption among middle-class people. They savoured the exploit of the Magyar nobles. They also could not help enjoying the thought that the police, alert to the Hungarian peril, were willing to stretch their authority. Communist agitators, in speech and print, stressed the obvious leniency with which the authorities treated 'White Guards' operating in Vienna. But the Socialist leaders, it may be safely assumed, were not sorry about the loss of funds the embassy had suffered. (Brandl succeeded in keeping the money returned to him in escrow.) They knew that all embassy funds were at the disposal of a special envoy Kun had sent to Vienna, a young lawyer by the name of Ernö Bettelheim.

Police headquarters was well informed on his movements, and kept the government in full knowledge of the progress of his inter-party reforms. Thus alerted, the Socialists redoubled their attention in watching the Communists' work in the ranks of the *Volkswehr*. The 'Committee of Revolutionary Soldiers' appeared to be growing more restless. The idea of yielding to the Allies' stepped-up demand for a reduction in the strength of the *Volkswehr* as a way of ridding it of dangerous troublemakers cannot always have been absent from the thoughts of the government in those days.

Vienna's middle-class population did not learn much of Bettelheim's work; the replacement of the party's central committee by a four-man *Direktorium* seems to have been a closely guarded secret at first. What was known of the discord within the committee had blunted middle-class sensitivity to its policies; and the polemical tone with which the *Arbeiter Zeitung* was reacting to the utterances of Communist publications only served to confuse even those middle-class men who made it their business to scan the Socialist journal.

True, a large section of the bourgeoisie, despite all denials published, had remained convinced that the Maundy Thursday riot had been set in motion by a Communist plot, with Hungarian Bolsheviks as its prime movers. But the image of the foreign schemers of world revolution had changed since that bloody day: Munich was no longer theirs; and Kun's army had retreated before the Czechs. Still, the uneasiness of middle-class people was growing as they became aware of what in lighter moments they might speak of as 'new Communist antics'. Those new fears did not paralyse bourgeois life in Vienna. Theatres did not lack for business. The drama critic of the *Neue Freie Presse*, reporting on 28 April on a new comedy presented at the Burgtheater, wrote, 'It seems that the great tragedy of contemporary events is inimical to the production of comedies. Yet everybody is yearning for entertainment, for having a good time in the theatre ... for something likely to take his mind off [the present misery] and make his spirit free once again.' On 31 May the Theater an der Wien (where *The Magic Flute* had had its première one hundred and twenty-eight years earlier) gave the first performance of a new operetta. *Nimm mich mit* ('Take Me Along') was an instantaneous hit. As reviewers pointed out, early in the war the composer had written the subsequently immensely popular 'Air Force March' and had also been the bandmaster of the same regiment whose band used to play under the baton of Franz Lehar. Josef Redlich noted on 3 June: 'The terms of the peace treaty have been published. The whole of Vienna is, so to speak, shattered.' One may wonder whether he had seen the long lines of people queueing up to buy tickets for the new operetta.

Nightclubs, despite their short hours, were crowded. (One of the rumours about them had it that inebriated patrons of one such place had compelled its orchestra to strike up the march of Vienna's 'own' infantry regiment of old.) Games of chance for high stakes, rare in pre-war Vienna outside exclusive men's clubs, were being organized in the large flats of some impoverished middle-class ladies. That particular use to which such women, mostly widows, put their last remaining asset – an apartment they were paying a pittance for, thanks to rent control and the decay of the Austrian *Krone* – was but one of the means by which they supported themselves. Advertisements of rooms 'in a quiet neighbourhood' to be rented by the hour for what no one doubted were assignations could be found daily in the press. More respectably, antiques, usually referred to as family heirlooms, were offered regularly for sale. And the *Neue Freie Presse* of 23 April carried an advertisement reading, 'Refined upper-class lady gives lessons in high-society manners and customs. Applications to be directed to the advertisement office of this paper under "New Wealth 27702".'

As early as March the *Neue Freie Presse* had from time to time discussed the inhospitality of the *Länder* and their resorts. The restrictions imposed on railway travel, boding equally ill for that year's summer vacation, became a steady feature of the paper in April. Summer vacations spent in Alpine valleys or on lake shores had been customary not only for wealthy people; even middle-class people of very modest means had regularly gone to the countryside for some weeks, if only to stay as boarders with a farmer. For them, the wholesome peasant fare had grown to be an additional attraction since the middle of the war; and as fewer and fewer of them could afford a change of air in summer, they had been complaining about those fellow townsmen who apparently could find this kind of money. Ignoring that aspect of the vacation problem, the *Neue Freie Presse* of 6 May 1919, urged the government to issue 'regulations with regard to vacation trips on the railways'. The great journal also continued to chide the *Länder* for cold-shouldering Viennese holiday-makers who had been 'such highly welcome guests for so many years and [were] hungry now for a breath of fresh air'.

The pitiful health of Viennese lower-class children had become a matter of concern to the town hall during the latter stages of the war. But not until the summer of 1918 had the municipality set up an organization which subsequently managed to take some to rural areas for a few weeks. It was said that the offspring of indigent Christian-Social voters had been favoured in the course of that welfare action. It was due to the single-handed efforts of a newspaperman of Liberal persuasion that in April 1919 the ambassadors of the neutral countries met under the chairmanship of the Nuncio to initiate a larger action. '40,000 children suffering from malnutrition, particularly from the homes of workers and those middle-class families who are in need, will be given the blessings of a summer vacation with sufficient food,' reported Vienna's press on 20 April. The mayor, knowing by then that his days in office were numbered, had urged the City Council to allocate a substantial sum to the action, and was also talking about a municipal tax that might be levied on theatre and cinema tickets for charitable purposes. The mayor also expressed Vienna's gratitude to the Argentine ambassador, who had supervised the organizational work. The name of his far-away country was to become a household word in Vienna that summer.

As it was, his action was not the first of its kind. In an article published in the *Neue Freie Presse* on 6 May Dr Klemens Pirquet, the foremost pediatrician of the Medical School, reported how a Col Summerhayes had arrived unannounced in Vienna in mid-December 'bringing with him from Italy the surplus foodstuffs of a British brigade ... to distribute them to our children'. A member of the medical corps, he 'intended to ascertain the true state of affairs without being influenced by local authorities. He did not call on any functionary, and made his investigations in Vienna without being known to anyone, a modern Harun al-Raschid ....' Only later 'did he come to me and then, guided by a volunteer lady of [my] pediatric clinic embarked on studying [conditions in] those outlying districts which are inhabited by the poorer part of the population.' Informed of the results of Summerhayes's inquiries,

> Herbert Hoover, the chairman of the Allied Council of Supply and Relief, sent a mission to Vienna, whose head ... visiting the over-crowded children's wards of the various hospitals, discussed with me the ways in which the misery might be checked. ...
>
> The Americans emphasize the fact that their government has decided to extend aid to a country which, the peace treaty not having been signed yet, must still be viewed as a hostile power. ... The Americans also insist on being certain, through strict control, that the foodstuffs actually reach the children. That can be achieved only by having prepared dishes fed them on premises to be opened for that purpose, and making sure that the dishes are consumed on the spot. ... Social motives will not influence the choice of children. They will be chosen solely with regard to their health ... and [the degree of] their malnutrition. ... Social considerations and those of local politics are matters of indifference to the American mission [Dr Pirquet felt it appropriate to add].

The massive American help extended to the children in Vienna, as well as in the country's other urban centres, restored some lustre to the tarnished image of Woodrow Wilson. Yet it was not after him, but after the Argentinians, that Vienna's city fathers some years later named the main street of the embassies' quarter.

The foreign aid did not particularly embarrass wealthy people. For one thing, money donations alone could not possibly have furnished food to the many thousands of

undernourished children. Besides, the feeling of injustice
suffered at the hands of the 'empire's destroyers' undid such
embarrassment as their own country's accepting alms might
have called forth in privileged circles. And finally, the
concept of having money was becoming problematic: by the
end of May, the Austrian *Krone* was traded at the Zurich
bourse for less than a sixth of the pre-war value of the
currency unit of the late Habsburg state.

The armistice of November, while clearly specifying the
future strength of the Austro-Hungarian armed forces, had
not considered a future German-Austrian army. Probably the
imperial messengers did not draw the victors' attention to the
steps the Germans of the Habsburg state had taken to
salvage from its break-up a country of their own; and the
triumphant Italians did not bother. Thus the strength of the
Volkswehr was from the beginning a matter of Allied acquiescence rather than of international obligation. The resulting
question had grown urgent for the Italians (who were having
their own problems with public order) when their mission in
Vienna continued to stress that the 'red spirit' of the
Volkswehr had survived the turmoil of the actual revolution.
The events in Munich and Budapest had deepened their
concern, which up to a point was shared by the other
Allies.

The Austrian government had been temporizing at first,
referring vaguely to its plan for reducing the strength of the
Volkswehr. In the last week of April however, the government yielded to the unceasing Italian pressure, and pledged
itself to start a twenty-five per cent reduction on 31 May.
Middle-class people were of two minds: on the one hand,
they were more than tired of the continuing extra-legal
activities of self-appointed *Volkswehr* commissions; on the
other, they could not help foreseeing that the dismissal of
every fourth soldier was bound to swell the unruly masses of
the jobless. As a matter of fact, Communist propaganda took
up the issue with a vengeance.

The *Direktorium* Bettelheim had set up was not the
streamlined command post his inter-party memoranda
declared it to be. For one thing, it did not succeed in
bringing in line the party's organ, *Die Soziale Revolution*. The

Communist party managed to organize a series of outdoor meetings of *Volkswehr* men in protest against the 'imminent decimation of the proletarian army' and castigate the role that the Socialist party bosses (allegedly conspiring with 'officer battalions', a nascent 'White Guard') were playing in the sinister scheme. Although even the Committee of Revolutionary Soldiers was not in consistent agreement with the *Direktorium*, its influence on the rank and file of the *Volkswehr* appeared to be growing by the hour. Julius Deutsch's appeals were losing their force. In a conference of Vienna's soldiers' councils on 28 May, he barely prevented the adoption of a Communist resolution rejecting any reduction of the force.

Discouragement was sweeping the Social-Democratic leaders. It was reflected in Bauer's speech to parliament of 7 June. Its topic was the 'death sentence' imposed on the republic at Saint-Germain. 'At this moment we know only certain parts of the economic terms of the treaty,' he said, 'but those parts suffice to picture the consequences that would be inevitable should we be forced to sign. . . .' Summing up, he referred to a 'fiscal collapse' certain to be followed by the gravest social disruptions, and, if one considered the chasm between Vienna and the *Länder* . . . their 'secession and thus German-Austria's dissolution'. His warnings were no mere rhetoric: in the *Land* of Lower Austria, whose valleys and plains surrounded Vienna, the farmers, disgusted by news from the 'red city', had tightened their partly armed associations. Now that Bavaria was purged of the Bolshevik plague, the idea of a great Catholic country to be formed consisting of Austria and the southern parts of Germany was being discussed in some provincial circles.

By the time Bauer delivered his speech, the government had gained a modest success in its negotiations with the chief of the Italian mission: he had informed Julius Deutsch that a postponement of the *Volkswehr* reduction until 15 June was acceptable, but that a quarter of the twenty-five per cent agreed on earlier must be discharged by that day. As the *Arbeiter Zeitung* pointed out, the original deadline had been revoked only thanks to the protests of large parts of the *Volkswehr*. That was not the wisest remark to make. Communist propaganda hastened to point out the powerful influence that the *Volkswehr's* protests could, as proved, exert to frustrate the baleful plans for disarming the proletariat.

'Workers, comrades, awake to the danger! The arms we took up to stand by socialism are still in our hands. In this twelfth hour this call goes out to you: close ranks with us to demonstrate for our sacred right.... Disarm the White Guard! Long live world revolution! Up with socialism! Forward to victory!' These were the salient lines of a poster calling for a mass meeting in front of the Votiv church less than a mile distant from Parliament House, which was to take place on the afternoon of 5 June.

Around 5 p.m. a press of curious people was to be noticed on the square between Ringstrasse and the Votiv church, [started the report in the 6 June issue of the *Neue Freie Presse*]. Shortly thereafter *Volkswehr* arrived, marching in formation, as were large processions of the unemployed. The soldiers did not carry rifles.... Their companies, flying red flags, were finally arrayed on one side [of the square], the unemployed and Communists on the other. Inscriptions such as 'Work and Bread', 'Down with Capitalism', or 'Down with the White Guards' could be made out on signs held aloft. Communist party members were distributing a handbill headlined 'Some Frank Words to the Social-Democratic Workers'.

The *Volkswehr* band had welcomed the processions of civilians as they entered the square. Toward 5.45 the *Marseillaise* was struck up, followed by the Workers' Anthem, which the multitude listened to with bared heads. At 6 p.m. the signal 'Attention!' was sounded by a trumpeter.... Soldiers' councilman Grüber was the first speaker. He declared it to be the purpose of this demonstration to drive home to the government the iron determination of the *Volkswehr* not to let itself be disarmed.... The Communist leader Toman, speaking next, said that Vienna's proletariat had no intention of obeying the commands of the bourgeoisie of the Allied countries.... Then the Communist Melcher said that the proletariat had joy-

fully followed the call of the *Volkswehr*. It was high time
to stop the reactionaries. . . .

The orations over, a resolution was read out. It opened by
affirming that 'the *Volkswehr* and Vienna's workers regard
the demand for a reduction in the strength of the former as a
counter-revolutionary assault on the proletariat. Conse-
quently, they do not recognize the plan of merely deferring
the reduction till 15 June.' The resolution, closing with the
declaration that it was 'incumbent on the *Volkswehr* and its
red soldiers . . . to complete the revolution', was adopted by
enthusiastic acclamations. Once more, the *Marseillaise* was
played. And then the demonstrators, the band heading the
procession, started out on their way to Parliament House,
where they were to dispatch a deputation to Secretary
Deutsch and any other cabinet members who might be in the
building. Street demonstrations had developed a routine of
their own since the *Umsturz*. What distinguished the demonstration of 5 June was the discipline of its participants. The
rally's speakers had warned them repeatedly of *provocateurs*.
'This manifestation against capitalism must remain dignified,'
Gruber had told them, 'and disturbers will be removed with
no fuss at all.'

Two days later *Der Abend* printed the text of a con-
gratulatory telegram that both the *Volkswehr* and the Communist party had received from Béla Kun. No doubt, the
self-assured mood of the *Volkswehr* blinded Bettelheim to
the power residing in the workers' councils. Probably he was
also unaware of the desperate efforts of the government to
deprive the Communists of their most effectual propaganda
weapon.

On the morning of 13 June the front page of the *Neue
Freie Presse* carried the following official announcement:

> The German-Austrian government, in a note addressed to
> the Italian Armistice Commission, copies of which were
> handed to Mr Allizé and Col Cunningham [the chiefs of
> the French and British missions], pointed out that the
> hostilities between the Czechoslovak and the Hungarian
> troops threaten to jeopardize the security of German-
> Austria. Those military operations are approaching our

borders, and one or the other [of the belligerents] may well attempt to use German-Austrian territory as an area of transit. The German-Austrian Republic is determined to uphold its strict neutrality. In order to do so under any circumstances, the republic must have [the necessary] military strength. Therefore the German-Austrian government is not, to its regret, in a position to continue [*sic*] the reduction of the *Volkswehr* initiated upon the request of the Italian Armistice Commission, and have it implemented by 15 June.

That announcement was followed by the news that the head of the French mission had notified 'the proper authorities that France did not, for the time being, wish to have the strength of the *Volkswehr* reduced. Moreover, the French mission, having convinced itself of the poverty in the homes of *Volkswehr* men, had decided for purely humanitarian reasons to deliver foodstuffs to the families and provide their children with milk.'

And on the same page Moritz Benedikt added his own views:

The *Volkswehr* did its duty on Maundy Thursday [his editorial opened]. It was thanks to its sober-minded intervention that the rioting, arson and armed attacks had no political consequences. That military body, almost [*sic*] the only one that German-Austria has, was born of the revolution. As a child of its excited days, it could not have been trained to practise the goose-step, to march in parades, or to suppress all of the men's [individual] volition. . . . The *Volkswehr*, particularly in its early days . . . was also eager to prove that men recruited from the masses had not shed their convictions in donning military garb. Moreover, the Socialist party wanted to increase its own political power through the *Volkswehr*. Only after engaging in a variety of actions beyond its proper field did the *Volkswehr* men realize that they had an obligation to all of the country's social strata, to all taxpayers who, after all, were supporting the armed force. The *Volkswehr* was thus on the way to raising itself from the rank of a party institution . . . to an institution of the state. Its relationship to ... people outside the barracks has improved markedly since the events of Maundy Thursday. But that is not enough. The *Volkswehr* must become popular. Now an action of the Italian government has deflected it from that goal. It is an untimely intervention. It greatly disturbs Vienna, this Niobe among the metropolises of the world. ... [The Italians] could not but realize that their action must foment revolutionary tendencies among the soldiers, bring about a grave social crisis in Vienna, encourage the *Länder* to secede, and deprive the sorely tried city of food supplies. ... The peace treaty will decide the strength of German-Austria's military establishment anyway. Surely Italy could have tolerated until then the 'danger' posed to her by the entire *Volkswehr*. ...

As it was, the Italian mission had accepted the government's representations by the time Benedikt's editorial was in print.

In the afternoon of that day the newly consolidated council of Vienna's workers assembled for its constituent session. Foremost on the agenda was the threatening putsch, for by then the whole of Vienna knew that the Communists had decided on an 'uprising' for the coming Sunday, 15 June. Even its starting hour, 10 a.m., was a secret to no one. The Socialist politicians addressing the meeting warned it of the disaster certain to befall the country should a republic of councils be proclaimed in Vienna. Once again they reminded the gathering of Austria's dependence on the goodwill of the Allies. Once again they stressed the separatist movements spreading in the *Länder*. Finally, Friedrich Adler put to the vote a resolution that declared the workers' council to be the sole body entitled to organize mass demonstrations of the working population. His self-confidence at that moment can hardly be taken for granted: to be sure, the majority of his audience consisted of veteran Socialists; but he could not possibly gauge the impact on them of Communist propaganda. The *Reichspost*'s Heinrich Funder, a severe critic of the Socialists and all they stood for, was to pay tribute in his memoirs to the determination with which Adler persuaded the meeting to adopt his resolution. Its text was published the following morning (14 June) by the *Arbeiter Zeitung*.

Vienna's labouring force [the closing sentences read] rejects the notion that its political future can be decided by people who are totally unfamiliar with conditions in German-Austria and have not for very long been familiar with Socialism. The council of workers hereby declares that it alone is responsible for the decisions of Vienna's labouring class. It expects the Communists to argue their cause within, not against, the workers' council.

During the night thousands of Communist posters had been put up in Vienna as well as in the industrial towns of the Wiener Neustadt area. Over the signatures of such groups as 'Free Association of Soldiers Facing Dismissal' or 'Organization of Revolutionary Invalids', those placards climaxed invariably in the ringing appeal, 'Union with the councils' republics of Russia and Hungary! Up with world revolution! Long live the German-Austrian republic of councils!' A call to arms issued by the Committee of Revolutionary Soldiers gave detailed instructions of the individual tasks of the various *Volkswehr* units at the start of the scheduled uprising. (The *Neue Freie Presse* was to print one of those directives verbatim some days later.)

The government had lost no time in informing the *Volkswehr* men of the open-end postponement of its disbanding. Earlier in the week the Department of Army Affairs had ordered them to stay in their barracks on 15 June; the vehement objections raised to that order now died down. Even the Committee of Revolutionary Soldiers pledged compliance; it had been swayed by Gilbert Melcher, a highly popular returned P.O.W. from Russia who, though a member of the *Direktorium*, had turned against Bettelheim. To complete the success of the government on 14 June, the commander of Battalion 41 solemnly promised to keep it confined to barracks. Nevertheless, Deutsch stationed an unquestionably loyal *Volkswehr* detachment close to the barracks of the notorious battalion, instructing the officer in command to prevent its egress, if necessary by force.

Unlike regular readers of Socialist publications, middle-class people knew nothing about the endless discussions, doctrinaire or tactical, which were in progress at the top

echelon of the Communists. Nor did they realize that the
Budapest government, which was directing the Communists,
was nearing the end of its tether. During the past months
of seemingly ceaseless street demonstrations, rallies, marches
and *Hungerkrawalle*, a frivolous witticism had become
popular at coffeehouse tables: paraphrasing the notice
customary on the announcements of outdoor festivities in the
grounds of suburban cafés or inns of pre-war Vienna, wags
suggested that 'in the case of rainy weather the revolution will
take place indoors'. Probably some cynics on that Saturday
reiterated that phrase. It was, incidentally, a brilliant late-
spring day, with the chestnuts along Ringstrasse in full
bloom.

Only in the late afternoon of Saturday did the authorities
learn that the Communists, contrary to their declarations
in the meeting of the workers' council, were planning a
violent action for Sunday, [the *Neue Freie Presse* of 16
June reported]. [The authorities learned further] that, to
discuss the plan the Communist leaders would assemble
that very night. Surveillance of the premises of their party
secretariat ... made it evident that no meeting was in
progress there. But it was also discovered that a number of
persons had some time earlier driven off in seven motor
cars. Shortly thereafter police headquarters was informed
that several automobiles had stopped in front of a building
on Pulverturmgasse in which the editorial offices of the
Communist party organ ... are located. Based on the
decision meanwhile arrived at to arrest the leaders of the
Communist party, police made the necessary arrangements to surprise the participants of the meeting.

By about 9.45 the street ... had been sealed off. Under
the command of several senior officials, 200 policemen, 100
Stadtschutzwache and 50 plain-clothes men had been
deployed. First to be apprehended were the drivers of
three motor cars parked in front of the building. ... Then
the officials, accompanied by 150 policemen, entered the
house, a modern four-storey structure ... which since last
February has housed the offices of *Der Weckruf*, now *Die
Soziale Revolution*. ... The meeting was taking place in

the spacious attic which, formerly leased to a photo-
grapher ... had been rented by the Communist party.
Meetings had been regularly held there, but never had so
many people participated in any of them as did that
Saturday night. . . .

Their surprise was complete. The resistance put up was
minimal. The participants attempted to rid themselves of
their weapons. Numerous handguns were subsequently
found under the tables and chairs, as well as in the corners
of the attic. . . .

The decision reached in the late afternoon of 14 June was to
become a matter of bitter controversy in the following weeks
and months. Obviously foreseeing the storm of recrimina-
tions, police headquarters, in a press release printed on
Monday, referred to the 'Communists' plan of bringing about
by force the proclamation of a republic of councils'. Police
could not help being 'convinced of the earnestness of that
plan by the flood of incendiary leaflets and placards ...
calling people out for a large Ringstrasse demonstration.
Headquarters, which knew that Hungarian agitators had
hatched and were fomenting the project of a putsch, thus
decided to thwart its execution, and as a first step apprehended about 120 Communists who had assembled for a
meeting. . . .' It was not known whether the chief of police
attached no importance to an article in the Saturday issue of
Der Abend which, printed as an announcement of the Communist party, forecast a peaceful demonstration 'unless reactionary forces should provoke the demonstrators', or
whether his informers' reports on the impending nocturnal
meeting simply panicked him into action. At any rate,
Johannes Schober made up his mind without informing his
superior, the Acting Secretary of the Interior, Socialist
Matthias Eldersch. There was an apologetic overtone in the
closing words of the press release, 'The arrests were made, on
the one hand, to get hold of the Hungarian agitators who had
been forcing their way into the [leading] circles of the
German-Austrian Communists; on the other hand, to identify
the individuals responsible for the projected putsch, and
block action due to take place that very night.' It would seem

that the intelligence Schober received on the rift in the *Direktorium* and the consequent muddle within the party's former central committee was sorely incomplete. He must have been astonished when Bettelheim turned out not to be among the seized conspirators brought under heavy escort from Pulverturmgasse to the police detention centre on Elisabethpromenade.

At dawn Eldersch was advised of the arrests – and his inaction in the following hours would earn him a great deal of opprobrium from many of his fellow-Socialists, as well as from the Communist publications. Middle-class people who learned of Schober's arbitrary decision were to sympathize with him; how often had the government stayed his hand in the past months! And not all of them refused to understand Eldersch's dilemma in the small hours of Sunday. As true Viennese, they could well picture a man hoping that things would somehow sort themselves out.

The following morning a man carrying a red flag informed a crowd of several thousand from the steps of the town hall that the leaders of 'our party' had been put under arrest. Demands that they should be released rose from the ear-splitting chorus of boos that met this announcement. And only a few minutes later the crowd had formed into a column to march to the District Court House. Responding to calls for a deputation to enter the building, ten or twelve men volunteered.

They were admitted to the court house, and the demonstrators, falling silent, gazed expectantly up at the windows. But soon impatient shouts began to break out again. At last the deputation appeared on a third-floor balcony, accompanied by a soldier, who indicated that he had something to say. (Apparently isolated *Volkswehr* men had slipped out of their barracks after all.) Prevailing over the din, the soldier said he had been advised that none of the arrested men was on the premises; they were being held either at police headquarters or at the detention house on Elisabethpromenade. 'To Elisabethpromenade!' roared the men as they broke ranks and started to move past the Votivkirche in the direction of Hörlgasse, a comparatively narrow street where flats in the buildings were tenanted by middle-class families. At the approach of the jeering, chanting, running mob they flung their windows open; and though they no doubt retreated from time to time, they became eyewitnesses to the events destined to mar this fateful Sunday.

With surprising speed mounted and foot police, some of whom were equipped with rifles, had blocked the various side streets leading to Elisabethpromenade. According to most later accounts, stones and pieces of metal were at once hurled at the police squads by the abusive mobs rushing from one cordoned-off side street to another. The security units did not budge even where dense knots of men concentrated to press against them. At that critical moment, 'a number of revolver shots are said to have been fired,' the *Neue Freie Presse* reported on Monday. 'And after repeated warnings had proved futile, and attempts to break through the security lines continued to be made, police and *Stadtschutzwache* fired blanks to discourage the assailants.' Most other accounts mention 'three salvoes of blanks'.

The crowd responded by hurling more rocks. 'Then the unmistakable whiplash sound of rifle shots could be heard.' There was some irony in the role that fell to the *Stadtschutzwache* in the ensuing massacre. In the earlier post-*Umsturz* months that auxiliary troop had frequently been made sport of, by radical proletarians and dismayed middle-class folk alike, on account of its lack of aggressive spirit and its less-than-martial appearance. It would appear that Schober had purged the *Stadtschutzwache* since Maundy Thursday of men tending to avoid head-on clashes. Certainly there were very few Socialists left among its members. *Stadtschutzwache* patrols had for the first time been seen carrying carbines in the days following the Maundy Thursday riot.

The first shots put the rioters in Hörlgasse to flight, while the reports of rifle shots mingled with the screams of wounded men lying in the street. For the security forces did not stop shooting. Indeed they redoubled their fire as some of the attackers turned round and concentrated once again on breaking through the cordon. 'The fighting lasted for at least three quarters of an hour.'

At last an unarmed *Volkswehr* soldier was lifted up on the shoulders of two men and announced at the top of his voice that nearly all the party leaders had been set free. The chorus of triumph that greeted this information was followed by cries suggesting a march back to the town hall, where, the soldier had added, the released leaders would address their comrades.

The seriously injured – some eighty of them (eight were to die within the week) – were lifted from the pavement and carried into doorways. The bodies of the twelve victims were removed to the coffee house on the corner of Hörlgasse. Witnesses disagree on the amount of assistance offered by the police.

None of the freed leaders was present in Town Hall Square when groups of exhausted fighters arrived from the Hörlgasse. A rumour began to circulate among the disappointed men that new instructions would be given at 1 p.m. in front of the Rossau barracks. Nevertheless Karl Toman, who spoke there at two o'clock, found himself addressing only a few hundred.

Enough blood had been shed, he said, and it would be senseless to risk more bloodshed. The leaders had not slept for several nights. They badly needed to rest, and would not be able to unless they could be certain that their followers were not exposing themselves to new danger. They should go home but remain in readiness to respond to a further call to action.

Toman's speech was received with subdued acclamations. And then his listeners moved on. One particular group deliberately passed through Hörlgasse once more. When they saw the strong police cordon still posted there, they stopped to taunt and revile them. People stood at the corner of the street, 'staring', as one reporter put it, 'at the large pool of blood in front of No. 6'.

The police report, published on Tuesday, emphasized that the 'heavy pieces of iron flung at the police had clearly been brought along for that purpose'. The report also identified the individual who had fired the first pistol shot as 'a young man in a brown suit and wearing a brown hat who, after he had tried to pull a mounted policeman from his horse and been shaken off . . . shot point blank at the officer, the bullet hitting him in the right arm and entering his abdomen'.

Seven other policemen had been seriously injured by revolver shots or missiles. According to the news release, the mounted police in their counter attacks had been 'forced to use their sabres'. Nothing was said of the bayonets that some of the *Stadtschutzwache* men were supposed to have fixed on their carbines and put to use – a grisly detail that was to be heard again and again in the long aftermath of the riot. As for the men apprehended in the attic on Pulverturmgasse, police headquarters stated that 'pending such criminal actions as may be brought against them, German-Austrian citizens among them were set free after they had been interrogated throughout the night and the morning hours. Several foreign agitators have been kept under arrest.'

While the bloody fracas had been in progress, the city was swamped by fantastic rumours. The dictatorship of the proletariat was said to have been proclaimed in Wiener Neustadt. (Actually the emissary Bettelheim dispatched there on Thursday or Friday had been rebuffed by both the workers and the local *Volkswehr*, and Melcher had subsequently recalled him.) The number of police said to have fallen victim to the fury of the mob was growing by leaps and bounds in the retelling. And the middle-class distrust of the *Volkswehr* erupted in a farrago of tales that referred to large groups of heavily armed soldiers breaking out of the barracks in defiance of orders. (According to Bauer's memoir, 'the Communists tried to get ... Battalion 41 out on the street, but soldiers' councilmen, revolvers drawn ... prevented its Communist men from leaving.')[4] The exemplary discipline displayed by the troops that the government had drawn up along parts of the Ringstrasse as soon as the shooting started had not assuaged fears. As soon as the stories had lost the horror of immediacy, people everywhere wanted to know who was responsible for the bloodbath.

The Socialist party executive, assembling only hours after the shooting stopped, had set up a committee charged with investigating that question. On the strength of the committee's report, Wednesday's *Arbeiter Zeitung* put the blame for the fatal riot squarely on the shoulders of the Communist party. Although in the past weeks the Socialist press had alluded repeatedly to the disarray of the Communist leader-

ship, it was not mentioned now. To a certain extent, the
Socialist leaders were justified in wondering who had been
the actual authors of the declaration printed in *Der Abend*
on the eve of the demonstration; and outsized posters urging
all disbanded soldiers to participate in it – and promising
each of them a 'severance payment of five thousand *Kronen*
once the enterprise has succeeded'[5] – were still on the walls
in working districts, and could substantiate the idea of
earnest preparations for a putsch. Thus the Socialist
spokesmen had their reasons for blaming the Communist
party alone for the fatalities. Otto Bauer was never to revise
that view. (Curiously, he was also to credit Eldersch with
having ordered the arrests and to call Schober's repute
among the bourgeois as Vienna's 'saviour from Bolshevism' a
'foolish legend'.)[6]

The report of the investigating committee met much
criticism among the rank and file of Labour. Critics within
the workers' council pointed out that the Pulverturmgasse
meeting had been about to decide to keep the Sunday
demonstration strictly peaceful when the police had burst
into the attic. Demands for a formal condemnation of police
brutality were raised in the stormy debates, as were demands
for Schober's and Brandl's resignation – and Eldersch's, too.
Finally the Social-Democratic executive managed to take
some of the heat out of the controversy by organizing a mass
memorial rally and thus making the 'martyrs of Hörlgasse'
their own.

The bourgeois press had not waited for the report of the
Socialist committee to pin the undivided blame for the bloody
events on the Communists. Although it referred to the
foreigners who had urged them on, it left unmentioned the
in-fighting, the intrigues, and the mutual jealousies besetting their decision-making body. As for Vienna's middle-
classes themselves, they were in the throes of ever more
bone-chilling stories. Not the least of those dealt with
Hungarian troops supposed to have stood ready for invasion
on the border during the fateful weekend. A detailed list the
Neue Freie Presse published on 18 June of the large sums of
money the Hungarian embassy had disbursed to Communist
party workers was the subject of much talk among Inner

City people and in the garden suburbs. And as late as 1952 Heinrich Funder would retell in his memoirs a story, in circulation in the summer of 1919, of 'twenty machine-guns and two lorries with ammunition seized in the police raid'[7] on Pulverturmgasse. Rumours of a threatening rift within the Socialist leadership that reached middle-class folk were not conducive to lessening the idea of a large-scale Bolshevik 'enterprise'. Their nervousness would abate only after Hungary's soviet regime had collapsed on 1 August, and Battalion 41, the *Volkswehr's* Red Guard of unaltered parlance, had been disbanded four weeks later with stunning ease. What the Viennese of all classes were not to realize for many months was that the bloodbath on Hörlgasse had signalled the virtual end of Communism as a political force in their country. While in years to come Germany's Communist party would be able to enroll masses of working people, Austria's Communists would never gather anything like such strength. (Even in the years when a Soviet army was in Vienna after World War II, the country's surviving Communist politicians, for all the support of the occupiers, would gain no great power.)

In March 1919, L. G. Namier had noted on a Foreign Office document, 'As far as I can gather from the Austrian press, in Vienna the Communists are just a joke, and their different attempts have always a touch of *opéra bouffe*.'[8] Had the Viennese been cognizant of that marginal note, they would have resented it as a supercilious observation. Yet the confusion-ridden incident of 15 June, its tragic outcome notwithstanding, had in fact had some farcical aspects.

On 22 June the *Arbeiter Zeitung* reported on the closing session of the consolidated workers' council and the speech delivered by Adler. He abstained from stressing once more the Communists' guilt. 'The problem we confront is complex inasmuch as not we, the workers, or the masses of reactionaries, or for that matter the Communists, determine [the future]. The fate imposed upon us is being shaped by psychological forces we have no influence on.' Did Adler in that enigmatic remark allude to decisions, present or future, of the Allies? Was the sobering thought of Austria's economic conditions in his mind? In any event the Friedrich Adler of 21 June 1919, appears to have been very different indeed from the man who, as Count Stürgkh's assassin, had impressed even his stern judges with the cogency of his ringing defence.

❧ *Epilogue* ❧

Vienna was not the first metropolis to be shorn of its role in world affairs. What was unique was the suddenness of its downfall. Nor had the malcontent components of an empire ever abandoned its ancient capital with similar ease.

The idea that Vienna must acquire an identity of its own, as must the 'leftover country' of Clemenceau's coinage, was from the first caught up in the political conflicts splitting the citizenry. To the two most forceful politicians of the inter-war period, Otto Bauer and Monsignor Seipel, the search for a viable *raison d'être* for the new republic in the strange new Europe was never detached from the pursuit of the doctri-nai goals they were pursuing at home. Moreover, Austria's foreign policies were played out against a sombre economic background. After the League of Nations in 1922 had taken over her financial reconstruction, a commissioner was appointed to supervise the finances of the country. Austria was sovereign only up to a point for nearly four years.

No sooner had the League's control been removed than the agitation in favour of *Anschluss* gained strength not only among workers. Radical German nationalism always had had its adherents in the middle classes of the *Länder* and their intelligentsia. Throughout the 1920s the antagonism between the bourgeois government and Vienna's Socialist town hall gathered momentum when, encouraged by a modicum of economic recovery, Vienna's masters pressed their ambitious reforms. They were not deterred by the incipient world depression.

At its depth (1931) the collapse of Austria's biggest bank – brought about as much by its inability to accommodate itself to the realities of the small country as by the sudden with-drawal of credits by French bankers – destroyed the very bases of the economic life of the country. The international loan granted it under a guarantee by the League of Nations was made dependent on Austria's pledge to forgo for twenty years political or economic union with the *Reich*. That agreement, killing plans for a custom union, roused a storm of protest. Ever since 1920, when the Socialist leaders left the coalition born in the *Umsturz* days, anti-government sentiments had been alive among the proletariat; they had strengthened immensely after the police of Vienna bloodily put down an arsonist riot of striking workers protesting a miscarriage of justice in a jury trial. Now, however, anti-government feelings were growing also among large sections of the peasantry and lower-middle-class people of the *Länder*. Futile attempts of succeeding governments to gain the co-operation of one or another of the new states of Central Europe had been straining public opinion. Sanguinary clashes between opposing factions, each fielding its private army, became increasingly frequent, with the government veering from acquiescence to suppression.

In those years of latent civil war and economic depression Vienna offered a curious spectacle indeed. Spreading unemployment had not fully dispirited the workers: the powerful opposition of their leaders in parliament, as well as the social achievements of the municipal administration, filled them with proud expectations. The Communists' rising power in Germany, while supposedly cooling the enthusiasm for *Anschluss* on the part of the Socialist politicians, disquieted Vienna's middle classes only slightly more than did Bolshevik dominance in distant Russia. Upper bourgeois had changed their life style only little since the *Umsturz*. Even while the economic crisis led many of them into risky investments, they continued to play their part as the cultural backbone of eternal Vienna. Neither the departure of the Habsburgs nor Vienna's divorce from what used to be the dynasty's most precious dominions impinged on the self-assurance of upper-class Viennese as denizens of a quasi-imperial city. Their Austrianness they took for granted. In actual fact, there was not much room for it beside their overweening love of Vienna. Their attitude toward the *Länder* contained, as it always had, a strong element of the attachment of urban tourists to rural beauty. There were hardly any Gay Twenties in bourgeois Vienna. But its way of living seemed frivolous to lower-middle-class families, who never had recovered from the ravages of inflation.

The upswing in Germany's economy following the Nazi triumph in the 1933 elections gave food for thought to those disinherited people. While not necessarily in favour of Austria's union with Hitler's totalitarian *Reich,* they were dazzled by the apparent blessings of totalitarian rule. So was the Christian-Social chancellor, Engelbert Dollfuss. When he suspended parliamentary government, most of Vienna's upper bourgeois condoned his dictatorial brand of Austrianism. The numerous middle-class Jews of Vienna relied, in addition, on the religious spirit of its Christian-Socials as a bulwark against *Anschluss,* and were reluctant to appreciate the waxing lure that Hitler's anti-Semitism exerted on the Little Man of Vienna who had never forgotten his Jew-baiting great tribune, Lueger.

At the same time, the new Germany's harsh anti-Socialist measures pleased Vienna's bourgeois. The bloody destruction of their own Socialist party by Dollfuss's government, which shocked the Western world in 1934, did not horrify them. They underrated the now leaderless workers' estrangement from the state that action was to cause. Vienna's proletariat stayed sullenly aloof during the attempt by a band of Nazis to seize power, in the course of which the chancellor was murdered. Still, the strong stand that Mussolini's Italy took in those hours reinforced the belief of many Viennese that Europe's powers would never tolerate Austria's Nazification. Factional agitation was abating somewhat under the rule of Dollfuss's successor, Kurt von Schuschnigg, and economic agreements with Hungary and Italy led to a slight improvement in the situation. But when, after modifying the anti-Habsburg laws of 1919, he publicly claimed his right to decide on the question of the dynasty's restoration, he provoked new acts of terrorism on the part of the Austrian Nazis. Soon the meanwhile Axis-bound Mussolini advised him that he had better make his peace with Hitler. Schuschnigg's dickerings with the Habsburg pretender had alienated the successor states, and frantic attempts he now made to find support in Prague and Paris were in vain. Was it, then, Mussolini's turnabout, combined with the virtual indifference of the great powers, that sealed Austria's doom?

Today it is the fashion to view the *Anschluss* of 1938 as simply a coup of Hitler's, and Austria as only a victim of his aggression. Indeed, the delirious enthusiasm that welcomed him in Vienna stunned foreign observers. They failed to realize that in the glare of his propaganda he appeared as saviour from the depression still holding Austria in its grip. They also did not understand that a great many of Vienna's middle-class people felt that, as citizens of the now powerful *Reich*, they would regain the gratifying self-importance that had been theirs at the hub of the empire of the Habsburgs. In the months after the *Anschluss*, the man in the street became convinced that the improvement in Austria's economic climate was due not least to the Jews' elimination. That notion has not totally been discarded after almost forty years, even though Austrians are eager to condemn the brutalities of the Nazi regime. In the seven years it lasted, they experienced, along with its power of seduction, some of Nazism's horrors themselves, in addition to the trials of warfare.

It may be argued that it was the *Reich's* ultimate defeat that disenchanted the hundreds of thousands who had greeted the *Führer* in the spacious courtyard of the Hofburg and on the streets of their city. In fact, those seven years had brought about what all the exhortations of the inter-war period had not accomplished: the Viennese had found their identity at long last. The present-day local phrase that lumps the Nazi era with the decade of Vienna's occupation by the war's victorious powers – 'seventeen years of foreign occupation' – may grate on the ears of the victors of '45; it does justice to the feeling, matured under Nazi overlordship, that the *Reich's* Germans were foreigners. They had abolished the very name of the country, reduced Vienna to the rank of a provincial city, and imposed their ruthless single-mindedness upon its people, thus reviving the Austrian anti-Prussianism which the Kaiser's ambassador used to complain about in World War I. Be that as it may, today's so-to-speak horizontal mobility between Vienna and the *Länder* began to develop as the Viennese during the Nazi era awoke fully to their Austrianness. Not its least manifestation was the upper-class use of broad-dialect expressions. It has continued to this day.

The resulting veneer of egalitarianism is deceptive. The class stratification of Vienna's population has not changed. The social prestige of aristocratic families has not been impaired by the absence of a royal court; no one pays any heed whatever to the law that abolished the titles of the nobility. Civil-service and even office titles are used as punctiliously as they ever were, and the republic's medals of merit are distributed in bewildering profusion. The old fascination with Vienna's cultural life has not diminished among its self-styled élite; but it has become intertwined with the country's interest in tourism, one of its economic mainstays.

Middle-class people still speak of Socialists as Reds. They in turn refer to the voters of the People's (formerly Christian-Social) Party as the Blacks. However, the fierceness of the old antagonism has gone out of those epithets. The rule of the Socialists in Vienna's town hall has never been challenged since the rebirth of their party upon the end of World War II. For a quarter of a century after that hour the republic itself was governed by Black-and-Red coalitions. Despite their internecine tension, something like a consensus appears to have come into being in those twenty-five years. It has been carried over into the subsequent era of Socialist governments with their cautious, pragmatic approach to Marxist doctrine. Full employment and generous welfare legislation have ensured a peaceful social climate that is the envy of many a greater country. The number of workers' sons to attain higher education is still small; bourgeois are not averse to contending that there is not much of a yen for it in workingmen's homes. Although lower-middle-class Viennese still love to grumble, their old annoyance at the modern world seems to be vanishing; they joke, but no longer fume, about innovations in their city. The Jews 'have gone', as the local parlance had it in the immediate post-Nazi years.

Nothing like the burst of scientific, philosophical and

literary talent, which we now realize constituted the true glory of turn-of-the-century Vienna, has occurred in the last four decades. Few of its citizens seem to mind. Nor do they pay much attention to the decreasing population of the city; small-town *Gemütlichkeit* was, after all, part of the myth of Old Vienna. That myth, if sometimes smiled at today, has not altogether faded. The fabled Viennese *joie de vivre* has been largely replaced by widespread contentment. It is not always easy to distinguish this from complacency. The apparent insouciance about the closeness of the Iron Curtain astounds the visitor, particularly when listening to the elderly recounting the rape and the spoliations engaged in by the Red Army a generation ago. But as it is, Vienna's geographical position is not the least important reason for the robust little republic's viability. Its people do not allow the danger from the East to dampen their recently regained self-confidence.

The memories of the *Umsturz* of 1918 have paled, even for the shrunken group of survivors. Whenever the thoughts of the tradition-minded turn to the Habsburgs it is the aged Franz Josef, not Emperor Karl, that such musings alight on. Postcards showing the Old Gentleman in his ceremonial robes or the Alpine sportsman's loden jacket are on sale in some shops in the Inner City. Whatever facile sentiments those likenesses may evoke, they are unlikely to conjure up nostalgic pictures of the vast realm that he tenuously ruled. 'Loss of empire' is not a phrase current in present-day Vienna.

On Sundays in clement weather people of all classes still flock to the wooded hills at whose base Roman soldiers built the *castellum* that grew to be Vienna. Gazing down upon the sprawling city skirted by the grey waters of the river that Viennese legend has transmuted into the 'blue' Danube, they must not be assumed to mourn the passing of the Habsburgs' deceptively glittering city. Rather the changes of the recent past have convinced them that their Vienna, in the words of a song of the days of waning Habsburg power, 'will remain Vienna'.

❧ *Notes* ❧

CHAPTER 1

1 Quoted in Z. A. B. Zeman, *The Break-Up of the Habsburg Empire 1914–1918* (London 1961), p. 96.
2 All quotations from Redlich's diaries are drawn from Fritz Fellner (ed.), *Schicksalsjahre Österreichs. Das politische Tagebuch Josef Redlichs* (Graz/Cologne 1954). Individual quotes are to be found under the dates referred to in the text.
3 Quoted in Arthur J. May, *The Passing of the Habsburg Monarchy 1914–1918* (Philadelphia 1968), p. 290.
4 Quoted in Julius Braunthal, *Victor und Friedrich Adler* (Vienna 1965), p. 208.
5 *Ibid.*, p. 211.
6 Friedrich Adler, *Vor dem Ausnahmegericht* (Jena 1923), p. 198.
7 Otto Bauer (ed.), *Die österreichische Revolution* (Vienna 1965), p. 66.

CHAPTER 2

1 Ottokar Czernin, *In the World War* (London 1919), p.146.
2 Quoted in May, *op. cit.*, pp. 332f.
3 *Heurigen* (literally 'of this year') means the previous autumn's vintage, as well as the premises of the vintner who was licensed to sell his own yield by the glass.
4 Actually, the enemy coalition was referred to as 'the Entente'.
5 Quoted in May, *op. cit.*, p. 296.

CHAPTER 3

1 Quoted in Albert Fuchs, *Geistige Strömungen in Österreich 1867–1918* (Vienna 1949), p. 60.

2 Bauer, *op. cit.*, p. 74.

CHAPTER 4

1 Quoted in Rudolf Neck (ed.), *Österreich im Jahre 1918: Berichte und Dokumente* (Vienna 1968), p. 32.
2 Police reports are drawn from Neck (ed.), *op. cit.*
3 Quoted in Zeman, *op. cit.*, p. 159.
4 Quoted in Robert A. Kann, *Die Sixtusaffäre und die geheimen Friedensverhandlungen Österreich-Ungarns im Ersten Weltkrieg* (Munich 1966), p. 23.
5 Quoted in *Die Fackel*, No. 481–9, p. 181.
6 Quoted in May, *op. cit.*, p. 717.

CHAPTER 5

1 Leuthner's speech is quoted from shorthand notes taken by one of his colleagues and printed in Neck (ed.), *op. cit.* pp. 54f.
2 Quoted in May, *op. cit.*, p. 438.
3 *Zentralen,* established in mid-war, were associations of commodity dealers functioning with government co-operation.
4 Edmund Glaise von Horstenau and Rudolf Kiszling (eds), *Das Kriegsjahr 1918*, vol. VII of *Österreich-Ungarns letzter Krieg* (Vienna 1938), p. 573.
5 *Ibid.*, p. 572.
6 Quoted in May, *op. cit.*, p. 720.

CHAPTER 6

1 Quoted in Neck (ed.), *op. cit.*, p. 39.
2 Quoted in Helmut Rumpler, *Max Hussarek* (Graz 1965), p. 102.

CHAPTER 7

1 Friedrich Funder, *Vom Gestern ins Heute* (Vienna 1952), p. 584.
2 Brandl's diary entries are quoted from his memoirs, *Kaiser, Politiker und Menschen* (Vienna 1936).
3 C. A. Macartney, *The Habsburg Empire 1790–1918* (London 1969), p. 808.
4 Quoted in Neck (ed.), *op. cit.*, p. 101.

CHAPTER 8

1 Bauer, *op. cit.*, p. 112.

2 Hellmut Andics, *Der Staat, den keiner wollte* (Vienna 1962), p. 13.
3 This episode is based on Karl Werkmann, *Der Tote auf Madeira* (Munich 1932), p. 19; May, *op. cit.*, p. 808; and Gordon Brook-Shepherd, *The Last Habsburg* (London 1968), p. 212.

CHAPTER 9
1 Bauer, *op. cit.*, p. 113.
2 *Ibid.*, p. 137.
3 Funder, *op. cit.*, pp. 597–8.
4 The Bosel episode is based on Brandl, *op. cit.*, pp. 334f.

CHAPTER 10
1 Quoted in Brandl, *op. cit.*, p. 301.
2 Quoted in Brook-Shepherd, *op. cit.*, p. 230.

CHAPTER 11
1 Bauer, *op. cit.*, p. 150.
2 *Ibid.*, p. 151.
3 Brandl, *op. cit.*, p. 311.
4 Quoted in Funder, *op. cit.*, p. 621.
5 Bauer, *op. cit.*, p. 153.
6 Brandl, *op. cit.*, p. 314.
7 Hans Hautmann, *Die verlorene Räterepublik* (Vienna 1971), p. 149. The rest of the paragraph is based on that well-documented study, pp. 150f.
8 Brandl, *op. cit.*, p. 321.

CHAPTER 12
1 Quoted in Karl R. Stadler, *The Birth of the Austrian Republic* (Leyden 1966), p. 48.
2 Bauer, *op. cit.*, p. 162.
3 Brandl, *op. cit.*, pp. 334f.
4 Bauer, *op. cit.*, p. 154.
5 Hautmann, *op. cit.*, p. 190.
6 Bauer, *op. cit.*, p. 155.
7 Funder, *op. cit.*, pp. 623–4.
8 Quoted in F. L. Carsten, *Revolution in Central Europe 1918–1919* (London 1972), p. 234.

Select Bibliography

Adler, Friedrich, *Vor dem Ausnahmegericht* (Jena 1923).

Andics, Hellmut, *Der Staat den keiner wollte* (Vienna 1962).

Bauer, Otto, *Die österreichische Revolution* (Vienna 1965).

Barea, Ilsa, *Vienna* (New York 1966).

Brandl, Franz, *Kaiser, Politiker und Menschen* (Vienna 1936).

Braunthal, Julius, *Victor und Friedrich Adler* (Vienna 1965).

Broch, Hermann, *Hofmannsthal und seine Zeit*, in *Gesammelte Werke* (*Essays*), I (Zurich 1955).

Brook-Shepherd, Gordon, *The Last Habsburg* (London 1968).

Carsten, F. L., *Revolution in Central Europe 1918–1919* (London 1972).

Czernin, Ottokar, *In the World War* (London 1919).

Demblin, August, *Czernin und die Sixtus-Affäre* (Munich 1920).

Deutsch, Julius, *Aus Österreichs Revolution* (Vienna 1921).

Deutsch, Julius, *Ein weiter Weg* (Vienna 1960).

Erényi, Gustav, *Graf Stefan Tisza* (Vienna 1935).

Fellner, Fritz (ed.), *Schicksalsjahre Österreichs 1908–1919: Das politische Tagebuch Josefs Redlichs*, 2 vols, (Graz/Cologne 1954).

Field, Frank, *The Last Days of Mankind: Karl Kraus and His Vienna* (London 1967).

Fischer, Fritz, *Griff nach der Weltmacht: Die Kriegszielpolitik des kaiserlichen Deutschland 1914–1918* (Düsseldorf 1964).

Frei, Bruno, *Die Matrosen von Cattaro* (Vienna 1927).

Fuchs, Albert, *Geistige Strömungen in Österreich 1867–1918* (Vienna 1949).

Funder, Friedrich, *Vom Gestern ins Heute* (Vienna 1952).

Glaise von Horstenau, Edmund, and Kiszling, Rudolf (eds), *Das Kriegsjahr 1918* (vol. vII of *Österreich-Ungarns letzter Krieg* (Vienna 1938).

Gulick, Charles A., *Austria from Habsburg to Hitler* (Los Angeles 1948).

Hantsch, Hugo, *Die Geschichte Österreichs,* II, 2nd edn. (Graz 1962).

Hautmann, Hans, *Die verlorene Räterepublik* (Vienna 1971).

Heller, Erich, *The Disinherited Mind* (London 1957).

Helmer, Oskar, *50 Jahre erlebte Geschichte* (Vienna 1957).

Hindels, Josef, *Von der ersten Republik zum zweiten Welt-krieg* (Malmø 1947).

Jásci, Oscar, *The Dissolution of the Habsburg Monarchy* (Chicago 1961).

Kann, Robert A., *Die Sixtusaffäre und die geheimen Friedensverhandlungen Österreich-Ungarns im Ersten Weltkrieg* (Vienna 1966).

Kessler, Harry Graf, *Tagebücher 1918–1937* (Frankfurt 1961).

Kleinwächter, Friedrich F. G., *Von Schönbrunn bis St. Germain* (Graz 1964).

Klemperer, Klemens von, *Ignaz Seipel* (Princeton 1972).

Macartney, C. A., *The Habsburg Empire 1790–1918* (London 1969).

May, Arthur J., *The Passing of the Hapsburg Monarchy 1914–1918,* 2 vols (Philadelphia 1966).

Neck, Rudolf (ed.), *Österreich im Jahre 1918: Berichte und Dokumente* (Vienna 1968).

Plaschka, Richard Georg, *Cattaro-Prag: Revolte und Revolu-tion* (Graz 1963).

Pollak, Walter, *Dokumentation einer Ratlosigkeit: Österreich im Oktober–November 1918* (Vienna 1968).

Renner, Karl, *An der Wende zweier Zeiten* (Vienna 1946),
Renner, Karl, *Österreichs Erneuerung* (Vienna 1916).

Rumpler, Helmut, *Max Hussarek: Nationalitäten und Nationalitätenpolitik in Österreich im Sommer des Jahres 1918* (Graz 1965).

Schorske, Carl E., 'Politics and Psyche in fin-de-siècle Vienna', *American Historical Review* (July 1961).

Sieghart, Rudolf, *Die letzten Jahrzehnte einer Grossmacht* (Berlin 1932).

Skalnic, Kurt, *Dr. Karl Lueger* (Vienna 1954).

Stadler, Karl R., *The Birth of the Austrian Republic* (Leyden 1966).

Taylor, A. J. P., *The Habsburg Monarchy: A History of the Austrian Empire and Austria-Hungary* (London 1948).

Wandruszka, Adam, *The House of Habsburg* (Garden City 1964).

Watt, Richard M., *The Kings Depart* (New York 1968).

Werkmann, Karl, *Der Tote auf Madeira* (Munich, 1923).

Wheeler-Bennett, John W., *Brest-Litovsk: The Forgotten Peace* (New York 1939).

Zeman, Z. A. B., *The Break-up of the Habsburg Empire* (London 1961).

Neue Freie Presse, Vienna (1916–19).
Arbeiter Zeitung, Vienna (1917–19).
Die Fackel, Vienna (October 1916–July 1919).

❧ Index ❧